PACIFIC
OCEAN

Equator

INDIAN
OCEAN

THE
CHARDONNAY
GRAPE

CHARDONNAY

Tim Atkin

Series editor: Harry Eyres

VIKING

VIKING

Published by the Penguin Group
Penguin Books Ltd, 27 Wrights Lane, London W8 5TZ, England
Penguin Books USA Inc., 375 Hudson Street, New York, New York 10014, USA
Penguin Books Australia Ltd, Ringwood, Victoria, Australia
Penguin Books Canada Ltd, 10 Alcorn Avenue, Toronto, Ontario, Canada M4V 3B2
Penguin Books (NZ) Ltd, 182–190 Wairau Road, Auckland 10, New Zealand

Penguin Books Ltd, Registered Offices: Harmondsworth, Middlesex, England

First published 1992
1 3 5 7 9 10 8 6 4 2

Set in 9/12 Linotron Janson Text 55 by Wyvern Typesetting Ltd, Bristol
Printed in Great Britain by Butler & Tanner Ltd, Frome and London

A CIP catalogue record for this book is available from the British Library

ISBN 0–670–82515–8

*For
Ron and Julie,
who enjoy
good wine,
but don't mind
the odd free
sample.*

CONTENTS

MAPS

FOREWORD

From a damp island in the middle of the Rhine to a cactus-haunted desert in mid-California, from the South Downs to South Australia, from the Niagara Falls to the valleys of the Andes – Chardonnay has travelled further and with more adaptability than any other grape variety. There is even a (rather successful) Chardonnay vineyard in China.

This global success is an extraordinarily recent phenomenon, as Tim Atkin explains – and he is well qualified to do so, having covered more miles in pursuit of Chardonnay than any previous wine writer. Even at the end of the 1970s there was practically no Chardonnay in Australia – for many now the country most closely associated with the grape – and very little in California, producer of some of the world's most sophisticated examples of the variety. In some ways Chardonnay's success is puzzling: according to many winemakers the grape does not have a very strong varietal character – indeed, it is the winemaker's grape *par excellence*, the one which cries out to be moulded, tempered by malolactic fermentation, enriched with lees contact, embellished with greater or lesser amounts of oak. When Tim Atkin compares Chardonnay to Madonna, he may not be thinking solely of the grape's star status: Chardonnay shares some of Madonna's Protean ability to change from blonde to brunette, sophisticate to slut.

Personally I think the chameleon-like nature of Chardonnay can be exaggerated. In Burgundy at least, Chardonnay has a fairly well-defined personality: flowery (sometimes also buttery and nutty) on the nose, quite rounded and generous on the palate (though there are wide variations from the steeliness of Chablis to the richness of Meursault), a splendid wine to drink with many kinds of food, especially fish cooked in French buttery sauces. But when people speak of Chardonnay these days, they are probably not thinking primarily of Burgundy. The full-blown oaky Chardonnays of the Hunter Valley, the ripe, melony Chardonnays of Riverland, the light, easy-drinking Chardonnays of Sonoma County – these are the wines which have taken the middle market by storm.

It is the New World countries which have brought the name Chardonnay into living-rooms, wine shops, wine bars and restaurants. The combination of the New World and Australia (in particular), the supermarkets and the use of a named variety on the label has been a great democratizing force in wine. Perhaps many of the winedrinkers who have latched on to New World Chardonnay would be much warier of tackling the complicated hierarchies of Burgundy. But Burgundy is where Chardonnay comes from, and where still, as Tim Atkin roundly and rightly asserts, all the greatest examples of Chardonnay are made.

Burgundy, as those who have been exploring Pinot Noir under Andrew Barr's tutelage may already know, is the world's most difficult and infuriating wine region. The situation with the white wines, made from Chardonnay, is marginally better than with the reds, but there is still the same labyrinthine subdivision of properties and variation in quality of wines from the same vineyard. In the end the only guarantee is the grower, and Tim Atkin has unearthed from their limestone cellars in the villages of Chassagne-Montrachet, Puligny-Montrachet and Meursault some of the world's supreme white-winemaking artisans. This is a task which required tact and diplomacy as well as tasting expertise (and excellent French): very important to know which Gagnard is likely to bite off your head and which will be charming, and the exact relationship between the *négociant* wines of Chartron et Trébuchet and the domaine wines of M. Chartron. A labour of love, then, and rewarded when you taste the sublime Meursaults of François Jobard or the majestic Chassagne-Montrachet Premiers and Grands Crus of Ramonet.

White Burgundy, contrary to popular supposition, need not burn a hole in your pocket. There are some excellent inexpensive Mâcon wines, and even on the Côte de Beaune, villages such as Saint-Aubin provide classy drinking at an affordable price (not for too long I fear).

A sound knowledge of Burgundy, then, is the Chardonnay-drinker's first requirement – if only so that he or she is aware of the original moulds from which the New World producers have taken their copies. The great success of Australian Chardonnay has been in providing reliable and immediately attractive flavours of ripe fruit, usually backed up with some toasty oak, at an extremely reasonable price. The sophisticated wine drinker may find these flavours a little too obvious: fortunately, the better Australian producers have been experimenting with cooler regions than the torrid Hunter and Barossa valleys, and coming up with excellent and more subtle wines from areas such as Padthaway and even Tasmania. Perhaps even these have not (yet at least) got close to the complexity and finesse of the great white Burgundies. It is possible that cooler, damper New Zealand may eventually emerge as the real class act in Antipodean Chardonnay – wines such as Cloudy Bay Chardonnay, even more sought after than the celebrated Sauvignon Blanc, give evidence of enormous promise.

California has not been quite as successful as Australia in providing the wine lover with reliable value for money, but the top California Chardonnays, for my money, beat those of Australia in terms of the very Burgundian qualities of subtlety and complexity. Acacia, Chalone, Saintsbury and Sonoma-Cutrer are four producers of great refinement and sophistica-tion, and individuality, whose standards would be hard to match anywhere outside the Côte de Beaune. Chardonnay is now *the* Californian grape, and (a remarkable fact among many in Tim Atkin's guide) a grape more widely planted in California than in its native France.

But Chardonnay's empire extends much further than just Australasia and California. Almost all the major European wine producers have produced their own version of the world's most fashionable grape. Some outstanding examples have emerged from Spain (the brilliant single-vineyard Torres Milmanda) and Italy (the super-refined versions from Angelo Gaja); the mass producers of Eastern Europe churn out large quantities of everyday Chardonnay (although the Bulgarian offerings, it must be said, are nothing like as successful as the same country's Cabernet Sauvignon), and perhaps, with the change to a market economy, will in time make some wines of exciting quality.

There is no sign of the Chardonnay boom slowing down. New countries keep appearing with acceptable, or more than acceptable, wines from the variety: to name two, Chile and South Africa, both searching for a recognizable style and hampered by political conditions and the lack of a sophisticated local market. The Chinese Chardonnay I mentioned earlier shows that Chardonnay can thrive in a very different political climate. In fact it is difficult to think of anything stopping this brilliant, adaptable grape.

Harry Eyres

PREFACE

Most books are written by a single person, sitting alone at a word processor, and this one was no exception. I take full responsibility for what follows but feel I must acknowledge a debt to the producers, merchants and individuals who shared knowledge, time and wines with me over the last three years, making Chardonnay such a pleasure to research. Whatever its drawbacks, the wine trade is not short of generosity. Many people extended hospitality to me on my travels, opening precious bottles and searching out snippets of information. They are too numerous to thank individually; but this book is as much their work as mine.

I am, however, especially grateful to the following: Susy Atkins; Nicolle Barnett of Lay & Wheeler; Andrew Barr; Barwell & Jones; Nelly Blau; Penny Bool of the Champagne Bureau; Jim Budd; Steve Burns of the California Wine Institute; Bob Campbell MW; Ellen Cartsonis; Oz Clarke; Claudine Cô of the Bureau Interprofessionel des Vins de Bourgogne; Sergio da Luca of Enotria; Luciann Flynn of Winecellars; Michael Fridjhon; Rosemary George MW; David Gill MW of Bulgarian Vintners; David Gleave MW of Winecellars; David Graves of Saintsbury; James and Suzanne Halliday; Tim Hamilton-Russell; Pam Holt of Penfolds UK; Jonquil Houghton; Brice Jones of Sonoma-Cutrer Vineyards, who allowed me to attend the 1990 Focus on Chardonnay; Robert Joseph; Tony Keys; Willy Lebus; Luciana Lynch; Giles MacDonogh; Catherine Manac'h of Food and Wine from France; Thierry Matrot; Richard Mayson; Manuel Moreno; Hazel Murphy of Wines of Australia; Lyn Parry; Mike Paul of Penfolds UK; Joe Rollo of the California Wine Institute; Mark Savage MW of Windrush Wines; Cordelia Sayers; Jean-Charles Servant of the BIVB; GCI Sterling; Rawlings Voigt;

Larry Walker; Dick Ward of Saintsbury; Jeremy Watson of Wines from Spain; Fiona Wild; Adam Wynn, who kindly allowed me to consult his thesis on Chardonnay production in Burgundy; Emily Nott, my long-suffering editor at Penguin; and, lastly, Matthew Fort and the staff of *Weekend Guardian*, who put up with my frequent trips abroad while I was researching this book.

A note on the organization of the book. Countries are listed alphabetically and broken down into individual regions. Thus, California appears under the United States, and Burgundy under France. Within each region or country, I have selected the best producers of Chardonnay. The most noteworthy (marked with an asterisk*) are covered in greater detail at the end of the section. To forestall cries of anguish and/or indignation, I should add that these are *my* favourite producers. I am well aware that the list has its eccentricities, but without eccentricity the world would be a dull place.

INTRODUCTION

Chardonnay is the world's most glamorous grape variety. It is Madonna, Princess Diana and Jerry Hall, all rolled into one. From Tokyo to Tijuana, Birmingham to Biloxi Beach, almost everyone has heard of Chardonnay. The great thing about Chardonnay is the breadth of its appeal. From the sublime heights of a great white Burgundy to the most humble, uncomplicated blast of tropical fruit and oak, it gives people a set of flavours they find easy to appreciate.

The grape's rise to prominence has been spectacular. Only twenty years ago, Chardonnay was virtually unheard of in Australia, California, Chile, New Zealand or South Africa. How things have changed. As Chardonnay's renown has increased, so plantings have multiplied like gerbils. Some of these have popped up in very unlikely places. Apart from the more obvious New and Old World sources, there are Chardonnay vineyards in England, Mexico, Japan, China, Egypt and even Holland. According to one story, someone is about to try his luck in Denmark. Wherever next? The Gobi Desert?

Despite this global proliferation, the finest Chardonnays are still produced in one country: France. The supreme examples of the grape come from Champagne, Chablis, the Corton hill and three world-famous villages on the Côte de Beaune: Meursault, Puligny-Montrachet and Chassagne-Montrachet. None of these regions has a divine right to make great Chardonnay – indeed much of what they produce is mediocre – but, at their best, Blanc de Blancs Champagne and white Burgundy are capable of a depth and complexity which others simply cannot match.

Nevertheless, the balance of power is shifting. The rest of the world is gaining in confidence, knowledge and expertise, and producing considerably more complex Chardonnays than it did a decade ago. Australia, New Zealand and the United States have emerged as principal pretenders to the French throne, but the claims of other countries, particularly Chile, Spain, South Africa and Italy, are gaining in stridency. France's grip on the crown is looking increasingly tenuous, as a number of tastings comparing white Burgundy with the best New World Chardonnays have demonstrated. The commoners are milling at the palace gates. Who knows, revolution may not be far away.

But whatever the present, uncertain state of affairs, the New World owes a considerable debt of gratitude to Burgundy. Winemakers outside France would be the first to acknowledge that the white wines of Chablis and the Côte d'Or were, and to a large extent remain, a source of tremendous inspiration. When New World pioneers started to plant Chardonnay in the sixties, they did so out of admiration for the wines of Puligny-Montrachet, Corton-Charlemagne and Meursault.

Not that the first New World Chardonnays were lifeless imitations of white Burgundy – far from it. California and Australian producers consciously rejected Burgundian methods in the youthful, if headstrong, belief that they could make better wines their way. Size was everything. California in particular set out to make bigger, brasher Chardonnays than everyone else. Grapes were picked ultra-ripe to maximize fruit character and alcoholic strength. Keen to extract colour and even more flavour from their grapes, winemakers also subjected Chardonnay to an extended spell on its skins, frequently at warm temperatures, before fermentation. A Burgundian would rather chew on his beret than countenance such a practice.

Restraint, in other words, became a dirty word among New World winemakers. Instead of fermenting their wines in barrel, as the Burgundians did, they fermented them in stainless-steel tanks, again to emphasize fruit flavour. The resulting wines were then aged in new oak barrels – another departure from Burgundian precepts. Often they were little more than an over-alcoholic cocktail of tropical fruit and sawdust that became undrinkable after two or three years of bottle age.

The Eighties was a decade of change for New World

Chardonnay. Slowly but inexorably, New World winemakers started to modify their opinions. Their tone became less arrogant, their sense of self-belief less assured. Increasingly, many of them started to adopt Burgundian winemaking techniques – vinification in barrel, lees stirring and (where appropriate) malolactic fermentation. Those wily Burgundians weren't so stupid after all.

At the top end of the scale, this has made it increasingly difficult to tell one Chardonnay from another. I once attended an international Chardonnay conference where a superstar Burgundian grower confidently identified a Simi Chardonnay as one of his own wines. The California producer sitting next to him placed his own in Italy. None of this was surprising. As Zelma Long, who had made the Simi wine, pointed out at the time: 'It's a myth that you can always tell California and French Chardonnays apart. Great Chardonnay has power, complexity and delicacy, and the French aren't the only ones who can make that kind of wine.'

This is not to say that all Chardonnays taste alike. There is a world of difference between the lean, knife-edge steeliness of a young Chablis and a big, well-upholstered brute from the Australian Riverland. All the same, in the New World there has been a definite shift away from the alcoholic, sledgehammer Chardonnays of old to a more subtle, balanced style, even in warm areas like the Napa and Barossa Valleys. The emergence of cool climate regions in Australia, California, New Zealand and South Africa, where the longer growing season produces finer, more complex wines, has produced Chardonnays which are more Burgundian in structure – that is to say with natural, rather than added, acidity and less emphasis on simple fruit flavours.

Not all the traffic has moved in one direction, however. The success of New World Chardonnay has, in turn, influenced wine-makers on the Côte d'Or. The proportion of new oak barrels has increased and there have been significant advances in cellar hygiene and temperature control, both areas where Burgundy has traditionally favoured a rather lax approach. The most important New World influence has been the promotion of the variety itself. Easy to identify (and, of course, pro-nounce), Chardonnay was the grape which launched the single varietal craze in California and Australia. It would not be an exaggeration to say that this phenomenon has changed the way many people buy wine. Rather than looking for the region of origin, or the name of the producer, on the label, they seek out the word Chardonnay, Sauvignon Blanc or Merlot instead. There is a certain amount of irony here. Chardonnay, the world's most patrician white grape, has made wine a more demotic product.

The grape's success has its down side, too. Chardonnay dominates the scene in Australia and California, and its influence is increasing in almost every wine-producing region. The reason is simple enough. Chardonnay grows well in most climates, providing large and consistent yields. It is also a lot easier to sell than less prestigious local varieties, such as Arneis in Italy or Petit Manseng in France. As a result, many growers are pulling out characterful, indigenous grapes in order to plant Chardonnay. Before we know it, the whole world will be covered with Chardonnay.

These new plantings carry the risk of a glut. One well-known Australian producer has predicted that much of the Chardon-nay which went into the ground in the late eighties will finish up as cheap bag-in-box wine, what he calls 'Château Card-board'. Chardonnay is in danger of becoming a generic white-wine style, the way 'Chablee' did in the Seventies. In the USA, Chardonnay is already on sale at/under five dollars a bottle. There is even, glory be, a 'pink' Chardonnay on the shelves, made by adding a few drops of red wine.

Surprisingly, such things do not appear to have damaged the image or prestige of Chardonnay. We have been 'Chardon-nayed to death', in the words of California winemaker Dick Arrowood, but still we clamour for more. Why? Reliability is a large part of the answer, with the possible exception of white Burgundy. Even to people who have no idea that Chardonnay is a grape variety, let alone the source of some of the world's finest white wines, the word is a guarantee of quality. Chardonnay has something for everyone, from the most exacting wine buff to the once-a-month tippler. This, more than anything, explains the strength and durability of its appeal. Make no mistake, Chardonnay is here to stay.

The Character of Chardonnay

To describe the essential character of Chardonnay is to attempt the impossible. Like the anti-hero in Woody Allen's film, *Zelig*, Chardonnay is something of a chameleon, supremely skilled at adapting to its surroundings. There is no one style of Chardonnay; the grape, to paraphrase the poet Walt Whitman, contains multitudes.

Pliable, deferential and eager to please, Chardonnay is a natural diplomat. If you taste unfermented Chardonnay juice, it does not have a particularly strong varietal character. As Bruno D'Alfonso, the winemaker at Sanford in Santa Barbara County, puts it: 'Chardonnay has rather simple fruit unless you do something to it or with it.'

Chardonnay may have less intrinsic personality than Riesling, Sauvignon Blanc or Gewürztraminer, but it is more adaptable (and reliable) than any of its competitors. Like a piece of putty, Chardonnay can be modelled by the individual winemaker into a number of different shapes and styles. It can be sparkling or still; sweet, medium or dry; oaked or unoaked; barrel-fermented or barrel-aged; full-bodied or (very occasionally) light and ethereal. Whatever form it takes, Chardonnay is rarely anything less than palatable.

More than any other white wine, Chardonnay is open to manipulation. It is sometimes described, with some justification, as a blank canvas on which winemaker and climate are free to make their mark. Chardonnay is an extremely forgiving variety, but it is not immune from bad winemaking. By the same token, it responds well to careful handling. Indeed, many of the flavours traditionally associated with Chardonnay are created or enhanced by winemaking practices: yeast selection, skin contact, lees contact and barrel-fermentation, to name but a few.

This highlights the main difference in emphasis between the New and Old Worlds. New World winemakers talk about modelling wines, whereas the French take what comes out of the soil and leave it that way. There has been a definite shifting of ground in the last decade, but the distinction is still valid.

Chardonnay is a great traveller. It copes well with a wide range of soils and climates, although it is at its most complex in cooler growing regions like Burgundy's Côte d'Or, Carneros in California and New Zealand's South Island. These areas have longer growing seasons, during which flavour develops more slowly in the grapes. As a result, the wines usually have a better balance of fruit and acid, which enables them to age more gracefully in bottle. In warmer climates, the flavours are broader and more pronounced – citrus tones are replaced by an overt blast of tropical fruit.

Having said that, Chardonnay is not as site-specific as a grape like Pinot Noir, even in Burgundy, where the greatest vineyard nuances are to be found. If vinified in the same way, it can produce broadly similar flavours in different parts of the world. After all, a François Frères oak barrel with medium toast has much the same character in New Zealand as it does in Meursault. Any Burgundian who tells you that innate breeding will always show is talking through the top of his beret. It is not always easy to spot white Burgundies in a tasting line-up. Cool climate wines from, say, the Yarra Valley or Tasmania (Australia), Marlborough (New Zealand) or Carneros (California) can be very Burgundian in structure.

Clones, too, have less influence on the character of Chardonnay than they do on that of Pinot Noir, the grape's Burgundian stable-mate. They may affect yield and resistance to disease, but, in general, their impact on flavour appears to be less important. The obvious exception is Chardonnay Musqué, which I discuss more fully in the section on the Chardonnay vine.

Most Chardonnay is dry, although some examples from the

New World, California in particular, are in effect medium-dry. The question of sweet Chardonnay is so vexed in California that wine competitions have begun to discriminate against Chardonnays with high levels of residual sugar. The argument is that such wines enjoy an unfair advantage in comparison with dry styles which are less immediate in their appeal.

Sweetness apart, most Chardonnay is distinguished by three main things: vinosity or 'mouth-feel', richness and fruit flavour. Generally speaking, the warmer the region, the more pronounced the combination, although early picking can alter the mix (see the Taste Spectrum). The character of the fruit may differ from region to region yielding grapes with higher levels of acidity and less sugar (and therefore alcohol), but it is always present. Yields have to be very high indeed before it disappears entirely.

Many people associate Chardonnay with the flavour of oak. So strong is the link that even experienced wine-tasters can mistake oak-aged Sémillon or Pinot Blanc for Chardonnay. Oak is a vital component of most Chardonnay, but there is oak and oak. As I discuss in my section on The Oak Factor, stainless steel, oak chips, oak-ageing and barrel-fermentation all produce different results.

Great Chardonnay is all about nuance and complexity and, whatever the climate in which the grape is grown, these are invariably the result of barrel-fermentation. Chardonnay is not over-endowed with varietal aromas, so an unoaked wine, even one that has been aged on its lees, will never attain the depth and complexity of a wine that has the added structure of oak fermentation. One or two Chablis producers come close – Louis Michel springs to mind – but it is surely significant that the appellation's two undisputed greats both use a percentage of barrel-fermented wine.

The other exception to the barrel-fermentation rule is sparkling wine, particularly Champagne. Krug's world-famous Clos du Mesnil is vinified in (old) oak, but most Blanc de Blancs Champagne derives its character not from barrels, but from ageing on its lees and bottle maturation.

Chardonnay is rarely made as a dessert wine. Late-harvest

styles are produced in Australia, New Zealand, France and California, some of which are very good, if seldom as exciting as a great Beerenauslese or Sauternes. The paucity of late-harvest Chardonnays has less to do with the grape's innate unsuitability for sweet wine (many producers are happy to use a small percentage of botrytis-affected grapes to add complexity to their Chardonnay) than with economic considerations. Quite simply, Chardonnay is more valuable as a dry wine.

THE TASTE SPECTRUM

UNRIPE	COOL CLIMATE	WARM CLIMATE	WINE-MAKING
Green apple	Lemon	Banana	Yeast
Herbaceous	Lime	Pineapple	Butter
	Grapefruit	Melon	Honey
	Fig	Peach	Toffee
	Pears	Apricots	Butterscotch
	Mineral	Honey	Popcorn
	Honeysuckle	Boiled sweets	Wet wool
	Acacia		Nuts
			Toast
			Spices
			Vanilla

The table is only a summary of the flavours and scents Chardonnay can produce. It may not have the distinctive, talcum-powder and rose-petal aroma of Gewürztraminer, or the grapey, orange-peel tang of Muscat but, with the possible exception of Riesling, Chardonnay is capable of a greater range of flavours than any other white grape.

Chardonnay ripens early in the growing season, so green, herbaceous characters are rare. A poor vintage in, say, Chablis or Tasmania, with insufficient sunshine, would be the obvious exception. In Champagne, on the other hand, where Chardonnay is used as a sparkling wine base, the grapes are deliberately picked before they are fully ripe, in order to preserve acidity. The resulting wine can taste extremely lean in its youth, but it is this austerity (among other things) that enables the wine to age so well in bottle.

Cool climate regions, such as the Côte d'Or and parts of New Zealand, California, Italy, South Africa and Australia, tend to bring out citrus fruit flavours in Chardonnay. This is the grape's most refreshing aspect. Chardonnays from warmer climates (Chile and most of Australia and California) are usually fuller in alcohol, with a preponderance of tropical fruit flavours. These are easy to appreciate, but can become a little tiring after more than one glass.

Many of the flavours we readily associate with Chardonnay are the result of winemaking techniques, rather than innate varietal personality. Lees contact, fermentation temperatures, barrel-fermentation, *bâtonnage*, partial or full malolactic fermentation, and the use of wild or selected yeasts can all have a marked impact on the character of Chardonnay. If the wine has been fermented in new oak, flavours of vanilla and toast are initially dominant. As it ages, flavours of nuts, butter and honey begin to emerge.

The History of Chardonnay

The precise origins of Chardonnay, like those of most *Vitis vinifera* grape varieties, are lost in the proverbial fug of antiquity. There are three main schools of thought, each of which has its passionate adherents and detractors.

The first theory, much favoured by inhabitants of the Mâconnais village of the same name, maintains that Chardonnay is indigenous to France. Whether the grape originated in the village of Chardonnay, however, is anyone's guess. The hamlet's Latin name of Cardonacum – which later became Chardonnay – is unenlightening. The literal translation ('the place of thorns') is not much help. Vines were definitely planted here by AD 986, but there is nothing, other than a bit of wistful marketing by the local cooperative, to support the theory that Chardonnay was among them.

The second theory, advanced by Claude Taittinger of the eponymous Champagne house, is that Chardonnay was brought to France by Thibaud Le Chansonnier, Comte de Champagne. It may not be entirely coincidental that Taittinger's headquarters in Reims are based in the ancient dwellings of the Comtes de Champagne. Thibaud certainly stopped off in Cyprus on his way back from the Crusades, where he tasted the local wine. He considered it so good (which just shows you how times and tastes can change) that he asked for some vine cuttings and carried them back to Champagne. If these were Chardonnay, as Claude Taittinger would have us believe, the coincidence is remarkable.

Theory number three, which is the most likely, is that Chardonnay came from the Middle East. Serge Hochar of the Lebanese Château Musar is convinced that two of the Lebanon's native white grapes, Merwah and Obaideh, are the ancestors of the grape we call Chardonnay. If so, Chardonnay-lovers could be in for a treat – all but five per cent of the Lebanon's 60,000 acres of vines are planted with these two varieties. Hochar's own blend of the two grapes, which he ages in Allier oak, certainly tastes something like Chardonnay – nutty, full-bodied and slightly buttery.

History would seem to support Hochar. According to wine authority Hugh Johnson, the first wines were made (around 8,000 BC) in the Middle East – in the countries we know as Turkey, Syria, Jordan and the Lebanon, as well as in the Soviet Republic of Georgia. The wine writer Jancis Robinson says that the vine species *Vitis vinifera*, which includes all of the best-known wine grapes, Chardonnay among them, originated in Transcaucasia, to the south of the Black Sea.

Whatever its origins, Chardonnay developed its worldwide reputation in France – particularly in Burgundy and Champagne. The first official mention of the grape (as 'Chardenet') did not come until 1855 in Dr Jean Lavalle's *Histoire et Statistique de la Vigne et des Grands Vins de la Côte d'Or*, but Chardonnay had almost certainly been around for some time before that. According to the Californian ampelographer Harold Olmo, it is extremely likely that Chardonnay was established (under a variety of pseudonyms) in France by the end of the twelfth century.

According to the Italian academics Antonio Calò and Angelo Costacurta, Chardonnay was cultivated around Orléans in France at this time, under the name of Muscat Gennetin or Melon Musqué. It was during the Middle Ages that the grape spread from Burgundy to other regions of France and to countries such as Italy and Spain.

Chardonnay's colonization of the New World is much more recent, as I have detailed in the individual introductions to California, Australia, South Africa and New Zealand. Suffice to say that Chardonnay was virtually unheard of outside France until the fifties. The New World varietal craze, which has carried Chardonnay to a position of pre-eminence, began in the late sixties, picked up speed in the seventies and was in overdrive by the late eighties. The rate of expansion has been spectacular – New World plantings of Chardonnay now exceed those of France by far. However venerable its origins, the spread of Chardonnay is very much a modern phenomenon.

Synonyms

Chardonnay is probably known by more synonyms than any other grape. It pops up under a wide variety of local names, some of which are rarely used these days. After all, if what you've got planted in your vineyards is Chardonnay, why sell it as Beaunois or Epinette?

Nevertheless, it is still possible to come across the following synonyms: Arnoison (Touraine), Arvoisier (Aube), Aubaine (Burgundy), Auvernat Blanc (Loire), Auxerrois Blanc (Lorraine), Beaunois (Burgundy), Chaudenet (Côte Chalonnaise), Epinette (Champagne), Gamay Blanc (Jura), Melon Blanc (Arbois), Morillon (Austria), Noirien Blanc (Burgundy), Petit Chatey (Jura), Petite Sainte-Marie (Savoie), Plant de Tonnerre (Chablis), Refay (Auxerrois), Rousseau/Roussot (Chablis), Weisser Clevner/Weiss Edler/Weiss Silber (Alsace), Weisser Ruländer (Germany).

Chardonnay was not officially recognized under its own name until the Congrès Viticole at Lyon in 1872. Since then, it has been confused (sometimes deliberately) with any number of lesser white grapes. As Chardonnay's popularity has increased, so the temptation to rechristen whole vineyards of Trebbiano, Pinot Blanc, Aligoté or Melon de Bourgogne has proved too strong for some. The most common case of mistaken identity is Pinot Blanc, a false synonym which is still used in the three great white wine villages of the Côte de Beaune. The term Pinot Chardonnay is still permitted in Burgundy for wines made with Pinot Blanc, Chardonnay or a combination of the two, which hardly simplifies matters.

Historically, Chardonnay was probably called Pinot Blanc in Burgundy simply because it made good white wine, and was therefore assumed to be a white version of Pinot Noir. Elsewhere in France, the name Pinot was given to other good-quality white grapes. Chenin Blanc, for example, is known locally as Pineau de la Loire.

Confusion between Chardonnay and Pinot Blanc still exists, even though, ampelographically, they have little or nothing in common. Indeed, in shape and form, the Chardonnay vine is closer to Gamay than it is to Pinot Blanc. It is more vigorous and buds earlier than Pinot Blanc; it also produces more interesting wines. In Italy and Austria, much of what is supposedly Chardonnay is in fact Pinot Bianco. In Australia, too, the grapes have traditionally been grouped together. Until very recently, the Hunter Valley winemaker Murray Tyrrell stubbornly continued to call his wine Pinot Chardonnay. These days, even he has admitted defeat.

The Chardonnay Vine

Like all the world's leading grape varieties, Chardonnay is a member of the *Vitis vinifera* family. *Vitis vinifera* vines grow wild in much of Europe and Western Asia, but the grapes which find their way into bottles of wine all come from cultivated varieties. There are three main groups of *vinifera* vines known, with no intended reference to George Orwell's *1984*, as proles. Chardonnay belongs to the group called *Proles occidentalis*, which includes all the best-known European varieties. These varieties are generally resistant to cold weather, produce small bunches of juicy, flavoursome grapes and are well suited to a comparatively short growing season. They have also adapted successfully to warm climates.

Chardonnay is a simple vine to recognize. Its leaf is medium-sized with a bright yellow/green colour shading to a golden hue in autumn. Virtually circular in shape, the leaf has shallow indentations that resemble a serrated edge. Chardonnay grape clusters are small, compact and cylindrical, with unusually short stems. They are dark green in colour initially, but develop a deeper golden green as they mature. The grape's skin is thin and easily broken, which can lead to problems with machine harvesting and bunch rot. The vine produces soft, juicy fruit of no pronounced flavour, but generally displays a good balance of sugar and acid.

It is also possible for a winemaker to adjust the balance of his Chardonnay by adding tartaric acid (in warm climates) or sugar (in regions where there is insufficient sunshine). These two processes are known, respectively, as acidification and chaptalization. If used skilfully, they are difficult to detect. All too frequently, however, this is far from the case, resulting in clumsy, unbalanced wines with too much tartaric acid, or an excess of alcohol.

CULTIVATION

Chardonnay is an easy grape to grow. It is one of the most winter-hardy of *vinifera* varieties, as demonstrated by its success in Chablis and Champagne. Chardonnay buds (and ripens) early, which can expose it to spring frost damage. Apart from its susceptibility to frost, Chardonnay's other main weakness is its vulnerability to powdery mildew, fan leaf and grey rot. On the positive side, Chardonnay is a relatively vigorous vine – a characteristic which makes it popular with growers – and can produce, without significant loss of character, yields of up to 70 or 80 hectolitres of juice per hectare.

The age of the vine is also significant. Young vines tend to be more vigorous, but produce grapes with less flavour. If we have not yet seen the best of the New World, it may be because so much of its Chardonnay is still in short trousers. According to one particularly revealing statistic, world plantings of Chardonnay have more than doubled since 1988. The reappearance of the phylloxera louse in California, which has forced many producers to grub up their vineyards and replant on disease-resistant rootstocks, may put back the cause of New World Chardonnay by a decade.

In Burgundy, the average age of a Chardonnay vine is considerably older than in the New World, although here too, there has been a good deal of expansion and replanting over the last thirty years. Unless you have the time to inspect a producer's vineyards, you have no way of knowing how old his vines are. It is worth looking out for wines with '*vieilles vignes*' on the label, but even this doesn't tell you what you really need to know. The term has no legal definition, but usually implies that the wine was made from vines that are at least ten years old.

PREFERRED SOIL AND TERROIR

Chardonnay is suited to a wide variety of soils and climates. It is a much better traveller than Pinot Noir or Riesling. Meursault in Burgundy and California's Napa Valley, for example, have little or nothing in common, but Chardonnay performs equally well in both places. It may produce different styles of wine, but neither is necessarily superior to the other.

According to the French, Chardonnay does best in soils with a high limestone content, such as those found in Champagne, Chablis and the Côte d'Or. This is an empirical observation at best. As Dick Graff of the California winery, Chalone, puts it: 'We know that limestone has important effects but we don't know why. We can't demonstrate the connection organoleptically.' For most New World winemakers the important factor as far as Chardonnay is concerned is poor soil with good drainage. Its precise chemical composition is less important.

Overly rich soil, or soil which does not drain easily, can result in water-logged vines and excessive yields. Poor soil, on the other hand, forces vines to struggle for a living. The vines grow roots that have to dig deep into the subsoil for their life-sustaining supply of mineral nutrients. This stops the vine getting fat and lazy – it restricts yields and leaf growth, producing more concentrated, flavoursome grapes as a result.

The French notion of *terroir* – a vague term covering everything from climate to soil composition – does not necessarily contradict the findings of wine-makers in California or Australia. Increasingly, both sides agree that good Chardonnay is made in the vineyard, and that a multitude of factors can affect the quality of the fruit. These would include the age and general health of the vines, the specific microclimate, the structure and depth of the soil, pruning and canopy management. The main difference in emphasis is that while the French talk about allowing the individual vineyard to express its personality, New World winemakers tend to rely more heavily on technology, vineyard management and winemaking techniques to create a style of wine. In many cases, they decide what sort of wine they want to make before they plant vineyards or buy grapes.

New World winemakers tend to be a little more receptive to modern ideas. As the Californian oenologist Zelma Long put it recently: 'The French are still locked into this *terroir* thing. When we started in California, we had no idea what we were doing, so we had to question everything. But now even the French are more questioning than they used to be.' The French, for their part, often accuse their New World colleagues of placing too much faith in technology, of lacking respect for the vineyard.

Vineyard distinctions certainly tend to be more marked in cool climates, such as Burgundy, where a few degrees of elevation can make an enormous impact on the structure of a wine. In marginal climates, the right exposure and altitude can make the difference between ripe and unripe grapes, or between a Grand Cru and Bourgogne Blanc. With the tendency to move to cooler vineyard sites in the New World, the concept of vineyard identity is starting to emerge. It is not uncommon these days to find producers selling as many as half a dozen vineyard-designated Chardonnays. In Burgundy, communal, regional and generic blends (Meursault, Mâcon Blanc, Bourgogne Blanc) account for the great majority of the Chardonnay produced, but all the best wines come from individual vineyard sites (the Grands and Premiers Crus). Perhaps the New and Old Worlds aren't so far apart after all.

ROOTSTOCKS

Ever since the phylloxera louse visited destruction on the vineyards of Europe, more than a century ago, most *Vitis vini-*

fera vines have been grafted on to phylloxera-resistant American rootstocks. Chardonnay is no exception, although ungrafted vines exist in Oregon, Washington State, Chile and parts of Australia. The choice of rootstock is determined by three main things: soil type, climate and desired yield. It also affects the longevity of the vines. Since it was discovered in California that one widely planted rootstock (AXR1) was no longer resistant to phylloxera, research has intensified into possible alternatives. SO4 (much used in Burgundy), Rupestris du Lot or Saint George, 3309C, 5BB, 161–49C and 41B are the most popular rootstocks worldwide for Chardonnay. Of these, SO4, 5BB and 41B tend to give the highest yields.

SUBVARIETIES AND CLONAL SELECTION

Apart from Chardonnay Blanc, there are two lesser-known variations of the grape. The first, Chardonnay Musqué, which probably originated in the Jura region but is now mainly planted in the Mâconnais, has a spicy, Muscat-like aroma. The second, found almost exclusively in the Côte d'Or village of Marsannay, is Chardonnay Rose. The difference between this and the classic Chardonnay grape is slight: the berries have a pinkish hue when ripe, but otherwise taste pretty much like classic Chardonnay.

Clonal selection, which is used to reproduce healthy vines and emphasize or play down certain varietal characteristics, is principally concerned with Chardonnay Blanc. The development of modern clones has not been as important for Chardonnay as it has for Pinot Noir, but it has still played a considerable part in the renaissance of Burgundy's vineyards. When Raymond Bernard, regional director of the Office National Interprofessionnel des Vins (ONIVINS) in Dijon, arrived in the region in the mid-fifties, the Chardonnay *vignoble* was in what he calls 'a pitiful state'. Many of the vines were affected with fan leaf, or *court noué*, a disease which causes premature degeneration, and yields were as low as 5 hectolitres per hectare in some vineyards. Bernard immediately instituted a programme of clonal research which, nearly forty years later, has saved Burgundy.

Bernard's primary concern was disease-resistant stock, but he found that the dozen clones he eventually developed displayed different characteristics. In a small vineyard, it may not be worth planting more than a single clone, as the differences in flavour are not that marked, but choosing the most suitable one is still important. Irrespective of where they are planted, each clone produces wines with a similar structure. 'We've found that a good clone in Chablis is a good clone in the Mâconnais,' says Bernard.

Clones can affect results like yields, alcohol levels and the balance of sugar and acid. Bernard divides his clones into four main groupings: (a) those that produce aromatic, complex wines (such as clones 76 and 96); (b) those that make richer, but less elegant wines (95 and 548); (c) those that are neutral and therefore best-suited to sparkling wine production (277, 75 and 78); and, lastly, (d) those that have a Chardonnay Musqué character (77 and 809). Despite these differences, Chardonnay is still a much more homogenous variety than Pinot Noir.

Clonal selection for Chardonnay has also been developed in California and, on a more modest scale, in Champagne, Australia, Germany, New Zealand and Canada. Worldwide there are now more than thirty recognized clones, the most important of which are 95, 96, 75, 76, 548 and 277 in France, and 8025 (Mendoza), 8129 (I10V5), UCD5 and 8127 (also known as I10V1 and UCD6) in the New World.

DENSITY OF PLANTING

The number of Chardonnay vines planted per hectare varies enormously. As a general rule, vineyards in France tend to be more densely planted than those in the New World. The highest density (10,000 vines per hectare on average) is found in Burgundy – a figure which is still half of what it was before phylloxera – followed by Champagne (8,000 vines per hectare). Vineyards with this number of vines virtually have to be hand-picked, and in fact machine harvesting is outlawed in Champagne and, outside the Mâconnais and the Hautes Côtes, rarely used in Burgundy.

New World producers use wider spacings for their Chardonnay, which results in a density of between 1,500 and 4,000 vines per hectare. There are exceptions – Piper's Brook, Robert Mondavi and Bannockburn all use much denser plantings – but they are rare. Wide spacing is used partly to facilitate machine harvesting and pruning, but also to avoid using up precious moisture in what are often highly evaporative climates. (Burgundian plantings pre-date the age of mechanization.) Experiments with Burgundian spacing in warm climates have proved unsuccessful, as irrigation will not compensate for the absence of humidity. With close planting, vines are forced to dig deeper for moisture and nutrients. The Burgundian argument is that the resulting wines develop more intense flavours. Irrigation is pointless with close planted vines, as it tends to encourage the development of surface roots denying them access to the trace minerals that feed the plant.

New World vines, in other words, generally have an easier time than their French counterparts. As individual units, they produce much larger crops, but they struggle less to do so. The effect this has on quality is open to question. It is widely accepted that moderate yields are a *sine qua non* of fine wine-making, but the number of vines needed to produce that yield is debatable. Naturally, the ideal ratio varies from vineyard to vineyard.

TRAINING, PRUNING AND CANOPY MANAGEMENT

Pruning a vine is essential in order to regulate its growth and achieve the desired balance between the age and vigour of the vine and the size of the crop that is required. Chardonnay vines are trained in a number of different ways for ease of cultivation and to suit local climatic conditions. In Burgundy alone there are three different cane-pruned systems: *taille à queue* in the

Mâconnais (where the fruit-bearing cane is looped over the upper wire); *taille du Chablisien* in the Yonne (where two or three canes are run along the lower wire); and *guyot simple* in the remainder of the region (where a single cane is used on the lower wire). The *guyot* system, or a variant known as *guyot double* (two canes rather than one), is also used in Chardonnay vineyards outside France, but in the New World, cordon-pruned vines are much more common. The main difference between the cane and cordon systems is that for the former the vine is pruned back each year to allow a new cane, or canes, to take its place. With a cordon system, one or two branches are permanently trained along the fruiting wire and its individual spurs are pruned each year.

More elaborate vertical training systems, intended to reduce vigour and allow sunlight to penetrate the grapevine canopy, or leaves, have been introduced in the New World over the last decade or so, largely as a result of the pioneering work of Australian viticulture expert Dr Richard Smart.

In the main, these are cordon-pruned systems. The most important ones, as explained to me by the New Zealander Michael Brajkovich of Kumeu River, are the Geneva Double Curtain (a split canopy with, as its name suggests, two hanging curtains of foliage); the Open Lyre system (a split canopy with two angled walls of foliage); the 'V' system (a large-scale structure shaped, unsurprisingly, like a 'V'); the Te Kauwhata Two-Tier (two vertical canopies superimposed above one another); the Scott Henry trellis (similar to the two-tier, but with the shoots in the upper canopy trained upwards and those in the lower canopy trained in the opposite direction); and, lastly, the Te Kauwhata Twin Two-Tier (a combination of two-tier and lyre systems with four walls of foliage trained on a large trellis). It is early days, but the Open Lyre and Scott Henry trellises seem to be particularly well suited to Chardonnay.

HARVESTING

Deciding when to pick is the most important choice a grower has to make. Should he allow the grapes to reach full maturity, even if it means losing acidity? Or should he pick early, sacrificing sugar levels (and therefore alcohol in the finished wine) but preserving natural acidity? Chardonnay is an early ripening variety so, unlike Cabernet Sauvignon or Mourvèdre, it generally gets enough sunlight, even in cooler years, to ripen.

Most of the world's finest Chardonnays are hand-picked. This gives producers more control over their grapes, enabling them to weed out rotten or unripe bunches. As long as picking proceeds at a reasonably brisk pace, it also cuts down the risk of oxidation – a potential problem where Chardonnay, with its thin skin, is concerned. If the juice is exposed to excessive contact with oxygen, it can lose fruit and aroma. Nevertheless, there are good reasons for harvesting Chardonnay by machine, particularly in hot climates. Machines enable producers to pick grapes at night and so deliver their Chardonnay cool to the winery. My own feeling is that premium-quality Chardonnay should be hand-picked, but that machine-harvesting can be useful and inexpensive for more commercial styles. The other point worth making is that machines are faster and generally more reliable than human beings. In the immortal words of David Hohnen of Cape Mentelle and Cloudy Bay: 'Machines don't get pissed on Saturday nights, they pick on holidays and they don't get bitten by redback spiders.'

The Making of Chardonnay

Stripped of glamour and mythology, winemaking is little more than a series of skilled decisions. At each stage of the process, a winemaker is faced with one or more options. His choices will, cumulatively, determine the character of the finished wine. The old winemaking cliché, that you cannot make good wine out of bad grapes, is essentially true – the winemaker cannot alter the basic structure and flavour of his grapes as they come out of the vineyard.

Nevertheless, some grapes are easier to mould than others. Chardonnay is a case in point. If winemakers are artists, then Chardonnay is the variety which gives their talents free rein. By deciding when to pick and by varying the amount of skin contact, barrel ageing, lees stirring and malolactic fermentation, the winemaker can have a huge impact on the style of his Chardonnay. In a world of big egos, Chardonnay can be a very flattering grape.

The winemaking practices described below are used more extensively in the New World than the Old, although there has been a certain amount of cross-fertilization, particularly in the last decade, as a new generation of globe-trotting Burgundian and New World winemakers has emerged. Nevertheless, Burgundians still believe in the primacy of *terroir*; New World winemakers, while recognizing the importance of climate and soil-structure, believe that while Chardonnay is made in the vineyard, it is mastered in the winery.

HANDLING THE GRAPES

Once the Chardonnay grapes have been crushed and (usually) destemmed, the first decision a winemaker faces is how to handle the juice. Should he bash it around, exposing it to potentially damaging oxidation? Or should he coddle and protect it like a vulnerable child? Both methods, described respectively as the 'brown' and 'green' schools of winemaking, have their advantages. The former process eliminates unstable proteins, which might oxidize later, but produces wines that take longer to develop. The latter retains more colour, aroma and fruit but may lose out in the ageability stakes. Chilling the must keeps oxidation to a minimum.

*

SKIN CONTACT

Described by the Australian winemaker James Halliday as a 'fly now, pay later technique', skin contact is used to extract short-term flavours in Chardonnay. It can only be used effectively with protective handling to prevent excessive oxidation. Even so, the wine may turn bitter and develop a prematurely golden colour with age. Everything depends on the length of time the juice spends on its skins. Rarely used in France, skin contact has also fallen out of favour (for Chardonnay at least) in California and (to a lesser extent) Australia. Not a technique for premium Chardonnay production, in my view.

JUICE CLARIFICATION

Before the juice is fermented, the winemaker has to decide on the level of grape solids he wishes to preserve. A high level of solids will produce a yeasty, 'leesy' flavour in the finished wine. Clarification, or *débourbage*, which cleans up the juice by removing solids, is usually total in the New World (with the exception of Burgundian-style producers like Mountadam) and partial in the Old. The effects of clarification, or the lack of it, are more marked if the temperature goes above 20 °C during fermentation. To be successful, hot fermentations of unclarified juice require grapes with a considerable intensity of flavour, otherwise they tend to produce flabby, neutral wines.

ALCOHOLIC FERMENTATION

There are a number of important options at this stage. The choice of fermentation vessel – stainless-steel, concrete, epoxy resin or oak – is one. Yeast selection (or the use of wild, indigenous yeasts) is another. But the most crucial decision of all, especially in warm climates, is fermentation temperature.

If they are well maintained, stainless-steel, concrete and epoxy tanks will produce identical wines. The main difference is that stainless-steel tanks are easier to cool and clean. Oak (discussed in more detail below) will impart a more-or-less woody flavour to the wine, depending on the age, size, origin and toast of the barrel. It is harder to regulate this type of fermentation as cooling a barrel is not as easy as cooling a stainless-steel tank.

Yeast selection can also affect the flavour of Chardonnay, particularly in its youth. Yeast strains are chosen for their ability to work at a desired temperature, for their readiness to convert grape sugars and for the aromas they can bring to a wine. These aromas are more pronounced if the wine is fermented cool (say, between 12 and 17 °C). Popular yeasts for Chardonnay are Montrachet, Prise de Mousse and Épernay B.

Wild yeasts, which occur naturally in the vineyard and the cellar, are less predictable, and carry the risk of off-flavours. None the less, they are widely used in Burgundy, where winemakers see them as an integral part of a wine's personality. Poor winemaking is often excused as a '*goût du terroir*', literally a flavour of the soil, but used to describe the stamp of an individual vineyard or area.

Cool fermentation temperatures are crucial for making fresh, early-drinking styles of Chardonnay. For wines that are intended to age, they are slightly less important. As a rule, the lower the temperature, the fruitier the wine. In Burgundy the ambient autumn and winter temperatures in the cellar tend to be cooler than in California or Australia, as anyone who has shivered through a mid-December cellar tasting on the Côte de Beaune will appreciate. In other words, temperature control is not as vital in Burgundy as it is in the heat of the Barossa Valley.

MALOLACTIC FERMENTATION

Malolactic, or secondary fermentation, is a natural process by which malic acid is converted to softer lactic acid. It usually occurs after the primary, alcoholic fermentation, although the two can be simultaneous. As well as softening a wine, it adds a buttery richness and complexity to it, albeit at the cost of varietal fruit flavours. In areas such as Burgundy and

Champagne, where malic acid levels are naturally high, malolactic fermentation is encouraged as a matter of course. In warmer climates, where producers often need all the malic acidity they can get, it is employed sparingly or prevented, usually by adding sulphur dioxide. New World producers who allow their Chardonnay to go through malolactic fermentation frequently add tartaric acid to correct the wine's balance.

Wines tend to be more stable after malolactic fermentation. If malolactic is not induced, there is risk of it occurring in bottle, especially if the wine has not been adequately filtered.

THE OAK FACTOR

The use of oak – whether as barrels or oak chips – is so widely practised in the making of Chardonnay that, for many people, the two flavours are virtually indistinguishable. As use of barrels, particularly French oak barrels, has grown in fashion, it has become increasingly difficult to tell one expensive Chardonnay from another. Barrels from 'super coopers' like François Frères, Nadalié, Demptos and Sirugue are ubiquitous. Each cooper has a house style and frequently this flavour is more prominent than the wine itself. If anything, cheaper (and generally coarser) American oak, which is used in Bulgaria, the south of France, Chile, Rioja and sometimes Australia, tends to be even more assertive. Significantly, all the world's leading Chardonnays are fermented in French oak.

Chardonnay is certainly well-suited to oak ageing – it is naturally high in extract and sugar (and therefore alcohol), and its structure and flavours are usually enhanced by barrel-maturation. Fermentation and ageing a Chardonnay in barrel allows oak, wine and oxygen (which enters through the pores in the wood) to interact in a more or less felicitous fashion, subjecting the wine to gentle, and usually beneficial, oxidation.

If the barrels are new or nearly new, they will also impart an oaky flavour to the wine. As a rule, the heavier the toast (or charring) on the inside of the barrel, the more pronounced the oak character. The origin of the oak (whether it be from the forests of Limousin, Tronçais, Allier or the Vosges) also has an effect on the character of the finished wine. The effect of new Limousin barrels, for example, is generally disliked by Chardonnay producers, as it tends to make the wine bitter. Most winemakers favour barrels from central France (Tronçais, Nevers and Allier).

Use of new oak is more prevalent in the New World than the Old, although the fashion may well have started in Burgundy. According to the Burgundian winemaker Thierry Matrot, it all began in the early sixties when, finding their wines difficult to sell, vignerons in the village of Meursault decided to clean up their act. Many customers complained of a lack of hygiene in the wines, and the first thing the growers decided to replace was their barrels. Inevitably, some of them overdid it, producing wines where oak flavours overwhelmed the fruit. Coincidentally, it was around this time that American winemakers started coming to France, and the style they chose to copy was not, strictly speaking, Burgundian. 'They saw the new oak here,' says Matrot, 'and they thought, "We can't make Meursault in the States, but we can buy new barrels".'

Whether this story is apocryphal or not, unoaked Chardonnay is rare these days. The best places to start looking are Italy, Bulgaria, Austria, Chablis, the Mâconnais, Champagne and the Loire Valley. In Australia, the United States and the Côte d'Or it would be like hunting for an ant in a bowl of caviare.

There are several different ways of using oak. The winemaker can ferment the Chardonnay entirely (or partly) in oak, ferment it in stainless steel and age it in oak, or employ a combination of these. Much of the pioneering work on the effect of oak was done by Robert Mondavi in California. The age and origin of a barrel, he demonstrated, can have a considerable effect on the style of a wine. After five vintages, for example, a barrel ceases to impart an oaky flavour to the wine.

To make cheaper Chardonnays, but keep a whiff of oak, producers often add oak chips during fermentation. Rather like skin contact, this can be effective in the short term, but is rarely satisfactory over a longer period of time. Other winemakers like to combine the freshness of unoaked Chardonnay with a proportion of barrel-fermented wine. To my mind, though, the best Chardonnays are fermented entirely in tight-grained oak from the central forests of France. Oak-aged Chardonnays never seem to taste as good.

The key to barrel-fermentation is achieving a balance between the oak and the wine. If the wine is full-flavoured and needs new oak, so be it. If it isn't big enough to deal with it, use older barrels. Oak should be a flavour component, not the flavour itself. As the American barrel-broker Mel Knox once said: 'There is no such thing as an over-oaked wine, just under-wined oak.'

BÂTONNAGE/LEES CONTACT

Sometimes described as a 'dirty French' technique, lees contact (where the wine is left on its fermentation lees) is now widely practised outside Burgundy. As long as the lees remain 'sweet', that is, clean, they can be left in contact with the wine for as long as two years. The lees have two main functions: they reduce the risk of oxidation, which in turn cuts down on the need for sulphur dioxide; and they give the wine a creamy, almost nutty flavour. Such a flavour is more pronounced in barrel-fermented wines, where a smaller volume of wine is left in contact with the lees. Some producers also stir their lees, in order to keep them in suspension. This technique, known as *bâtonnage*, is more common in Burgundy than the New World.

RACKING, FINING, FILTRATION AND MATURATION

Most of the top Burgundian winemakers believe in disturbing their Chardonnay as little as possible while it matures in barrel. They will rack the wine (transfer it to clean barrels or tanks) when necessary, fine it (clarify it), top up their barrels and (sometimes) filter it before bottling, but that's about all. Commercial Old World Chardonnays tend to be treated a little more rigorously. This makes them cleaner, but generally less interesting.

As a rule, the longer a quality wine is aged the more complexity and richness it develops. The temperature and humidity of each cellar will affect the rate at which wine matures. For unoaked Chardonnays, most of which are bottled within three months of the harvest, this is a less important consideration. Few New World producers age their wines in barrel for as long as the best Burgundian growers, but even in technology-obsessed places like California and Australia, there is an encouraging trend towards extended lees contact. Some wineries have even stopped filtering their Chardonnays.

Chardonnay in the Cellar

Like most white wines, the majority of Chardonnays are not built to last. Where longevity is concerned, everything depends on the structure of the wine. If your cellar is packed with Chardonnays from the Alto Adige and the Barossa Valley, you'd be well-advised to drink them sooner rather than later. On the other hand, if it's full of white Burgundies and cool-climate Chardonnays from the New World, you should resist the temptation to drink the wines too young.

The life expectancy of a basic, unoaked Chardonnay, with the honorary exceptions of Chablis and Champagne, is short. Chardonnays from northern Italy, Spain, the Loire, the Ardèche, Savoie and Eastern Europe generally fall into this category. Most of these wines need six months in bottle to reach their peak, but will not improve with age; some of them may start to tire after a year or two.

It is often said that New World Chardonnays do not age well. This is certainly true of warm-climate wines from California, South Africa, Chile, New Zealand and Australia that lack natural acidity. A Chardonnay with pronounced oak character may take a year or two to marry in bottle, but it is still best drunk before its fifth birthday. (Remember that Southern Hemisphere Chardonnays are actually six months older than Northern Hemisphere wines from the same vintage.) After that, the wine will probably start to taste heavy and alcoholic. Wines that have been judiciously acidified (by adding tartaric acid during fermentation) may hold up slightly better in bottle. New World Chardonnays that have undergone malolactic fermentation do not necessarily age less well, though this is often the case.

Cool-climate viticulture is a comparatively recent development in the New World, so the question of the ageing potential of wines from areas such as Tasmania, Russian River Valley, Oregon, Marlborough and Carneros is still in its infancy. (The problem with viticultural and oenological research is that you only have one, or possibly two, harvests a year to play with.) My own empirical studies are inconclusive. Much depends on the style of the individual producer, not to mention the vintage. I have had Chardonnays from Carneros that were still sprightly after a decade in bottle, just as I have tasted wines that were tiring after three years.

The best candidates for your cellar are also, sadly, the most expensive. The leading Chardonnays from Corton Charlemagne, Meursault, Puligny- and Chassagne-Montrachet will certainly reward patience. Once again, it pays to know your producer and, more important, his attitude to quality. How high are his yields? Where are his vines? Does he filter his wines? If you find a producer whose wines you enjoy, stick with him.

Not all white Burgundy ages gracefully. The wines of the Côte Chalonnaise and the Mâconnais (with the possible exception of Pouilly-Fuissé) should be drunk in the first two to five years. For basic Mâcon Blanc, that would be an overestimate. Village-level Chardonnay from the Côte de Beaune, on the other hand, can stand as much as eight years in bottle, depending on the vintage. By and large, the less prestigious the village, the sooner you should drink the wine. The top Premiers Crus and Grands Crus are something else altogether. Provided a wine has been well stored, there is no reason why it shouldn't last for thirty years or more. When you drink it depends on how you like your Chardonnay. The older it gets, the more it will develop that sweet, honeyed, almost rancio character.

Blanc de Blancs Champagnes can also develop great complexity after a decade or so in bottle. In my experience, they do not age quite as successfully as Pinot Noir-based Champagne, but their natural acidity keeps them fresh and elegant. With age, the wines take on a creamy, almost nutty flavour. Taittinger's Comtes de Champagne, Dom Ruinart and Krug's Clos du Mesnil are your best bets for the long haul.

Chardonnay with Food

In a decade when alcohol consumption assumed the status of a minor perversion in the USA, the only way to escape neo-Prohibitionist suspicion was to drink wine with a meal. Hence the curious term 'food wine' – a tautology if ever there was one. With the possible exception of sparkling wines and Champagne, which are best drunk as aperitifs, there are very few wines that do not partner at least one or two dishes. It might not be easy to come up with the perfect foil for Thunderbird, but there must be something that would work.

Food-and-wine combinations are a modern obsession. There are a few basic rules – subtle dishes are easily overwhelmed by head-banger wines, oaked wines demand robust flavours – but otherwise, personal preferences are more important than fashion. With Chardonnay, particularly dry Chardonnay, you are on safe ground. The wine goes well with almost everything, including 'difficult' dishes like asparagus.

There is nothing worse than someone who is afraid to experiment: the most exciting partnerships are frequently born of serendipity. The received wisdom is that similar flavours are compatible – in other words, a buttery wine will work with a hollandaise sauce. This is true, but only up to a point – such combinations are safe but rarely exciting.

As far as Chardonnay is concerned, here are a few guidelines:

Blanc de Blancs Champagne or Sparkling Wine. Probably best as an aperitif, particularly if the wine is young and acid. Make an exception for oysters. Older wines can work with light and simple fish or white-meat dishes. A sparkling wine is a refreshing way to cut through a certain amount of oiliness, but is rarely successful with strong or spicy flavours.

Unoaked, Light-bodied Chardonnay. Good aperitif material. Also very drinkable with a wide range of dishes because of its relative neutrality. Try it with chicken, fish, cream or butter sauces, savoury pies and vegetables. A safe bet, but don't overwhelm the subtle flavours of a good wine.

Oaked, Light- to Medium-bodied Chardonnay. Less suitable as an aperitif. Make the most of the oaky, more robust fruit by matching it imaginatively with food. Smoked salmon works well, complementing the toasty oak character. Full-flavoured white meats, such as turkey or pork, shellfish and creamy pasta dishes all have the right intensity to balance the wine.

Oaked, Medium- to Full-bodied Chardonnay. This is your chance to throw out the precept that white wine never goes with red meats. Some Chardonnays do. Big, oaky wines need bold, richly flavoured dishes. Match Burgundian Chardonnays with juicy meats like game, steak or pork. New World Chardonnays, with their sweeter tropical-fruit flavours, combine well with creamy curries, red meats and barbecue sauces.

SERVING TEMPERATURE

Most white wine is served too cold. Chilled wines are fine, ice lollies are not. Cooling a wine to the point of frost-bite will dull its flavours and numb your taste buds. Champagnes and crisp, light-bodied Chardonnays, such as those from north-east Italy or the Loire, should be served at a cooler temperature than richer wines from Burgundy or the New World, but don't overdo it. The ideal temperature range for Chardonnay is between 12 and 18 °C.

GAZETTEER

KEY TO RATING SYSTEM

Quality

    indifferent

    average

    good

    very good

    outstanding

Price

★   cheap

★★   average

★★★   expensive

★★★★   very expensive

★★★★★   luxury

ARGENTINA

| Total vineyard area: 855,000 acres
| Area planted to Chardonnay: 3,000 acres

Argentina is an enigma to most winedrinkers. It is the world's sixth largest producer, dwarfing the output of neighbouring Chile, but consumes so much of its own wine that comparatively little is exported. A minor contretemps with the United Kingdom in 1982, memorably described by the writer Jorge Luis Borges as a case of 'two bald men fighting over a comb', didn't help, but Argentina is still some way behind the rest of the New World, especially where Chardonnay is concerned. Argentina's greatest successes to date have been with red wines. Its most interesting white variety is not Chardonnay but Torrontes, a mutation of the Spanish Malvasia, which can make flavoursome dry whites. Most of Argentina's Chardonnay is planted in Mendoza, the region which accounts for 75 per cent of the country's *vino*, although there are a few acres 500 miles to the south, in northern Patagonia. (see map on p. 94).

As in Chile's central valley, it would be impossible to make wine in the heat of Mendoza without irrigation from the Andes. Yields are high and as a result many of the Chardonnays lack concentration. It is difficult to discern an Argentine style – some wines are fermented in *raulí*, or beechwood, some in stainless steel and a couple in oak barrels. There is also a bit of fizz – Moët & Chandon and Mumm both make local sparkling wines which include Chardonnay in the blend.

The best Chardonnays are made by Peñaflor, Argentina's largest winery, and marketed under the Trapiche label. Peñaflor have been experimenting with different levels of barrel toast and origin – Allier, Nevers, Tronçais and Limousin – and make two styles of Chardonnay. At the moment, the unoaked

Andean Vineyards is better than the oak-aged Trapiche
Reserve, first made in 1990, but both wines demonstrate that
the grape has good potential in Argentina.

Best producers: La Agricola, Finca Flichman, José Orfila,
Pascual Toso, Roblevina, Suter, Trapiche/Peñaflor, Viña
Esmeralda

AUSTRALIA

Total vineyard area: 149,000 acres

Area planted to Chardonnay: 3,800 acres (New South Wales); 2,000 acres (Victoria); 5,400 acres (South Australia); 520 acres (Western Australia); 170 acres (Tasmania); 25 acres (Queensland)

Despite its modern, hi-tech image, Australian wine has a surprisingly long and varied history. The first vines were planted down under by First Fleet convicts, at Sydney's Farm Cove, as far back as 1788. Captain Arthur Phillip brought the original cuttings from Rio de Janeiro and the Cape, so it is highly unlikely that Chardonnay was among them. These vines, like most of the colony's initial attempts at agriculture, were unsuccessful. Subsequent plantings, away from the subtropical conditions around Sydney, were more propitious, and from these shaky beginnings the Australian wine industry began to expand – more, it must be said, by accident than by any great viticultural foresight.

Chardonnay probably arrived in Australia some forty years after the First Fleet. The cuttings that James Busby, the so-called father of Australian wine, brought back from a trip to Europe included something called Pineau Chardonnay, allegedly from Clos de Vougeot. What happened to these early vines is unclear, although Chardonnay does not appear to have been regarded as a particularly suitable variety for the (principally warm-climate) vineyards which developed over the next century. (It is sometimes forgotten that not until 1971 did the production – and presumably consumption – of table wine surpass that of fortified wine in Australia.)

For most of the next century, Chardonnay went underground. Officially, it did not pop up again until the early 1960s,

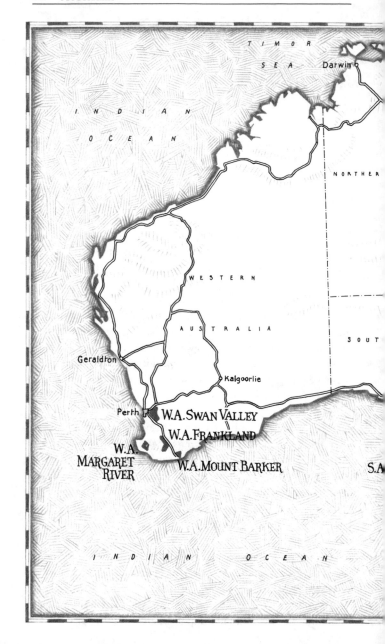

GULF OF CARPENTARIA

CORAL SEA

RRITORY

QUEENSLAND

PACIFIC OCEAN

USTRALIA

Brisbane

NEW SOUTH WALES

N.S.W MUDGEE
N.S.W.HUNTER VALLEY

S.A.
ARE VALLEY

S.A.RIVERLAND
N.S.W.MILDURA
S.A.RIVERINA

Adelaide
Newcastle
Sydney

S.A.
BAROSSA VALLEY

Wollongong

ERN VALES
LAREN VALE
ORNE CREEK

VICTORIA

V.GREAT WESTERN
YARRA VALLEY

A.COONAWARRA

Melbourne

TASMAN SEA

LAUNCESTON

TASMANIA

Hobart

when it was identified in Alf Kurtz's Mudgee vineyard by an understandably excited French ampelographer, Dr Denis Boubals. The grape, known as White Pinot, had arrived *chez* Kurtz by a circuitous route. According to Dr Phillip Norrie, in his book *Vineyards of Sydney*, this small patch of pre-phylloxera Chardonnay can be traced directly to Busby's own Kirkton vineyard in the Hunter Valley. From Kirkton, cuttings found their way to Ambrose Laraghy's Kaluna vineyard, thence to Bill Roth's Westcourt vineyard and, finally, to Alf Kurtz.

Boubals shared his discovery with the Australian viticulturist Bob Hollick, who subsequently secured cuttings from Kurtz and sold them to Mildara, among others. Even so, Chardonnay took some years to develop any sort of following in Australia. By 1968, for example, there was still no Chardonnay in South Australia, the state which now accounts for nearly half of Australia's plantings of the variety.

The first commercially produced Australian Chardonnay was made by Murray Tyrrell in the Hunter Valley, and was to have a huge influence on the grape's future development. 'White Burgundy' and 'Chablis' had been popular for some time before the release of Vat 47, but these two styles rarely contained Chardonnay. To this day, an Australian 'Chablis' is far more likely to be made from Sémillon than Chardonnay.

By the mid-eighties, Chardonnay had become the country's most sought-after grape variety, with substantial vineyards in virtually every viticultural region in Australia. It had been a truly remarkable rise to prominence: ten years earlier there were fewer than five hundred acres. It is no exaggeration to say that Chardonnay was instrumental in establishing Australia's reputation as a wine-producing country. Australia may have more characterful, indigenous styles – its Shirazes, Sémillons and Liqueur Muscats, for instance – but it was Chardonnay from down under which really captured the attention of the wine-drinking consumer.

Perhaps Australia's greatest success lies in its ability to produce well-made, quaffable Chardonnay at inexpensive prices – something that California has never quite managed, despite its greater production (Gallo alone makes nearly twice as much wine as the whole of Australia). Wines like Seppelts' Queen Adelaide, Orlando's RF and Lindemans' Bin 65 are among the best possible introductions to the grape.

Land is cheaper in Australia, and so are production costs, but this is far from being the whole story. Australia leads the world in wine technology, and this, as much as anything, has enabled it to process large quantities of good-to-excellent wine. Techniques like night harvesting and cool-temperature fermentation are practised almost as a matter of course. As Dr Terry Lee, director of the Australian Wine Research Institute, comments: 'We have the technology to overcome very warm climates, and we're the best at understanding the components responsible for varietal flavour.'

The production of Chardonnay in Australia is still dominated by warm-climate styles from the Riverland, Sunrasia, Murrumbidgee Irrigation Area, and the Hunter and Barossa Valleys. These wines are usually at the ripe, come-and-get-it end of the scale, emphasizing flavours of sweet oak and tropical fruits. As Robin Day, chief wine-maker at Orlando puts it: 'Chardonnay produces high-quality wine from these areas because it ripens before the hottest part of the summer. It is by far the best warm-area varietal we have and can be relied upon to produce perfectly acceptable wines each vintage at a moderate cost. These are the backbone of Chardonnay consumption within Australia.'

This is not to say that all warm-climate Chardonnays are basic quaffing wines, although many are made for immediate consumption. Some of them, particularly those from producers like Krondorf, Penfolds, Rosemount and Tyrrell can be fantastic wines in their own right, with rich, buttery concentration, great fruit and surprising longevity. For many consumers, this style is the essence of Australian Chardonnay, and winemakers, they feel, should seek to refine it at their peril.

Such people are worried by a second, more elegant style of Chardonnay which has begun to emerge from cool-climate areas like the Yarra Valley, Mornington Peninsula, Mount Barker, Adelaide Hills, High Eden Valley, Tasmania, Geelong and Padthaway. These wines are often closer in flavour to white

Burgundy than to the Barossa and, to my palate, this is not necessarily a bad thing. Chardonnays which have been adjusted with citric or tartaric acid, and fermented with oak chips, are superficially appealing but can get tiring after more than one glass. If I have a criticism to make of much Australian Chardonnay, it is one of overexuberance, of too much flavour. In general, though, even warm-climate Chardonnays have developed greater subtlety in the last few years. The oak is less blatant, the fruit a little more restrained.

The hallmark of top-notch Chardonnay is balance, and cooler-climate grapes make more complex, nuanced wines, especially when enhanced by lees contact, barrel-fermentation and partial or (in a few cases) total malolactic fermentation. They may not have the power of a steamroller Chardonnay, but what they lack in impact they make up for in finesse. In Australia, the best of these wines (names like Piper's Brook, Dromana, Mountadam, Coldstream Hills, St Hubert's, Plantagenet, Cullen's and Leeuwin spring to mind) are challenging (and sometimes beating) the top French and California Chardonnays.

Cooler climates have also given rise to a new generation of Chardonnay/Pinot Noir sparkling wines which have the potential to compete with Champagne. The Australian investments of Bollinger, Moët & Chandon and Louis Roederer serve to underline the potential. Names to look out for are Petaluma, Seppelt, Yalumba, Yellowglen, Domaine Chandon, Heemskerk and Seaview.

As far as Chardonnay is concerned, it is unwise to generalize about regional identity in Australia – and for two main reasons. The first is that many of the big wineries blend wines from several sources. For example, nearly three-quarters of the wine produced in the Barossa Valley is not made from Barossa fruit. The second is that some areas have not yet had time to develop a recognizable style of their own. It is easy to forget that, despite its historical pedigree, the modern Australian wine industry is still in its adolescence.

Nevertheless, regional differences do exist. As Andrew Pirie of Piper's Brook puts it: 'In the next few years, people will see that Australia has a diverse set of regions that can produce a full spectrum of wine styles.' Two areas in particular produce very distinctive Chardonnays: McLaren Vale (in the peachy/buttery camp) and Padthaway (in a crisper grapefruit-and-lemon style). But regions such as the Yarra Valley, the Hunter, Margaret River and Tasmania also have their own discernible Chardonnay character.

Grapes from areas like Padthaway and McLaren Vale are frequently used as part of a blend. This sort of assemblage typifies the Australian approach to rules and regulations. There are appellation systems of sorts in Mudgee, the Hunter and Tasmania, but otherwise, anything goes. The Australian way is extremely practical. If a Hunter Chardonnay tastes better blended with one from Padthaway, so be it. This approach is reflected in the vineyard and the winery. If a vine needs irrigating, Australians irrigate. If a wine needs acidifying, they acidify. Nevertheless, as in California, there is a growing concentration on vineyard location and a realization that technology alone cannot make great wine. This explains the gradual move away from traditional areas like the Barossa, Swan and Hunter Valleys (though these regions still produce a lot of wine) to sites which are more suited to premium Chardonnay. Areas like Padthaway, Mount Barker, Coonawarra, the Yarra Valley and Mornington Peninsula (the leading cool-climate vineyards as far as Chardonnay is concerned) are already extremely promising. But as these vines mature, I think the Chardonnays they produce will increasingly be numbered among the most exciting in the world.

At a less rarefied, but arguably more important, level Australia will continue to turn out inexpensive, technically proficient Chardonnay. As the mass of new plantings made in the late eighties come on stream, prices may fall even further. Don't be surprised in the next few years if Chardonnay turns up as bag-in-box wines – what John Brown Senior of Brown Brothers calls Château Cardboard. Could anything be more democratic?

*

Best producers: Bannockburn* (VA), Jim Barry (SA), Berri
  Renmano* (SA), Best's (VA), Wolf Blass (SA),
Briagdong Estate Brown Brothers* (VA), Grant Burge
  (SA), Cape Mentelle* (WA), Chittering* (WA),
  Coldstream Hills* (VA), Cullen's* (WA), De Bortoli
  (VA), Diamond Valley (VA), Dromana* (VA),
  Giaconda* (VA), Jeffrey Grosset (SA), Thomas Hardy*
  (SA), Heemskerk (TA), Houghton* (WA), Krondorf*
  (SA), Lake's Folly* (NSW), Leasingham* (SA),
  Leeuwin* (WA), Peter Lehmann (SA), Lindemans*
  (NSW), McWilliam's* (NSW), Geoff Merrill (SA),
  Mitchelton (VA), Moss Wood* (WA), Mountadam*
  (SA), Mountarrow* (NSW), Mount Mary (VA),
  Orlando* (SA), Penfolds* (SA), Petaluma* (SA),
  Petersons* (NSW), Pipers Brook* (TA), Plantagenet*
  (WA), Rosemount* (NSW), Rothbury* (NSW), St
  Huberts* (VA), Saltram* (SA), Sandalford (WA),
  Seppelt's* (SA), Shaw and Smith, Tarrawarra (VA),
  Tisdall* (VA), Tyrrell's* (NSW), Wynn's* (SA),
  Chateau Xanadu (WA), Yalumba* (SA), Yarra Yering*
  (VA), Yellowglen (VA), Yeringberg* (VA)

Australian Vintages

The following notes are intended as a guide only. Australia's
vineyards cover a vast area – roughly the size of Europe – so
general conclusions are difficult to draw.

1991. Generally a warm, dry, early vintage. First indications
were that this could be a classic Chardonnay year, with ideal
weather conditions in many regions. The wines tend to be ripe,
concentrated and full-bodied, if a little short of natural acidity,
but this is a worthy successor to 1990.

1990. A late, slow-ripening year. Good, balanced Chardonnays were produced in most regions. Some areas (particularly McLaren Vale, the Barossa, the Yarra Valley, Margaret River and North-Eastern Victoria) made exceptional wines. Not a great year in the Hunter or Mudgee.

1989. A mixed year. A mild, wet winter, followed by a warm, humid summer in many areas, led to an early harvest. Rain during vintage caused problems in Mudgee, the Lower Hunter, Milawa and the Yarra Valley. Margaret River, Geelong, the Upper Hunter, Clare and Coonawarra produced good, if not outstanding, Chardonnays.

1988. An above average vintage for Chardonnay, but generally less successful than 1987 or 1986. Hail (in the Barossa), poor fruit set (in the Yarra) and frost (in Coonawarra) reduced the size of the crop, while rain made the harvest difficult in the Hunter. The best Chardonnays were made in McLaren Vale, Mudgee, Tasmania and the Mornington Peninsula.

1987. Generally an excellent vintage, with lower-than-average yields in the Barossa, Geelong and McLaren Vale, and good-quality fruit. The summer was one of the coolest on record, producing Chardonnays with elegance, intense flavours and fresh acidity. Some areas, such as the Hunter and Swan Valleys, made even better wines than in 1986. The Yarra Valley and Mount Barker were notable exceptions.

1986. An extremely good vintage for white wines, possibly the best of the decade in South Australia and New South Wales, producing intensely flavoured, high-quality Chardonnay all over Australia. A cool growing season, with a wet spring and a long, dry summer, produced balanced wines, many of which are still drinking well.

BANNOCKBURN

Midland Highway, Geelong, E2311 Victoria

Chardonnay vineyard: 13 acres

Production of Chardonnay: 30,000 bottles (Bannockburn);
6,000 (Clyde Park)

Labels: Bannockburn; Clyde Park

Quality: 🍇🍇🍇/🍇🍇🍇🍇   Price: ★★★

Best vintages: 1986, 1988, 1989

Melbourne businessman Stuart Hooper planted his first vines in the tiny one-kangaroo town of Bannockburn, 25 km north-west of Geelong, as long ago as 1974, but has supplemented them with further vineyards since, maintaining an impressive level of investment. The winery produced its first varietal bottlings in 1978, but delayed release until 1981. Bannockburn like to sell their wines with at least two years' bottle age.

Today, this modern, well-appointed operation produces an impressive range of wines (Chardonnay, Pinot Noir, Cabernet Sauvignon, Shiraz and Rhine Riesling) from more than 40 acres, as well as a string of lesser varietals under the Clyde Park label. The wines are made by Gary Farr, who joined Bannockburn in the late seventies and owns Clyde Park in his own right.

A self-confessed Burgundophile, Farr has worked several vintages at Domaine Dujac in Morey-Saint-Denis. The experience has served him well – in the cool, variable climate of Geelong, his success with Chardonnay and Pinot Noir has been impressive. Yields are very low here, even with the support of irrigation (in dry years). The vines are planted on rich brown and black volcanic loam over limestone – another Burgundian parallel.

Limestone or no limestone, Bannockburn's complex Chardonnay is certainly made in a consciously Burgundian style. It is fermented in one-third new French *barriques*, goes through at least 25 per cent malolactic fermentation and spends as much as a year on its lees. The wine can be quite restrained in its youth as, by Australian standards, Bannockburn's

Chardonnays are built to last. My only complaint is that, in some vintages, the wines can seem too alcoholic.

BERRI RENMANO

PO Box 238, Berri, 5343 South Australia

Production of Chardonnay: 600,000 bottles

Labels: Lauriston; Chairman's Selection

Quality: 🍇/🍇🍇   Price: ★/★★

Best vintages: 1987, 1988, 1990

Berri Renmano's Chardonnays were once described as Dolly Parton wines: a big, blowsy, up-front style with bags of attractive tropical fruit flavours. This massive cooperative in the irrigated Riverland region, which accounts for between 10 and 15 per cent of Australia's entire production, draws fruit from a total of 600 members and produces remarkably consistent, if undemanding, Chardonnays. Most of the vines are young, and the majority of the fruit is machine-picked at night to preserve acidity and keep the fruit cool. The first half of the fermentation is done in stainless steel; the latter half in wooden hogsheads with some lees contact. The wines have some oak character, considerable body and a touch of residual sweetness. Berri's best Chardonnays are bottled under the Lauriston label.

BROWN BROTHERS

Glenrowan–Myrtelford Road, Milawa, 3678 Victoria

Chardonnay vineyard: 105 acres

Production of Chardonnay: not released

Labels: Whitlands; Family Reserve; King Valley; Koombahla (Australia only)

Quality: 🍇–🍇🍇🍇   Price: ★★/★★★

Best vintages: 1985, 1988, 1989, 1990

This substantial family-owned winery, which recently celebrated its 100th anniversary, produces a bewildering range of more than thirty varietal and blended releases, including everything from Chenin Blanc to Tarrango. It is a credit to the Browns – father John and three sons Ross, Peter and John Junior – that the quality of their wines is consistently good.

Until 1967, described by John Senior as a 'wipe-out vintage', most of Brown Brothers' fruit came from its home base in Milawa. Fearing a repeat of that year's devastating frosts, Brown began to plant vineyards in other areas of Victoria. The Browns now own vines in the King Valley, Mystic Park, Hurdle Creek and (most excitingly) Whitlands, but supplement their own production with purchased fruit, which accounts for around 75 per cent of their needs.

There are three main Chardonnays here, all of which spend some time in a combination of French, American and German oak. The King Valley is the most commercial of the trio, with a fruity, boiled-sweets and lychee character almost reminiscent of Gewürztraminer. The Whitlands Chardonnay, first released in 1987, is more interesting. This vineyard, situated in the cool foothills of the Victorian Alps at a height of nearly 800 metres, produces grapes with excellent balance. The 1987 and 1988 vintages were both rich in promise, although I find the latter a little over-oaked.

The Browns' top Chardonnay, at least as far as they are concerned, is their Family Reserve. This is usually produced in a riper, rather alcoholic style and is entirely barrel-fermented. For my money, it lacks the finesse of the Whitlands wine. As the emphasis has moved to cooler vineyard sites in the King Valley and at Whitlands, Brown Brothers' Chardonnays have improved considerably. The establishment of a Kindergarten Winery, designed to handle small, experimental lots, in 1989, should stimulate further developments.

CAPE MENTELLE

Wallcliffe Road, Margaret River, 6285 Western Australia

Chardonnay vineyard: 10 acres

Production of Chardonnay: 26,000 bottles

Quality: 🍇🍇/🍇🍇🍇   Price: ★★★

Best vintages: 1988, 1990

Cape Mentelle is the home of David Hohnen, one of Australia's most iconoclastic wine-makers. Hohnen has pulled off the rare feat of making award-winning wines in New Zealand (at Cloudy Bay) and in Australia. Cloudy Bay is better known for its whites, while at Cape Mentelle it is the red wines (Cabernet Sauvignon, Shiraz and Zinfandel) which have won most of the praise.

Chardonnay is a comparatively minor variety at Cape Mentelle, but David Hohnen's magic touch has produced some good, broad pineappley wines. The Cape Mentelle Chardonnay is released a year before the Cloudy Bay Chardonnay, and tends to be a much more forward easy-drinking style. The wine is fermented for two to three days in stainless steel then racked to barrels, where it remains for six to nine months. About 25 per cent of the wine goes through malolactic fermentation.

The 1988 and 1990 Cape Mentelle Chardonnays are both ripe, full-throated, alcoholic wines that should be drunk within three to five years. Enjoyable certainly, but I prefer the finer acid balance of the Cloudy Bay wine.

CHITTERING ESTATE

Chittering Valley Road, Lower Chittering, 6084 Western Australia

Chardonnay vineyard: 24 acres

Production of Chardonnay: 45,000 bottles

Quality: 🍇🍇🍇   Price: ★★★

Best vintages: 1987, 1988, 1989, 1990

A self-confessed GUAVA (Growing Up And Very Ambitious), Steven Schapera is the appealing, street-wise owner of Chittering Estate, which must be among the world's most picturesque wineries. These are the highest vineyards in Western Australia: the Gatsby-esque homestead, with its sculpted lawns and gambolling boxer dogs, sits incongruously amid the wild Darling Ranges, 40 km to the north-east of the Swan Valley.

The money behind the venture, which produced its first wines in 1987, comes from two fishing-industry families, the Schaperas of South Africa and the Kailis of Australia. Steven Schapera and partner George Kailis decided to plant vines in the cooler Chittering Valley, on the site of an old sheep station, following the advice of a well-known viticultural consultant. Chittering is the only winery in the valley.

In the meantime, Schapera took himself off to California to study oenology. Appropriately, his wine-making is 'essentially Californian' and most of the winery's sales are to the United States.

Chittering produces three wines: a red Bordeaux blend of Cabernet Sauvignon and Merlot and white and a complex, toasty Chardonnay that eschews the fat, buttery wines of the Swan Valley. The style is evolving here, but the Chardonnay is already very good. The wines are barrel-fermented, spend nine months on gross lees and are stirred fortnightly. Schapera is an intelligent, questioning wine-maker and he is currently experimenting with different types and ages of oak, trellising and increased malolactic fermentation. A winery to watch.

COLDSTREAM HILLS

Lot 6, Maddens Lane, Coldstream, Yarra Valley, 3770 Victoria

Chardonnay vineyard: 15 acres
Production of Chardonnay: 60,000 bottles
Labels: Coldstream Hills; Reserve; Steels Range
Quality: 🍇_🍇🍇🍇🍇   Price: ★★/★★★
Best vintages: 1986, 1988, 1990, 1991

James Halliday is a phenomenon, seemingly fuelled by some prodigious, almost supernatural, source of energy. He was still a young Sydney solicitor when he founded Brokenwood, one of the Hunter Valley's leading small wineries, with two colleagues back in 1970. But until he gave up practising law, in 1988, he somehow managed to juggle the demands of a full-time job with an expanding career in wine – as a taster, writer, show judge and hands-on wine-maker. Halliday has never conceded that there are only twenty-four hours in a day.

It was while researching a book on the wines of Victoria that Halliday first visited the Yarra Valley, surely the most beautiful wine region in Australia. 'I decided that the Yarra was the place I would retire to,' he says. Halliday came to the Yarra sooner than he anticipated. His law firm wanted to set up an office in Melbourne and he jumped at the chance to move to Victoria.

In 1985, Halliday and his wife, Suzanne, bought a piece of land in the Yarra Valley and planted it with vines. That year he purchased grapes from local Yarra growers and made a few hundred cases of wine at Elgee Park in the Mornington Peninsula. In 1986 and 1987 Halliday vinified his wines, again with bought-in fruit, at Yarra Ridge, but by 1988 his own custom-built winery was ready for occupation. The original vineyard was supplemented with further plantings, financed by a public share issue, in 1988.

Coldstream Hills continues to buy in two-thirds of its needs, even though its steep, densely planted vineyards are now approaching full production. Halliday says he likes the greater flexibility this affords him. He makes three different Chardonnays: a regular Coldstream Hills release, a Coldstream Hills Reserve and a second label, called Steels Chardonnay. Until 1990, Halliday's Chardonnays were vineyard-designated, with the names of one or more vineyards listed on the label, but this rather confusing practice has now been dropped. As a rule, the regular Chardonnay is released six months before the Reserve, and tends to be a little less complex, while the Steels Chardonnay is the lightest, least oaky of the trio.

Halliday's approach to the variety emphasizes careful handling and lean wine-making: juice clarification, cold settling and only a small percentage of grape solids during fermentation. He combines 10–15 per cent stainless steel with fermentation in French, mainly Vosges, barrels. Malolactic is used sparingly.

Coldstream's Chardonnays have improved with each vintage, but have yet to fulfil their full potential. Initially high prices have been moderated, and the 1990s were undoubtedly the best Coldstream Chardonnays yet. As one would expect from James Halliday, the Reserve and Coldstream Hills Chardonnays are subtle, elegant wines that take a year or so to settle into their stride. They are not built for the long haul, but should drink well for three to five years. As Halliday's own vineyards mature, expect further improvements.

CULLEN'S

Caves Road, Cowaramup, 6284 Western Australia

Chardonnay vineyard: 15 acres

Production of Chardonnay: 15,000 bottles

Quality: 🍇🍇🍇🍇   Price: ★★★

Best vintages: 1985, 1987, 1988, 1989, 1990

Cullen's is a remarkable family winery. It's a relaxed, friendly place where women are very much in charge: Di and Vanya run the winery and Shelley Cullen the cellar-door sales operation. It was set up in the late sixties by Kevin Cullen – a local doctor and aspiring television scriptwriter – but he leaves most of the day-to-day decisions to his wife and two daughters.

Di Cullen is living proof that great wine-makers can be self-taught. She made the wine at Cullen's from 1974 to 1988, despite the fact that she had no formal oenological training, and was voted Australasian wine-maker of the year in 1987. Today the wine-making is done mainly by Vanya, who studied in California and France before returning to Margaret River. She is already making her presence felt, introducing, among other things, vertical trellising for Chardonnay vines in order to increase yields.

Cullen's produces a highly individual range of wines, which includes a Chardonnay, a Sauvignon Blanc and a Spätlese Cabernet Sauvignon. The style of the Chardonnay emphasizes honeyed elegance rather than oak and tropical fruit, although the wine sees a high percentage of new barrels. Cullen Chardonnays do not go through malolactic fermentation, but spend up to twelve months on their lees. The Chardonnay usually takes at least four years to come together, but is usually good, and sometimes spectacular, when it does.

DROMANA ESTATE

Harrison's Road, Dromana, 3936 Victoria

Chardonnay vineyard: 2.75 acres

Production of Chardonnay: Dromana, 8,000 bottles;
  Schinus Molle, 30,000 bottles

Labels: Dromana; Schinus Molle

Quality: 🍇🍇🍇_🍇🍇🍇🍇🍇   Price: ★★/★★★

Best vintages: 1988, 1990, 1991

Garry Crittenden is a trained horticulturist who, in his own words, 'drank my way to the top of the Australian tree and then discovered France'. In the late seventies, he tasted a number of bottles from Tasmania, and was convinced that Australia could produce wines which combined elegance with good fruit flavours.

The area he chose for his initial vineyard was the cool Mornington Peninsula, although he has subsequently set up a thirty-acre estate in Tasmania. As well as running Dromana

Estate, Crittenden works as a viticultural consultant to other producers in Victoria, giving advice on nutrition, pest control, pruning and irrigation.

Crittenden's viticultural expertise is reflected in the quality of his own wines. Since its first vintage, in 1985, Dromana has established itself as one of the leading small wineries in Australia. Recent releases of Pinot Noir, Cabernet/Merlot and especially Chardonnay have been superb and very reasonably priced.

Crittenden makes three Chardonnays: Dromana Estate, from his own vineyard, Schinus Molle, which is made from purchased fruit, mainly from McLaren Vale and the Yarra Valley, and is intended for earlier drinking; and a cheaper South Australian blend called The Briars. Crittenden also produces a creamy 60 per cent Chardonnay Schinus Molle Brut sparkling wine.

The Dromana Chardonnay has 30 per cent malolactic and is entirely fermented in French oak. It has gained in complexity as Crittenden has moved away from cool-temperature fermentation to what he calls 'more cavalier handling'. The Dromana Chardonnays need at least three years to show at their best – the 1991 is Crittenden's best wine yet.

GIACONDA

RMB 6481, Eldorado, 3746 Victoria

Chardonnay vineyard: 2 acres

Production of Chardonnay: 5,000 bottles

Quality: 🍇🍇🍇🍇   Price: ★★★

Best vintages: 1986, 1989, 1990

I came across Rick Kinzbrunner's Chardonnay at dinner one night in northern Victoria and set off immediately to pay him a visit. It was a serendipitous discovery. I did a barrel-tasting of his Chardonnays at ten o'clock at night, increasingly convinced that these were great wines.

Kinzbrunner has an impressive wine-making pedigree, having worked at Simi, Matanzas Creek and Stag's Leap in California before setting up in Australia. The first vintage of Giaconda Chardonnay was in 1985, and the wine is still made in a deliberately Burgundian style. It is fermented in a mixture of new, one- and two-year-old French barrels, spends a year on its lees and goes through full malolactic fermentation.

Kinzbrunner's Chardonnay is planted on gravel and clay soil with a cool, southerly exposure. This contributes significantly to the style of the wine. The vines are still young, but the wine is extremely promising, with powerful, concentrated flavours and a lean, almost austere structure. The 1989 and the 1990 are among the leading examples in Victoria. Shame there's so little wine.

THOMAS HARDY

Reynell Road, Reynella, 5161 South Australia

Chardonnay vineyard: 54 acres

Production of Chardonnay: approximately 3 million bottles

Labels: Nottage Hill; Siegersdorf; Bird Series; Château Reynella; Hardy Collection; Eileen Hardy

Quality: 🍷–🍷🍷🍷🍷🍷   Price: ★–★★★

Best vintages: 1986, 1987, 1988, 1989, 1990

'Nowadays,' according to Hardy's white-wine-maker, Tom Newton, 'if you don't have a Chardonnay, you aren't really a winery.' Not an accusation that could be levelled at Hardy's; this large family-run operation, which also owns Houghton in Western Australia and Stanley/Leasingham in the Clare Valley, produces a string of Chardonnays, varying from fruity quaffers like Nottage Hill and Siegersdorf to Eileen Hardy, one of Australia's finest wines.

Hardy's buy fruit from four main areas: Padthaway (where they have important vineyards in their own right), Clare Valley, McLaren Vale and Riverland. But all of its white wines are made at Château Reynella, the group's historic headquarters near Adelaide.

The two best Chardonnays – Hardy Collection and Eileen Hardy, named after the late mother of the company's chairman, Sir James Hardy – are both made with a substantial portion of Padthaway fruit. The Hardy Collection is oak-aged, while the Eileen Hardy is (French) barrel-fermented, with 5–10 per cent malolactic, six months on the lees and a total of twelve months in barrel. The former is a fresh, nuanced wine with peach and citrus-fruit flavours; the latter, first produced in 1986, tends to display a bit more depth and weight, although it has a similar underlying fruit structure. The 1987, 1988 and 1989 releases have all been first-rate.

HOUGHTON

Dale Road, Middle Swan, 6056 Western Australia

Chardonnay vineyard: 52 acres

Production of Chardonnay: 300,000 bottles

Quality: 🍇🍇_🍇🍇🍇   Price: ★/★★

Best vintages: 1989, 1990

Houghton is the colossus of Western Australian wine production, crushing nearly two-thirds of the state's entire output. Its presence in the warm Swan Valley, an hour's drive from the centre of Perth, dates back to 1859, the year it produced its first wine. Since 1975, the winery has been part of the Hardy group.

Houghton draws grapes from all over Western Australia; it has substantial plantings in the Swan, at Moondah Brook, a little way to the north of Perth, and at Frankland River in the Lower Great Southern, the isolated but viticulturally promising region which includes Mount Barker.

The fruit that goes into White Burgundy, Australia's best-selling dry white wine, comes mainly from the Swan Valley. Despite its name, the wine is not a varietal Chardonnay. In fact, Chardonnay did not pop up in the blend until 1987; even now it only accounts for 20 per cent, with Chenin Blanc, Muscadelle and Verdelho completing the line-up. You can almost see the Burgundians going purple in the face. To make things worse, Houghton also produces a 'Chablis'.

Houghton makes a number of varietal Chardonnays – Moondah Brook, Margaret River, Gold Reserve and a small amount of Show Reserve – with varying blends of Swan and Frankland fruit. Eventually, all of the Chardonnay will come from cooler areas in the south of the state; for the time being, only the Show Reserve grapes are entirely from Frankland River.

Wine-maker Peter Dawson uses as much as ten hours' skin contact on his Chardonnay to enhance its body and flavour. The top wines are fermented in (one-third new) oak, have up to 20 per cent malolactic and stay on their lees for eight to ten months. Gold Reserve is the most enjoyable Chardonnay here with good balance, peach and pineapple fruit and integrated oak flavours. As the percentage of Frankland grapes increases, this wine is going to get better and better.

TIM KNAPPSTEIN

2 Pioneer Avenue, Clare, 5453 South Australia

Chardonnay vineyard: 14.5 acres

Production of Chardonnay: 72,000 bottles

Quality: 🍇🍇🍇🍇   Price: ★★★

Best vintages: 1989, 1990

Tim Knappstein's swish modern winery is housed in the old stone buildings of the Enterprise Brewery, and produces some of the best Chardonnays in the Clare Valley. The brewery had seen service as a soft-drinks factory before Knappstein took it over in 1976. Since 1986, the company has been owned by Wolf Blass, now part of Mildara, although Tim Knappstein has kept 123 acres of vineyard and remains very much in charge of the winemaking.

Knappstein, a tall blond Australian who bears a remarkable resemblance to the late English writer Bruce Chatwin, draws Chardonnay from two very different sources: the Clare Valley and Lenswood, in the much cooler Adelaide Hills. The latter vineyard has only been in full production since 1990.

As well as his own fruit, Knappstein buys grapes from growers in Clare. In fact, this is where most of Knappstein's Chardonnay comes from. In the future, he will produce Chardonnay under two separate labels but, for the time being, the main blend contains 30 per cent Adelaide Hills fruit. In 1991 Knappstein also released a small quantity of Lenswood Chardonnay.

The structure of Knappstein's Chardonnay has changed radically in recent vintages, moving from a crisp, lean, aromatic style to a more generous, well-upholstered wine with greater complexity. The Chardonnay is given twelve to fifteen hours' skin contact to extract the maximum flavour and weight; Knappstein also adds some fully oxidized juice to the blend. The wine starts its fermentation in stainless steel, but finishes it in (mainly new) French and American oak. A small percentage of the wine goes through malolactic, and it remains on its lees for seven to eight months. The addition of Adelaide Hills fruit should bring extra concentration and depth to what is already a very fine Chardonnay.

KRONDORF

Krondorf Road, Tanunda, 5352 South Australia

Chardonnay vineyard: 50 acres

Production of Chardonnay: 300,000 bottles

Labels: Krondorf; Limited Release; Show Reserve

Quality: 🍇🍇🍇🍇   Price: ★★

Best vintages: 1983, 1984, 1988, 1989, 1990, 1991

Krondorf has been quietly established in the Barossa Valley, under a number of different, mainly Germanic-sounding names, since the 1860s, but its rise to prominence is comparatively recent. The Lyndoch-based winery had nothing much in the way of a reputation when it was purchased by two young wine-makers, Grant Burge and Ian Wilson, in 1978. But this dynamic partnership revitalized Krondorf, so much so that the business went public five years later. In 1986, Burge and Wilson sold the company to Mildara, although the new owners continued to use their names on labels for a while. Krondorf is run as a separate operation within the Mildara-Blass group (as it is now called), with its own wine-maker and 60 acres of vineyard.

Under Burge and Wilson, Chardonnay became a speciality at Krondorf. The wines are made with a combination of fruit, both purchased and home-grown, from all over South Australia (principally the Barossa, Eden Valley and McLaren Vale). There are three of them in all – a basic tank-fermented wine; a Limited Release, some of which is vinified in barrel; and a fuller, more oaky release called Show Reserve. The best Show Reserves are big, buttery and concentrated, but also age extremely well. The 1984, made by Burge and Wilson, was still showing superbly after six years in bottle, but the Chardonnays produced after their departure, particularly the 1988 Show Reserve, have been well up to standard. If you want to taste Australian Chardonnay at its most exuberant, Krondorf is the place to start. Krondorf's top Chardonnays are also commendably inexpensive.

LAKE'S FOLLY

Broke Road, Pokolbin, 2321 New South Wales

Chardonnay vineyard: 10 acres

Production of Chardonnay: 20,000 bottles

Quality: 🍇🍇🍇🍇/🍇🍇🍇🍇🍇   Price: ★★★

Best vintages: 1981, 1986, 1988, 1989

Surgeon, musician, philosopher, author and all-round *bon viveur*, Max Lake is a crucial figure in the history of Australian wine. He it was, back in the sixties, who launched what was arguably the country's first boutique winery. Other people may have joined the bandwagon since, but Lake set it rolling.

Like all the best pioneers, Lake combined bravery with dogged self-belief when he started his 'Folly' in 1963. He was the first person to plant Cabernet Sauvignon in the Hunter Valley in over twenty years, and then went on to produce an elegant Bordeaux-style wine that was highly original (in Australia) at the time.

Chardonnay came later – the vines were planted in 1969, with the first release in 1974. Lake says this was Australia's second Chardonnay (after Tyrrell's 1971 Vat 47). 'Most people couldn't even spell the word Chardonnay then,' says Lake, who originally intended to use his grapes to make sparkling wine. 'Actually, I would have made a Chardonnay before Tyrrell, but I couldn't get the bloody thing to ferment.'

In the best boutique tradition, the quality of the wine has varied over the years, but Lake's Folly Chardonnay, now made by Max's son Stephen, can be brilliant, if restrained by Hunter standards. It is fermented (at low temperatures) in a combination of stainless steel and French oak, then aged in barrel, with some lees contact. As Max Lake himself puts it, with characteristic honesty: 'We're not interested in making a tits-up-front Chardonnay, with planks of wood suspended in the tanks, which will be dead a few months after release.'

His Chardonnay, like his Cabernet Sauvignon, is mainly sold by mail order. The winery continues to command a considerable following. Whether the wines, particularly the Cabernet, deserve their high reputation is open to debate, but I have had some extremely good bottles of Lake's Folly Chardonnay over the years. The 1989 is excellent, and wines like the 1981 have aged brilliantly.

LEASINGHAM WINES

7 Dominic Street, Clare, 5453 South Australia
Chardonnay vineyard: 37 acres
Production of Chardonnay: 170,000 bottles
Quality: 🍇🍇   Price: ★
Best vintages: 1989, 1990

The Stanley Wine Company, to give it its full title, was bought by Hardy's in 1988, but has retained a certain degree of autonomy since the takeover. Its substantial vineyards in the Clare Valley provide fruit for some of the Hardy's blends, but most of its production is bottled under the Leasingham label. A much larger operation, specializing in bag-in-box or 'bladder pack' wines under the Stanley label, has now moved to Mildura.

The Leasingham Chardonnay, made entirely with Clare Valley grapes, offers superb value for money. With Lindemans' Bin 65, it is one of Australia's leading inexpensive Chardonnays: easy to drink, with pleasant flavours of melon and fig, good acidity and pronounced, but not obtrusive, French and American oak character; 1989 and 1990 were both excellent Chardonnay vintages at Leasingham.

LEEUWIN ESTATE

Gnarawary Road, Margaret River, 6285 Western Australia
Chardonnay vineyard: 42 acres
Production of Chardonnay: 48,000 bottles
Quality: 🍇🍇🍇🍇🍇   Price: ★★★★★
Best vintages: 1982, 1985, 1987, 1988

Leeuwin is a showpiece winery. Its lush green lawns have played host, *à la* Robert Mondavi, to jazz singers, operatic divas and even the London Philharmonic. Leeuwin is a no-expenses-spared sort of place; in this case the man who foots the bill is

Perth millionaire Denis Horgan. It was Horgan who got Robert Mondavi involved in the initial vintages at Leeuwin, and Mondavi's influence affected more than the choice of jazz artistes.

Leeuwin was one of the first Australian wineries to ferment its Chardonnay in barrel, for example. 'Our 1980 marked the dawning of a new age of Australian Chardonnay,' says wine-maker Bob Cartwright. 'It really caught people's imagination.' The Leeuwin Chardonnays are fermented entirely in new French oak and aged in barrel for up to twelve months. About 30 per cent of the wine goes through malolactic fermentation, although the first two vintages (1980 and 1981) had no malolactic character at all.

Along with Cabernet Sauvignon, Chardonnay is the top variety at Leeuwin, consistently producing some of the most complex, age-worthy wines in Australia. Often surprisingly reticent in their youth, with age they develop into rich con-centrated wines of great depth. The 1982 is the finest Anti-podean Chardonnay I have ever tasted, and is fit to stand alongside the top Burgundies.

In 1991, Leeuwin bowed to commercial pressure and intro-duced a cheaper, second label Chardonnay, called Prelude. A sign of the times?

LINDEMANS

634–726 Princes Highway, Tempe, 2044 New South Wales

Chardonnay vineyard: see Penfolds

Production of Chardonnay: 6.8 million bottles

Labels: Padthaway; South East Australian; Bin 65/Premier Selection; Hunter River Reserve; Leo Buring; Rouge Homme

Quality: 🍇🍇_🍇🍇🍇🍇   Price: ★–★★★

Best vintages: 1985, 1986, 1989, 1990

The success of Australian wine has much to do with the high standards of the largest companies. Lindemans, just like its group partners Penfolds and Seppelt, produces good wines at every level. It is equally strong in reds and whites, with production facilities in the Coonawarra (Rouge Homme), the Hunter and at Karadoc in Victoria. Its most important plantings are in the Hunter, Lindemans' original nineteenth-century stamping-ground, Coonawarra and Padthaway, the last being one of the most sizeable single vineyards in Australia.

Lindemans produces a number of different Chardonnays, ranging in quality (and ambition) from the inexpensive, wonderfully drinkable Bin 65 (called Premier Selection in Australia) to its Padthaway, Hunter and Coonawarra (Rouge Homme) wines. Bin 65 is a blend of 25 per cent Padthaway and 75 per cent warm-area fruit, topped off with a bit of lees contact and oak character. The basic Leo Buring blend, like Penfolds' Killawarra Chardonnay, is also a very good varietal wine at the bottom end of the market.

Higher up the quality ladder, the Chardonnays see more oak fermentation and tend to be made from cooler climate grapes. The Rouge Homme and Leo Buring Reserve wines are partially barrel-fermented, while the Hunter River Reserve and Padthaway Chardonnay get the full treatment. The Padthaway Chardonnay has got better and better since 1985, when winemaker Greg Clayfield changed the style of the wine to introduce French oak and partial malolactic fermentation, but the Rouge Homme Chardonnay, which tends to be a little leaner in style, can also be extremely fine. Don't overlook the Leo Buring Reserve wines either.

McWILLIAM'S

Mount Pleasant Wines, Marrowbone Road, Pokolbin, 2321 New South Wales

Chardonnay vineyard: 50 acres

Production of Chardonnay: 85,000 cases

Labels: Homestead; Mount Pleasant

Quality: 🍇🍇🍇   Price: ★★

Best vintages: 1986, 1987, 1989

McWilliam's is among the largest half a dozen wineries in Australia, with vineyards in the Hunter Valley, Cowra and Riverina supplemented by enormous quantities of bought-in fruit. Its best wines come from Mount Pleasant in the Hunter Valley, a property which the family purchased in 1932.

There are over forty wines produced here, with the standard of the whites a good deal more consistent than that of the reds. The Sémillons are outstanding, the Chardonnays reliable (and improving under wine-maker Phil Ryan).

McWilliam's has only been producing commercial quantities of Chardonnay since 1984, but the late eighties produced a string of promising wines. The style here favours barrel-fermentation, with up to eight months' lees contact, but no malolactic fermentation. There are two Chardonnay releases: Mount Pleasant and the more expensive Homestead. Both wines are given two to three years' bottle age before release, allowing the Homestead Chardonnays to develop considerable complexity. The 1986 has delicious flavours of nuts, citrus fruit and honey. These are definitely wines that age gracefully.

MOSS WOOD

PO Box 52, Busselton, 6280 Western Australia

Chardonnay vineyard: 2.5 acres

Production of Chardonnay: 6,000 bottles

Quality: 🍇🍇🍇/🍇🍇🍇🍇   Price: ★★★

Best vintages: 1983, 1985, 1987, 1989, 1990

Moss Wood is one of a trio of Margaret River wineries founded by doctors in the 1960s (Cullen's and Vasse Felix being the other two). Dr Bill Parnell planted vines in 1969 and made his first 250 cases of wine in 1973, but Moss Wood really began to take off with the arrival of Roseworthy-trained oenologist Keith Mugford in 1979. Mugford and his wife Clare subsequently bought the winery – in reality an unprepossessing shack with no cellar-door sales area – and continue to produce some of the most intense wines in the area.

Moss Wood is best known for its stunning Cabernet Sauvignons, but it also produces a small amount of Chardonnay, Pinot Noir and Sémillon. The standard is uniformly high. The first Chardonnay was made in 1980, but not released. The next two vintages were destroyed by wind (a persistent problem in Margaret River) and frost, so it was not until 1983 that a Moss Wood Chardonnay finally hit the market.

The 1983 was part-fermented in barrel but had no lees contact; subsequent Chardonnays have been made in a more Burgundian style, although in ripe vintages, like 1989, the wine is not put through malolactic fermentation. Mugford does at least two pickings of Chardonnay, in order to achieve a balance of ripeness. The Moss Wood style emphasizes rich, creamy, honeyed fruit and barrel complexity, but never seems overblown. The wine can age for at least five years.

MOUNTADAM

High Eden Ridge, Eden Valley, 5235 South Australia

Chardonnay vineyard: 70 acres

Production of Chardonnay: 160,000 bottles

Labels: Mountadam; David Wynn; Eden Ridge

Quality: 🍇🍇🍇🍇🍇   Price: ★★★

Best vintages: 1984, 1987, 1988, 1989, 1990

Mountadam was set up in 1972 by David Wynn, who grew bored with sitting behind a desk, sold off the successful Coonawarra company which still bears his name (Wynn's) and went looking for somewhere to plant Chardonnay, then a comparatively minor grape variety in Australia. After visits to

Tasmania, Victoria and Western Australia, he plumped for the cool High Eden Ridge in South Australia, 400 metres above the Barossa Valley. His five acres of Chardonnay were the first commercial plantings in South Australia.

Between 1979 and 1983, Mountadam's wines were made by Roseworthy Agricultural College, Australia's top oenology school, but since 1984 the winery has been run by Adam Wynn, David's witty, barrel-chested son. Adam trained at the Universities of Bordeaux (where he came top of his year) and Dijon, as well as working at some of Burgundy's most prestigious domaines. Appropriately, his approach is 'a bit more *laissez-faire* than most Australian wineries'.

Mountadam produces Pinot Noir, Riesling and a small amount of Cabernet Sauvignon, but its main focus is Chardonnay. It also has a range of second wines, sold under the David Wynn and Eden Ridge labels. The Chardonnay is picked ripe – the excellent 1989 had 13.7 per cent alcohol – and is characteristically full and creamy. Wynn ferments the unclarified juice in a mixture of new and old Tronçais oak. The wine is left on its lees for four months, racked, and then returned to barrels for another seven months. Up to 40 per cent of the wine is put through malolactic fermentation, but to prevent it being too rich, Wynn adds 10 per cent of crisper, tank-fermented Chardonnay to the final blend. The result, which combines Australian fruit and semi-Burgundian techniques, is amongst the finest Antipodean Chardonnays. A wine for hedonists.

MOUNTARROW

Arrowfield Winery, Denman Road, Jerrys Plains, 2330 New South Wales

Chardonnay vineyard: 100 acres

Production of Chardonnay: 210,000 bottles

Labels: Simon Whitlam; Simon Gilbert; Arrowfield Reserve; Arrowfield Premium; Chardonnay Sauternes; Simon Whitlam Brut

Quality: 🍇🍇🍇   Price: ★★–★★★★
Best vintages: 1988, 1989, 1991

Mountarrow, as it is now known, is an amalgam of two Hunter Valley wineries: Arrowfield and Simon Whitlam. Arrowfield had its problems in the seventies, as prevailing tastes swung away from red wines, but under its new (predominantly Japanese) management, the revitalized group appears to be back on course.

Wine-maker Simon Gilbert, who spent eleven years at Lindemans before moving to Arrowfield (as it was then) in 1985, produces an intriguing range of Chardonnays. The top wines are Simon Whitlam (from the Simon Whitlam estate in the Lower Hunter) and Simon Gilbert (anything Brian Croser can do at Petaluma ...). But the more basic Arrowfield Chardonnays, made with mainly purchased fruit from all over New South Wales are very drinkable too. Simon Whitlam tends to be the broadest in style; Simon Gilbert (the wine, not the wine-maker) is more elegant and refined with less residual sugar and more pronounced oak – the result, I suspect, of a significant percentage of Padthaway grapes.

Gilbert also makes a creamy Chardonnay sparkling wine and (more controversially) a freeze-concentrated botrytis Chardonnay called Chardonnay Sauternes. There are very few late-harvest Chardonnays in the world, but this is probably the most interesting: peachy, raisiny and pleasantly honeyed with a marked flavour of new oak. So far, Gilbert has made his 'Sauternes' in 1985, 1986 and 1990.

ORLANDO

PO Box 943, Rowland Flat, 5352 South Australia
Chardonnay vineyard: 150 acres
Production of Chardonnay: 1.8 million bottles
Labels: RF; Gramp's; Saint Hilary

Quality: 🍇🍇/🍇🍇🍇   Price: ★—★★★
Best vintages: 1986, 1987, 1989, 1990

Orlando is one of Australia's most dynamic companies, turning out vast quantities of reliable, eminently drinkable wine; only the Seppelt/Penfolds/Lindemans group is larger. For many consumers, Orlando's Jacob's Creek range provides an introduction to Australia and, while it is not a varietal wine, the successful Jacob's Creek white does contain 10 per cent Chardonnay.

Orlando produces three different Chardonnays: RF (named after its enormous Rowland Flat winery); Gramp's (a tribute to Orlando's German founder, Johann Gramp, who planted the first vines in the Barossa Valley); and Saint Hilary, the most expensive of the trio. It sources its grapes from all over South Australia. In addition to the Chardonnay it purchases, Orlando has vineyards of its own in Padthaway and the Barossa.

The three wines are made with fruit from different sources: RF from all over South Australia; Gramp's from the Barossa; and Saint Hilary from McLaren Vale, Padthaway and Coonawarra, with an increasing emphasis on cool-climate fruit. RF tends to be the most forward of Orlando's Chardonnays, with sweet, tropical-fruit flavours. Gramp's is big and, to my palate, a little coarse, while Saint Hilary has greater complexity and finesse. These wines are good, rather than wildly exciting – Orlando's use of skin contact produces wines that are easy to drink young, but do not age particularly well – although the increasing percentage of Padthaway fruit in Saint Hilary is a promising development.

PENFOLDS

Tanunda Road, Nuriootpa, 5355 South Australia

Chardonnay vineyard: The Penfolds Wine Group, which now includes Lindemans, Penfolds, Seppelts, Wynn's, Rouge Homme, Tulloch and Hungerford Hill, owns Chardonnay vineyards in Mildura (75 acres), Barooga

(310 acres), Padthaway (435 acres), Coonawarra (250 acres), Riverland (300 acres), Clare (100 acres) and the Hunter Valley (62 acres)

Production of Chardonnay: Penfolds Eden Valley Chardonnay, 36,000 bottles; Penfolds Chardonnay, 240,000 bottles; Penfolds Padthaway, 24,000 bottles; Killawarra Chardonnay, 200,000 bottles; Tollana, 84,000 bottles; Seaview, 720,000 bottles; Tulloch, 48,000 bottles

Quality: 🍇_🍇🍇🍇🍇   Price: ★/★★

Best vintages: 1988, 1989, 1990, 1991

It is Australia's good fortune that its largest wine company is also one of its best. Penfolds produces some of the finest red wines in the world – including Bin 707 and the legendary Grange Hermitage – and in recent vintages its white wines have begun to catch up, spurred on by the acquisition of Lindemans, some of whose Padthaway fruit is used in Penfolds' own Chardonnays. (In November 1990, Penfolds was itself purchased by South Australia Brewing Holdings, owner of leading sparkling-wine producer Seppelt, and this has strengthened the group even further.)

The Penfolds side of the renamed Penfolds Wine Group produces a good range of Chardonnays in a number of different styles (Wynn's Coonawarra Estate is dealt with separately), using fruit from a variety of vineyard sources, both owned and under contract. At the company's base in Nuriootpa, white-wine-making is now handled by Neville Falkenberg, who is experimenting with a range of different viticultural and oeno-logical techniques for Chardonnay. 'I reckon we make as many as twenty different styles,' he says, 'and then evaluate them at the end of the vintage.'

The cheapest and most approachable Chardonnays here are Seaview and Killawarra, with the latter among the best-value white wines in Australia. Most of the grapes for Killawarra come from the Barossa and Riverland and, as you would expect, the emphasis is on (largely unoaked) varietal flavour. Seaview, which is made at the winery of the same name in McLaren

Vale, is richer, more complex and influenced by old (American, French and German) oak maturation.

Penfolds' top Chardonnays (excluding Tulloch's, located in the Hunter Valley) are the three wines released under its own label: Clare Estate, Padthaway and Penfolds' South Australia Chardonnay. The Clare and Padthaway wines are more restrained than the full-throttle, blockbuster South Australia blend. This is made with the ripest fruit from Clare, Barossa, Langhorne Creek and the Southern Vales, with a substantial proportion (50–60 per cent) undergoing barrel-fermentation and six months on its lees. The entire blend is aged for ten to twelve months in oak, and in years like 1988 and 1990 is a rich, oaky monster of a wine.

If you like flavour in your Chardonnay, buy a bottle of Penfolds. This is a wine best drunk within a year or two of release. The 1990 was only the sixth commercial release, so I expect further improvements. In a different style, the Clare Estate Chardonnay is also developing into something exceptional.

PETALUMA

> Spring Gully Road, Piccadilly, 5151 South Australia
>
> Chardonnay vineyard: 12 acres (Clare), 7.5 acres
> (Piccadilly), 12.5 acres (Coonawarra)
>
> Production of Chardonnay: 120,000 bottles
>
> Quality: 🍇🍇🍇🍇🍇   Price: ★★★
>
> Best vintages: 1980, 1982, 1987, 1988, 1989, 1990

In a country where most Chardonnay is intended for immediate consumption, Petaluma stands out as a producer of subtle, structured wines that can take at least five years to show at their best. Petaluma's wonderful Chardonnays have few rivals in Australia (Leeuwin, Lake's Folly, Pipers Brook and Mountadam spring to mind), although they do not always perform well in blind tastings when young.

Brian Croser is a methodical, supremely gifted wine-maker who leaves very little to chance. There is always a sense of Croser gently guiding the wine, rather than the other way round. After the grapes have been pressed, for example, Croser stores his Chardonnay juice at low temperature for four months until he is ready to barrel-ferment the wine (with his own yeast culture) in September. Croser is not a man to be rushed.

The source of Croser's Chardonnay has changed considerably since Petaluma produced its first wine in 1977. The early vintages were sourced from Cowra in New South Wales and have aged extremely well. Coonawarra fruit joined the blend in 1980, followed by Clare and Piccadilly four years later. The percentage of Piccadilly fruit has increased steadily from 5 per cent in 1984, to 50 per cent in 1987, to nearly 100 per cent in 1988: the first vintage that Croser was really happy with. Croser is a great believer in the fundamental importance of vineyard location. And in the cool Adelaide Hills he believes he has found the ideal spot for Chardonnay.

Croser intervenes as little as possible in the wine-making, which is ironic given his reputation as a technocrat. His Chardonnay is fermented in new French oak and spends eight to fourteen months on its lees. In all this time, it is not racked or fined. The fermentation is cool and slow (at 10–12 °C), and as a rule the wine does not go through malolactic – the 1982 saw malolactic as well as skin contact and is the most opulent of the Petaluma Chardonnays.

The late eighties saw a string of brilliant Chardonnays from Petaluma, with restrained, well-integrated citrus and oak flavours. The 1986, 1987, 1988, 1989 and 1990 all have great length and finesse, with the 1987 and 1990 the pick of the bunch. Petaluma also produces an excellent Pinot Noir/ Chardonnay sparkling wine called, appropriately enough, Croser. As one wit commented on its release – 'at least it isn't called Brian'.

PETERSONS

PO Box 182, Cessnock, 2325 New South Wales

Chardonnay vineyard: 15 acres

Production of Chardonnay: 18,000 bottles

Quality: 🍇_🍇🍇🍇🍇   Price: ★★★

Best vintages: 1983, 1986, 1989

Ian Peterson planted his first vines in Mount View, to the south of Pokolbin, in 1971, but sold his grapes to neighbouring wineries until the 1981 vintage. 'People were winning trophies with our grapes,' remembers Peterson, 'so I thought, why not have a go myself?' Peterson did just that in the initial vintage, using his wife Shirley's tights as a filter. From 1982, the wines have been made (without the help of Mrs Peterson's under-wear) by Gary Reed, formerly of Tulloch's Glen Elgin winery, and have won an impressive string of medals.

Wine is produced under at least eight labels (including a sparkling wine called 'Fiona'), but it is Petersons' Chardonnay which has won the greatest acclaim. From 1983 to 1986, the wines were immaculate, though recent vintages have been more uneven, partly due to poor weather.

The style of wine generally reflects its Lower Hunter Valley origins, with rich, oily, unctuous fruit overlaid with subtle French oak. In good vintages, Peterson Chardonnays can age for up to five years. The 1989 Chardonnay was more restrained, with minerally melon and grapefruit flavours. The 1987 and 1990 are best avoided.

Since 1989, the Petersons have been installed in a new winery in Pokolbin, and are now producing a second range under the Calais label. The Calais Chardonnay is cheaper but a good deal less interesting than the Peterson bottling.

PIPERS BROOK

Via Lebrina, 7254 Tasmania

Chardonnay vineyard: 35 acres

Production of Chardonnay: Pipers Brook, 30,000 bottles;
Tasmania Wine Company, 33,000 bottles

Quality: 🍇🍇🍇–🍇🍇🍇🍇🍇   Price: ★★–★★★★

Best vintages: 1984, 1986, 1988, 1989, 1990, 1991

Dr Andrew Pirie was once described as the 'thinking man's wine-maker'. Scientist, academic and expert in vine physiology, Pirie took himself off to France in the early seventies and did wine-making stints in Alsace, Bordeaux, Burgundy and Provence. On his return to Australia, he sought out a cool climate in which to grow European varieties, finally settling on the comparatively humid north-east corner of Tasmania, Australia's former penal colony, in 1974. The harvest here takes place up to two months later than it does in the Hunter Valley. Pirie was far from being the first to plant vines in Tasmania – that honour belongs to a nineteenth-century ex-con called Bartholomew Broughton – but he has become the island's most respected spokesman.

Pirie also makes Tasmania's best wines, with that Burgundian duo, Chardonnay and Pinot Noir, to the fore. Everything about the winery is stylish, from the handsome labels to the carefully tended vineyards and immaculate modern facilities. The style of Chardonnay, first produced in 1981, emphasizes elegance and cool-climate fruit. In a good vintage, the wine can age for up to eight years in bottle. Pipers Brook is one of the most complex Chardonnays produced in Australia, with crisp natural acidity, citrus and tropical fruit, toasty oak and excellent structure and balance. A perfect antidote to the blowsy 'Dolly Parton' styles of Australia's warmer areas.

Andrew Pirie also produces a second-string Chardonnay under the Tasmania Wine Company label and, since 1990, a super-premium Pipers Brook Chardonnay called Summit. This is fermented in new oak and goes through full malolactic – the ordinary Pipers Brook Chardonnay has a lower percentage of malolactic (40–60 per cent) and less pronounced oak character. The first release was an extremely impressive début, with rich, buttery oak flavours, refreshing acidity and a sweet, toffee'd finish.

PLANTAGENET

PO Box 122, Mount Barker, 6324 Western Australia

Chardonnay vineyard: 5.5 acres

Production of Chardonnay: 42,000 bottles

Labels: Bouverie; Plantagenet; Western Australian Chardonnay

Quality: 🍇🍇🍇🍇   Price: ★★—★★★★

Best vintages: 1989, 1990

Tony Smith, a pink-cheeked English aristocrat, left his native land more than thirty years ago because he felt 'uncomfortable with upper-class people'. His original intention was to become a farmer in Australia, but he got bitten by the wine bug and planted some of the first vines in the Mount Barker region of Western Australia in 1968.

Plantagenet has now established itself as one of the country's leading smaller wineries, producing a superb range from a cramped, converted apple-packing shed. Smith has been served by two excellent wine-makers: Rob Bowen and, since 1988, John Wade, who used to work at Wynn's in the Coonawarra.

Wade specializes in red wines, but his Chardonnays are also first-rate. Plantagenet buys fruit from local growers as well as producing its own Chardonnay. There are three distinct styles made here: an unoaked Western Australian Chardonnay, a lightish, barrel-fermented Chardonnay with up to 90 per cent malolactic, and a richer Bouverie Chardonnay, which spends eight months on the lees and goes through full malolactic.

In a country where unoaked Chardonnays are rare, it is a

delight to come across the perfumed, lemony style of Planta-genet's stainless-steel-fermented wine. The barrel-fermented Chardonnay has the same complex fruit structure, with well-integrated, perfumed oak. I find the Bouverie wine expensive and less convincing.

ROSEMOUNT ESTATES

Rosemount Road, Denman, 2321 New South Wales

Chardonnay vineyard: 700 acres

Production of Chardonnay: 7.6 million bottles

Labels: Yellow Label; Show Reserve; Giant's Creek; Roxburgh

Quality: 🍇–🍇🍇🍇🍇🍇   Price: ★★–★★★★★

Best vintages: 1984, 1987, 1989, 1990

Rosemount is one of the Australian wine industry's great success stories. Since the early eighties, it has produced a string of award-winning Hunter Valley Chardonnays, which have influenced a generation of Antipodean wine-makers. For many wine-lovers outside Australia, Rosemount's Show Reserve provided a first glimpse of down under – a flavour-packed blast of oak, tropical fruit and alcohol.

Rosemount's enigmatic wine-maker, Philip Shaw, is responsible for a range of wines that covers everything from Traminer/Riesling to Tawny 'port'. But Chardonnay is his main interest, and the winery's heart and soul.

Rosemount makes four different Chardonnays. Yellow Label, the cheapest, is commercial, if undemanding. More interesting are the Show Reserve and Rosemount's two single-vineyard Chardonnays, Giant's Creek and Roxburgh.

Roxburgh is the richest of the four wines, a quality which comes from the vineyard itself, not oenological tinkering. Surprisingly, Shaw has never used skin contact on Roxburgh. The wines are well balanced and are more long-lived than many Australian Chardonnays. The 1984, the first Roxburgh wine, is still in comparatively fine fettle. The Show Reserve resembles Roxburgh in style, with less fruit intensity. The 1989 is exceptional.

Giant's Creek is an altogether subtler wine. It is lighter and takes longer to develop than Roxburgh, and Shaw uses less new oak, so as not to swamp the wine. The 1987 and 1989 both have citrusy, aniseedy flavours which are closer to Chablis than Meursault. The difference between Giant's Creek and Roxburgh is all down to vineyard location, according to Shaw. After only five vintages, it is difficult to say how the Giant's Creek wines will develop, but they have the potential to take their place alongside Australia's finest Chardonnays.

ROTHBURY ESTATE

Broke Road, Pokolbin, 2321 New South Wales

Chardonnay vineyard: 30 acres (Herlstone); 55 acres (Brokenback); 20 acres (Rothbury); 84 acres (Denman Estate); 42 acres (Cowra)

Production of Chardonnay: 750,000 bottles

Quality: 🍇🍇🍇   Price: ★★/★★★

Best vintages: 1984, 1986, 1989, 1990

The irrepressible Len Evans, raconteur, ex-golf pro and Australia's best-known wine personality, set up this large venture in the Lower Hunter Valley, with the support of ten investors, in the late sixties. Rothbury has had its problems since, but the energy, enthusiasm and sheer bloody-mindedness of its founding figure have helped it through the bad times.

Early plantings here consisted of (predominantly) Shiraz, Sémillon, Pinot Noir and Cabernet Sauvignon, but the emphasis of the winery has shifted to white wines (especially Chardonnay) in the last decade, to the point where Chardonnay now accounts for 50 per cent of the estate's 1.5 million bottles.

Most of Rothbury's best Chardonnay comes from two sources: sixteen-year-old plantings at Cowra and ten-year-old plantings at the picturesquely named Brokenback vineyard. Yields vary, depending on soil structure, but still tend to be on the generous side.

Rothbury makes three different Chardonnays: an inexpensive Brokenback Chardonnay, a basic Rothbury Chardonnay and a more concentrated Reserve, selected from the best barrels. Fermentation is carried out in a combination of oak and stainless steel, with a maximum of 25 per cent malolactic and up to six months on the lees. The Reserve bottling has a higher percentage of barrel-fermented wine. Rothbury uses new, one- and two-year-old barrels, and its Chardonnays are certainly at the oakier end of the spectrum.

Rothbury's Chardonnays, even its Reserve wines, are intended to be drunk young. These are some of the richest, ripest, most deeply coloured Chardonnays in Australia – short on subtlety but long on tropical-fruit flavour. The truly great Rothbury whites are its Sémillons – a 1979 was still extremely lively when tasted more than a decade later. The Chardonnays are good, if rather obvious, but lack the depth and individuality of the Sémillons. The 1990 Reserve is Rothbury's best Chardonnay yet.

ST HUBERTS

St Huberts Lane, Coldstream, 3770 Victoria

Chardonnay vineyard: 12 acres

Production of Chardonnay: 18,000 bottles

Labels: St Huberts; Andrew Rowan; Kies Estate

Quality: 🍇🍇🍇🍇   Price: ★★★

Best vintages: 1984, 1988, 1990

Against a background of considerable financial insecurity, St Huberts' wine-maker Brian Fletcher has produced a string of excellent wines in recent vintages. This is one of the largest and most venerable wineries in the Yarra Valley, crushing fruit for a number of other producers on a contract basis as well as producing its own wines under three separate labels.

Fletcher has been at St Huberts since 1988, although he won his wine-making spurs at Seppelt, and his impact on the range has been considerable. Fletcher claims that his greatest problem with Chardonnay is to get the grapes to ripen. In 1988 and 1990, he freeze-concentrated the juice to give it more intensity.

Fletcher admits that he'd rather obtain the same results in the vineyard, but this bit of technological manipulation does not appear to have harmed the wine. The superb 1988 Chardonnay deservedly won a gold medal at *Wine* magazine's exacting International Challenge in 1991. The wine has complex, subtle citrus fruit and oak flavours. It is a comparatively elegant, almost lean Australian Chardonnay, made without skin contact or malolactic fermentation.

The encouraging news from Australia is that St Huberts has a new owner, Goodman Fielder, who has put the company on a more secure financial footing. Long may this state of affairs continue.

SALTRAM

Angaston–Nuriootpa Road, Angaston, 5353 South Australia

Chardonnay vineyard: 5 acres

Production of Chardonnay: 460,000 bottles

Labels: Saltram; Mamre Brook; Pinnacle

Quality: 🍇🍇🍇   Price: ★/★★

Best vintages: 1986, 1988, 1989

Rather like Krondorf, Saltram is an old Barossa winery which has stirred from slumber in the last decade. Since the Canadian multinational Seagram took over in 1979, the quality of Saltram's wines has improved dramatically, and this is now one of the best medium-sized companies in Australia, producing an excellent value-for-money range that covers everything from fortifieds to sparkling wines. Who could resist the delightful charm (and alliteration) of Mr Pickwick's Particular Port?

Saltram buys grapes from all over Australia – 95 per cent of its fruit is purchased. Its Chardonnay comes from Riverina, McLaren Vale, Eden Valley, Barossa and even the Hunter in good years. There are three different releases: the basic Saltram bottling, Mamre Brook (named after the firm's original nineteenth-century plot) and Pinnacle Chardonnay, in effect a single vineyard wine from one grower in McLaren Vale. All three wines finish their alcoholic fermentation in (French and American) oak, 25 per cent of which is new. Saltram use skin contact, but generally avoid malolactic on their Chardonnays.

These are big, oaky, flavoursome wines that are best drunk young, although the Mamre Brook and Pinnacle Chardonnay can hold up surprisingly well in bottle. The 1986 Pinnacle is an irresistible wine, a rich, golden, buttery mouthful with toasted oak, good acidity and considerable complexity, and the lighter 1988 Mamre Brook is not far behind. In the Barossa Valley few large companies produce such consistently good Chardonnay. If you like your wines stuffed with brash oak and fruit, Saltram's basic release is a true bargain.

SEPPELT

PO Box 221, Tanunda, 5352 South Australia

Chardonnay vineyard: see Penfolds Wines

Production of Chardonnay: not released, but certainly in excess of 1.5 million bottles

Labels: Queen Adelaide/Gold Label; Gold Label; Clover Ridge; Show Chardonnay; Blanc de Blancs

Quality: 🍇🍇–🍇🍇🍇🍇   Price: ★–★★★

Best vintages: 1986, 1988, 1989

When Seppelt's parent company, South Australian Brewing Holdings, took over the powerful Penfolds/Lindemans axis late in 1990, someone described it as a case of a minnow swallowing a whale. In fact, this substantial operation, with wineries in three locations, was an important producer in its own right (even before the events of November 1990), turning out some of the best fortified, sparkling and table wines in Australia. As the wine writer James Halliday put it, with some justification, 'Seppelt simply does not know how to make an indifferent wine.'

At one point in the mid-eighties, Seppelt owned nearly 75 per cent of Australia's total plantings of Chardonnay. It still turns out bottles of very drinkable Chardonnay in remarkably large volumes, including Queen Adelaide, Australia's best-selling Chardonnay. 'Sydney practically floats on the stuff,' an Aussie friend of mine told me. If so, Sydney is the right place to drink one of the world's great benchmark Chardonnays. It is impossible not to like this wine – it's commercial, sure, but in the best sense of the word: gluggable, off-dry and a pleasure to drink.

Since the Penfolds takeover, there has been a bit of label rationalization at Seppelt. Gold Label, the next step up from Queen Adelaide, is going to have its name all to itself in future; and Black Label, Seppelt's third-tier Chardonnay, has been rechristened Clover Ridge. Both awful names, in my view, but the wines are splendid. Unlike Queen Adelaide, Clover Ridge and Gold Label both have some oak character. It is most pronounced on the Clover Ridge, the more elegant wine, which spends a total of nine months in French barrels.

Clover Ridge combines grapes from three different states and four sources: Barossa, Barooga, Padthaway and Great Western, the last being the home of Seppelt's sparkling-wine facility, where wine-maker Mike Kluzkco is producing most of Australia's leading fizz, including a very decent Blanc de Blancs. Seppelt also make small amounts of a more pricey Show Chardonnay: 100 per cent barrel-fermented from Padthaway and Barooga fruit. Since 1986, this wine has been toned down a bit, a move which has increased its complexity and ageing potential.

*

TISDALL

19 Cornelia Creek Road, Echuca, 3149 Victoria

Chardonnay Vineyard: 353 acres

Production of Chardonnay: 100,000 bottles

Labels: Tisdall; Mount Helen; Mount Helen Brut

Quality: 🍇🍇/🍇🍇🍇   Price: ★★

Best vintages: 1986, 1989, 1990

Like Lake's Folly in the Hunter Valley and a trio of well-known Margaret River producers, this medium-sized Victoria winery was founded by a doctor – in this case, Peter Tisdall, who has since sold the winery to Timbercorp. In its initial vintages, Tisdall sold grapes to other Victoria producers, including Brown Brothers, but from 1979 it has bottled wine under its own label. The results are consistently good.

Tisdall takes grapes from two vineyard sites: Rosbercon in the Victorian Riverlands, where they planted their first vines in 1972; and Mount Helen in the cooler Central Victorian Strathbogie Ranges. Some Mount Helen fruit is used in the basic Tisdall wines, blended with grapes from Rosbercon, but most of it is bottled separately.

There are three Chardonnays here: a light, elegant sparkling Brut, an American and German oak-aged Tisdall bottling and a superior (French) barrel-fermented Mount Helen wine, which has a restrained, but attractive, minerally quality to it. The Mount Helen Chardonnay also ages well in my experience.

TYRRELL'S

Broke Road, Pokolbin, 2320 New South Wales

Chardonnay vineyard: 100 acres

Production of Chardonnay: 576,000 bottles

Labels: Vat 47; HVD; Chardonnay/Sémillon

Quality: ♥♥_♥♥♥♥   Price: ★—★★★
Best vintages: 1973, 1977, 1984, 1986, 1987, 1989

There have been Tyrrells in the Hunter Valley since the 1850s, though the size of the current operation might surprise its founder, Edward Tyrrell, who cleared the firm's original wooded vineyard by hand. This great wine-making dynasty has played an important role in the development of the Australian wine industry, not least in the creation of the country's first commercial Chardonnay, the famous Vat 47.

Murray Tyrrell obtained his first Chardonnay cuttings from two sources: Alf Kurtz's vineyard in Mudgee; and a local Penfolds planting, which was used for a wine called Bin 365 Pinot Riesling, in reality a blend of Chardonnay and Sémillon.

The first Chardonnay – which the Tyrrells stubbornly continued to call Pinot Chardonnay, in the face of ampelographical evidence, until 1990 – was produced in 1971, one of the worst-ever vintages in the Hunter Valley. This and the 1972 were both unoaked, but in 1973, on the advice of English Master of Wine John Avery, Tyrrell produced a barrel-aged Chardonnay. The result was a critical disaster. 'In its first wine show, the judges gave it five marks out of twenty,' says Murray's son Bruce. 'At that time in Australia, if you didn't drink red wine you were a fairy. The judges had simply never come across anything like it.'

Undeterred, Tyrrell persevered with his Pinot Chardonnay. The style of the wine has changed a bit over the years, but some of the old wines are still superb. The slightly sweet, concentrated 1973 had fading, but delicious creamy, oaky flavours of coconut and honey when I last encountered it in 1990. The wine got bigger and bigger in the early 1980s, almost to the point of being overblown, before the Tyrrells introduced a leaner, more restrained style in 1984. In the last few vintages, Vat 47 has been trimmed down even further – the grapes are picked earlier to avoid excessive acid adjustment and the wines did not go through malolactic fermentation in 1989 or 1990. The musty 1988, on the other hand, was extremely disappointing.

In addition to Vat 47, Tyrrell's also produces two other Chardonnays: HVD, named after a vineyard which the company bought, with neat historical circularity, from Penfolds, and a predominantly Chardonnay blend, called Chardonnay/Sémillon, which contains bought-in Riverland fruit. Vat 47 is the only one of the three wines which is oak-fermented, and it is by far the most complex of the trio. A tribute to Murray Tyrrell's perseverance.

WYNN'S COONAWARRA ESTATE

Memorial Drive, Coonawarra, 5263 South Australia

Chardonnay vineyard: 250 acres

Production of Chardonnay: 240,000 bottles

Quality: 🍇🍇🍇 Price: ★★

Best vintages: 1982, 1985, 1987, 1990

'If you don't get on with other people in the wine industry down here,' says Peter Douglas, the engaging, larger-than-life wine-maker at Wynn's Coonawarra Estate, 'you've got no one to talk to but your dog.' The wines that Douglas produces at Wynn's, the largest producer in the Coonawarra district and, since 1985, part of the giant Penfolds group, must earn him a few dinner-party invitations in this quiet, somnolent corner of South Australia.

The top wines at Wynn's, unsurprisingly given the area's pre-eminence as a red-wine-producing area, are the densely textured Cabernets and Shirazes, but under its previous wine-maker John Wade, now at Plantagenet, the winery had also begun to develop a reputation for Rhine Riesling and Chardonnay. Douglas has built on that reputation.

Chardonnay was first planted here, on an experimental basis, in 1972, according to Douglas, but Wynn's did not release a varietal Chardonnay until 1981. The grapes are planted, like all of Wynn's fruit, on the Coonawarra's fabled rust-red Terra

Rosa soil which, significantly for Chardonnay, has a high limestone content.

There is only one Chardonnay release at Wynn's. Made from ripe grapes, it is a rich, powerful, hedonistic wine with lots of sweet, oaky fruit. The style here is very un-Burgundian – Douglas does not like to ferment his Chardonnay with a high proportion of grape solids, and favours American, and even German, oak for maturation. Wynn's Chardonnay spends as long as twelve months in 80 to 90 per cent new barrels, half of it on its lees. This may sound excessive, but the wine usually has the structure to cope. All the same, this is not a Chardonnay for pallid, retiring types.

YALUMBA

Eden Valley Road, Angaston, 5353 South Australia

Chardonnay vineyard: 180 acres

Production of Chardonnay: 850,000 bottles

Labels: Hill Smith Estate; Heggies; Signature Reserve; Family Reserve; Oxford Landing

Quality: 🍇_🍇🍇🍇   Price: ★★/★★★

Best vintages: 1988, 1989, 1990

By its own admission, this substantial Barossa Valley winery was a late entrant in the Chardonnay stakes, producing its first example of the grape in 1985, nearly 140 years after it was founded by expatriate Dorset brewer, Samuel Smith. S. Smith & Son, the holding company which bears his name, has quickly righted the omission and now releases as many as six different Chardonnays – seven if you count its New Zealand brand, Nautilus – under the Hill Smith, Yalumba and Heggies labels.

Yalumba is a considerable South Australia vineyard owner, with more than 1,000 acres, but supplements its large production of still, sparkling, fortified and bag-in-box wines with fruit purchased from all over South Australia. There are several different styles of Chardonnay here, from the lightly oaked Oxford Landing to the two top releases, Heggies and Yalumba Signature.

Signature tends to be the softer and more buttery of the two, and I am unconvinced of its ability to age. Heggies, on the other hand, has the potential to become one of the finest Chardonnays in Australia. First made in 1985, Heggies Chardonnay comes from a high-altitude (500 metres) vineyard in the Barossa Ranges, which the Hill Smith family bought and planted in the early seventies. The wine has no skin contact, very little malolactic fermentation and is fermented and aged in a combination of (50 per cent new) French and German oak. The appointment of chief wine-maker Brian Walsh in February 1988 has had a beneficial effect on all of the company's white wines, but the 1989 Heggies – crisp, peachy, well-structured and judiciously oaked – is a most exciting development.

As well as its table wines, Yalumba produces some very good fizz. Angas Brut Classic, Yalumba Pinot Chardonnay and the (top of the range) 1988 Yalumba 'D' all contain significant percentages of Chardonnay.

YARRA YERING

Briary Road, Coldstream, 3770 Victoria

Chardonnay vineyard: 3 acres

Production of Chardonnay: 3,600 bottles

Quality: 🍇🍇🍇   Price: ★★★/★★★★

Best vintages: 1982, 1986, 1990

'I always make wine for myself, and I can't stand vulgar, blowsy Chardonnay.' Dr Bailey Carrodus is a peculiar, opinionated cove who wanders around his small Yarra Valley winery in a butcher's apron and crumpled hat. He was present at the modern renaissance of the Yarra Valley, planting his first vines in 1969. Some of his Chardonnay vines date back to the founding of Yarra Yering.

Carrodus makes a range of eccentric, flavoursome wines. He specializes in red wines, particularly Pinot Noir, but his Chardonnays can be superb, too. They often seem lean and acid in their youth – Carrodus hates fat, tropical-fruit character in his Chardonnay – but are some of the longest-lived in Australia.

Carrodus emphasizes secondary rather than primary fruit flavours in his wine, believing that Chardonnay develops its most interesting characteristics in barrel and bottle. He is usually the first grower in the Yarra to pick his Chardonnay. The wine is fermented in stainless-steel-lined vats, but aged entirely in new French oak, with full malolactic fermentation. The Chardonnay, first produced as a varietal in 1981, was initially unoaked, but the style has evolved since. The quality of Carrodus's Chardonnay is variable – I did not much care for the 1987 – but the 1982 and the 1986 were both wonderful wines. The 1990, which Carrodus calls the first he is really happy with, is very good, too.

YERINGBERG

Maroondah Highway, Coldstream, 3770 Victoria

Chardonnay vineyard: 1.25 acres

Production of Chardonnay: 3,000 bottles

Quality: 🍇🍇🍇🍇   Price: ★★★★

Best vintages: 1984, 1987, 1988, 1990

Yeringberg was among the first wineries to be established in the Yarra Valley. It enjoyed a lofty reputation in the late nineteenth century, but had fallen into disuse by the early 1920s. The current owner, Guillaume de Pury, is the grandson of the wealthy founder, and it was he who replanted a small five-acre portion of the original vineyard in 1969. De Pury grows Chardonnay, Pinot Noir, Marsanne, Roussanne, Cabernet Sauvignon, Cabernet Franc, Malbec and Merlot but, despite the long list of varieties, Yeringberg's production is an exiguous 1,000 cases. There is no lack of space here –

with over one thousand acres of unplanted land – but de Pury shows no inclination to increase the size of the vineyard.

The Yeringberg Chardonnay is one of the best in the Yarra Valley, with a good balance between oak, fruit and acidity. Yields are low and all of the vines are at least eleven years old. The grapes are picked ripe and fermented first in stainless steel, then in (mainly Vosges) oak. De Pury usually acidifies his Chardonnay, and does not put the wine through malolactic fermentation. These are Chardonnays that will age for at least five years, with concentrated but elegant fruit – the excellent 1988 still tasted young two years after the vintage.

AUSTRIA

Total vineyard area: 156,600 acres
Area planted to Chardonnay: 675 acres

Chardonnay has existed in Austria, under various *noms de cépages*, since the 1890s. However, its origins may be even more ancient – Weissburgunder, or Pinot Blanc, which has long been confused with Chardonnay, was first planted in the 1820s. Growers called their best Pinot Blanc Feinster Weissburgunder (finest Pinot Blanc) and it seems likely that what they were really describing was Chardonnay. Modern ampelography has enabled growers to distinguish between the two grapes, but confusion persists.

Chardonnay is now grown in every region of Austria (plantings stand at about 675 acres), and the best growers are often the top producers of other varieties, too. Austria has three main styles. The first is a traditional, unoaked version, known as Morillon, which has been made in Styria for over a century. The wines are crisp and fresh, with low alcohol and firm acidity, somewhere between a Chablis and a Chardonnay from the Alto Adige. The leading exponent of Morillon is Willi Sattler.

The second is a more international style, with new oak and more weight. These are produced in warmer regions like Burgenland and Thermenregion. These are less individual than Morillon, but can still achieve considerable complexity. The best barrel-aged wines are made by Willi Bründlmayer (Kamptal–Donauland), Josef Jurtschitsch (Kamptal–Donauland), Johann Reinisch (Thermenregion) and Georg Stiegelmar (Burgenland).

The final style, which is more unusual as far as Chardonnay is concerned, is Robert Wenzel's Ausbruch (the Austrian term for a wine whose sweetness levels fall between a Beerenauslese and a Trockenbeerenauslese). The 1989 is a raisiny, botrytis-affected dessert wine made entirely from Chardonnay grown in the Burgenland.

Best producers: Bründlmayer, Jurtschitsch, Mayer, Reinisch, Sattler, Stiegelmar, Wenzel

BULGARIA

Total vineyard area: 459,000 acres
Area planted to Chardonnay: 7,560 acres

The success of the centralized Bulgarian wine industry has been one of the wonders of the post-war economic world, demonstrating foresight and levels of efficiency rarely seen in Eastern Europe. But as the Bulgarian economy enters a tailspin in the early nineties, the future structure of its cooperative-based wine industry is unclear.

If Bulgaria had concentrated on white wines, instead of reds, it would not enjoy the reputation it does today. For most Bulgarian whites (made from Mehana, Riesling, Rkatsiteli, Muscat Ottonel, Sauvignon Blanc and Chardonnay) are bland, light and over-sulphured. Chardonnay has not proved as successful as its international travelling partner, Cabernet Sauvignon, but it still looks the most promising of Bulgaria's white wine varieties.

Chardonnay was first brought to Bulgaria, probably from France, in 1915 by Professor Nedelcho Nedelchev, the father of modern Bulgarian viticulture. The first commercial plantings were not made until the 1960s, however. Today, there are Chardonnay vineyards all over Bulgaria, from Perushtitza in the warm south to Varna on the Black Sea coast. The largest and most successful plantings are in the cooler north-east, between the Danube and the Black Sea. The top areas are Ruse, Shumen, Preslav, Khan Krum, Novi Pazar and Varna.

There are several styles of Chardonnay produced in Bulgaria. The cheapest is a Country Wine blend of 60 per cent Chardonnay and 40 per cent Misket from Sungurlare. Next come two Reserve Chardonnays (Varna and Khan Krum), both of which are fermented in stainless steel, but aged in new American oak.

The Khan Krum Special Reserve – ironically, the village is named after a ninth-century king who banned alcohol – is entirely barrel-fermented. All three of these Reserve wines have been clumsily over-oaked in the past, but the 1988 and 1989 vintages were a good deal less sawdusty. Further refinements are needed, although the 1988 Khan Krum Special Reserve looks promising.

For the time being, the best Bulgarian Chardonnays are those that use old oak, or no oak at all. In most vintages, the fruit is simply not weighty enough to stand up to the impact of new barrels. The Controliran Chardonnay (Bulgaria's top wine category) from the Varna cooperative is fresh and citrusy, the Novi Pazar Controliran Chardonnay (aged in old Bulgarian oak) is buttery and slightly earthy. But, overall, Bulgaria's Chardonnays are no match for the wines of France, Italy or the New World.

| Best producers: Khan Krum, Novi Pazar, Shumen, Varna

CANADA

Total vineyard area: 16,300 acres

Area planted to Chardonnay: 500 acres

The majority of Canada's *vinifera* vines are concentrated in the Niagara Peninsula, on the southern shore of Lake Ontario, where the microclimate is (just) warm enough for the cultivation of premium white varietals. The first Canadian Chardonnay was made here in the mid-fifties by Brights, up the road from Niagara Falls, but several other local wineries are now producing Chardonnay, the most successful being Inniskillin and Château des Charmes, both of whom planted in the seventies.

Château des Charmes Chardonnays have been patchy recently, although its Le Roi Estate can be extremely good. More consistent wines are produced by Inniskillin. This winery, which took its name from an Irish regiment that fought in the area during the 1812 war, makes four different Chardonnays – one partially and three entirely barrel-fermented. The first is called Reserve, the other three Seeger Vineyard, Schuele Vineyard and Montague Vineyard respectively. The Seeger Vineyard, which comes from Inniskillin's original plantings, is the most interesting of the three, with firm acidity, good toasty fruit and reasonable ageing potential, but the Schuele Vineyard, made from younger vines, also looks like a wine to watch. The 1988 is the best recent vintage I have tasted from this producer.

CHILE

Total vineyard area: 270,000 acres
Area planted to Chardonnay: 4,050 acres

Chardonnay is a comparative parvenu in Chile, where the most-planted white grape is the dull, usually over-cropped Sauvignon Vert, or Sauvignonasse. It was introduced on a commercial scale by Cousiño Macul in 1974, and most of the dozen leading wineries have since followed suit. Nearly all of Chile's Chardonnay is to be found in the fertile, irrigated Central Valley, between Santiago and Curicó, but the most promising source of Chardonnay is Casablanca, situated to the north-west in a coastal range between Santiago and the port of Viña del Mar. Rainfall is higher here (which does away with the need for irrigation), soils are poorer, and yields are comparatively low. At least one Chilean wine-maker thinks Casablanca could be Chile's answer to the Napa Valley, give or take the coach parties.

As yet, there is no discernibly Chilean style of Chardonnay. Examples range from the fresh and unoaked (made by Australians Nick Butler and Martin Shaw at Viña Canepa), to full, tropical fruit and vanilla wines at Caliterra. Most producers are moving towards a greater percentage of barrel-fermentation, though so far only Santa Rita's Medalla Real has gone all the way. Errázuriz Panquehue, Santa Rita and Concha y Toro (for their Marqués de Casa Concha) make the best-balanced wines, but Chilean Chardonnay in general lacks complexity. As the average age of the vines increases, and wineries continue to experiment with new, cooler sources of fruit, this should change.

Thierry Villard, a Frenchman who used to make the wine at Orlando in South Australia, and Cavas del Maipo (whose

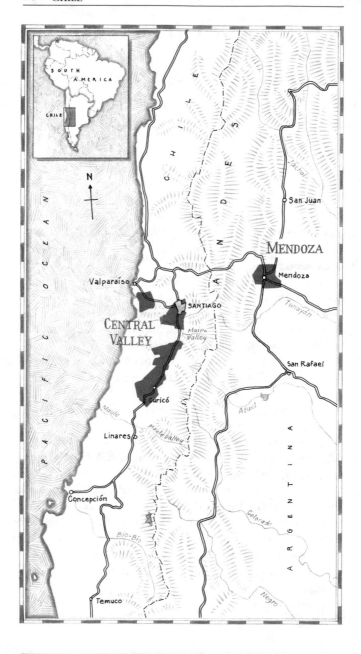

light, elegant sparkling Chardonnay I tasted in a Polynesian-style night-club in Santiago) are smaller producers worth keeping an eye on, as is William Fèvre, one of the top names in Chablis and a recent arrival in Chile. Château Lafite's three-year-old participation in Los Vascos may also yield interesting results.

Best producers: Caliterra*, Cavas del Maipo, Concha y Toro*, Cousiño Macul, Errázuriz Panquehue*, Los Vascos, Santa Rita*, Torres* (see section on *SPAIN*), Villard, Viña Canepa

CALITERRA

PO Box 2346, Santiago

Production of Chardonnay: 300,000 bottles

Quality: 🍇🍇–🍇🍇🍇   Price: ★/★★

Best vintages: 1989, 1990

Caliterra is a slick joint-venture between California's Franciscan Estates and the leading Chilean producer, Errázuriz Panquehue. The wines produced in tandem by Greg Upton (of Franciscan) and Ernesto Jiusan (of Panquehue) are appropriately Californian in style: full-throttle Cabernets and intense, oaky Chardonnays. Only the prices are authentically Chilean.

Unlike Errázuriz Panquehue, Caliterra has no vines of its own. Instead, it buys grapes from long-term-contract growers in Maipo and Curicó. The partnership must be choosing its grapes well, because in only six years, it has established itself as one of Chile's most consistent producers.

There are two styles of Chardonnay: the Curicó Chardonnay, 50 per cent of which is fermented in American and French oak; and the bigger, more buttery Maipo Reserva, fermented in French oak and aged on its lees. The Reserva is the more complex wine, but the Curicó blend is very good, basic Chardonnay.

CONCHA Y TORO

Fernando Lazcano 1220, Santiago

Chardonnay vineyard: 197 acres

Production of Chardonnay: 840,000 bottles

Labels: Concha y Toro; Casillero del Diablo; Marqués de Casa Concha

Quality: 🍇🍇/🍇🍇🍇   Price: ★★

Best vintages: 1989, 1990

Concha y Toro is Chile's largest producer, better known for its reds than its whites. The general quality of its white wines is certainly nothing to jump up and down about (the Riesling and the Sauvignon Blanc are fairly unexciting), but wine-maker Goetz von Gersdorff does appear to be on the right track with Chardonnay.

Concha y Toro makes three different styles of Chardonnay. The basic unoaked Chardonnay is clean and peachy; the oak-aged Casillero del Diablo is slightly over-splintered; but the more selected Marqués de Casa Concha is extremely promising. The 1989 was fermented in stainless steel and then aged for six months in French Allier and Vosges *barriques*; but von Gersdorff was so impressed with the result that in 1990 he fermented 10 per cent of the wine in oak. Further encouraged, he increased the figure to 50 per cent in 1991.

The development of this elegant, well-balanced wine is worth watching. It has the potential to become one of the Southern Hemisphere's finest Chardonnays.

ERRÁZURIZ PANQUEHUE

> Bandera 206 OF, 601, Casilla 2346, Santiago
>
> Chardonnay vineyard: 135 acres
>
> Production of Chardonnay: 190,000 bottles
>
> Quality: 🍇🍇🍇   Price: ★/★★
>
> Best vintages: 1989, 1990

The Errázuriz family is one of the most powerful in Chile, with a distinguished history of public service. Its business interests include brewing, malting, whisky distribution and bottling Coca-Cola under franchise. Errázuriz Panquehue, its wine company, is named after the original Panquehue vineyard, 130 km north of Santiago in the Aconcagua Valley. This was planted with red French grapes in 1870 by Don Maximiano Errázuriz Valdivieso, and at one point was the largest single vineyard in the world. It has subsequently dwindled from more than 6,600 acres to fewer than fifty.

There is no Chardonnay in the Aconcagua vineyard, though Errázuriz has plantings further south in the Maule region's Mataquito Valley. The first Chardonnay vineyards were grafted over from Cabernet Sauvignon and Sémillon in 1984, but these were supplemented with further plantings throughout the eighties. Errázuriz is also looking at developing Chardonnay in the cooler Casablanca region.

The Chardonnays made at Errázuriz are among the best in Chile, though so far the company has not established a consistent house style. It is currently experimenting with barrel-fermentation and with ageing wines on their fermentation lees, in an attempt to develop a greater range of flavours. The wines are more European than those produced by Caliterra, the joint-venture between Errázuriz and the Californian Franciscan Estates. The top wine is the Reserva, 90 per cent barrel-fermented and aged *sur lie*.

*

SANTA RITA

Gertrudis Echeñique 49, Santiago

Chardonnay vineyard: 42 acres

Production of Chardonnay: 210,000 bottles

Quality: 🍇_🍇🍇   Price: ★/★★

Best vintages: 1989, 1990, 1991

Santa Rita is one of Chile's most dynamic producers, combining traditionalism with a clear-sighted view of the future. It has invested an enormous amount of money in new technology over the last five years, and the quality of the bodega's white wines has improved dramatically. (The only blemish occurred in 1989, when above average levels of sorbitol, a harmless, but illegal additive, were found in some of the company's wines.) Riesling, Sauvignon Blanc and Chardonnay are all good, with well-defined varietal characteristics, a quality often lacking in Chilean whites.

Santa Rita made its first Medalla Real Chardonnay in 1987, with 20 per cent barrel-fermentation in Vosges and Allier oak. The style of the wine has jigged about a bit in subsequent vintages. The 1989 and 1991 were entirely barrel-fermented, whereas the crisp, slightly ungainly 1990 saw a mixture of barrels and stainless-steel tanks.

With the 1991 vintage, things appear to have settled down. Santa Rita has introduced a second, complementary style of Chardonnay, and this seems to have solved the identity crisis. The new Reserva is 60 per cent barrel-fermented, while the Medalla Real has reverted to 100 per cent barrel-fermentation.

Until 1989, all Santa Rita's Chardonnay came from the irrigated Maipo Valley, but in the last three vintages the wine has included an increasing proportion of grapes from Casablanca, Chile's up-and-coming white-wine region. Santa Rita is an ambitious operation, but its Chardonnay has yet to realize its full potential.

CHINA

Total vineyard area: 35,000 acres
Area planted to Chardonnay: 100 acres

Records of Chinese wine production date back more than 2,000 years, but wine-making as most consumers understand it is comparatively recent. As well as an intriguing list of native varieties (including Tiger's Eye and Cow's Nipple), China also has a few patches of more familiar *vinifera* vines. The majority of China's plantings are in Shandong Province. Qingdao, where the only Chinese Chardonnay is made, is one of five wine-producing districts in the area; the other four are Chefoo, Weifang, Heze and Jinan. Tsingtao is well suited for Chardonnay. It lies on the same latitude as the Napa Valley and enjoys a relatively cool, dry climate. Cool breezes from the Yellow Sea help to keep the temperature down.

The Cognac house Rémy Martin produces a reasonable white wine (made from a blend of Muscat and local varieties), but it is not a patch on the Huadong winery's Chardonnay. This is produced from vines planted in the early eighties under the supervision of the late English entrepreneur, Mike Parry. The area, in particular the port of Qingdao, has strong historical links with Germany and it was Lutheran ministers who introduced Welsch Riesling, but not Chardonnay, in the late nineteenth century. Parry smuggled in cuttings from France and set up a new, hi-tech winery with the help of Rosemount Estate.

The top Hunter Valley winery got involved with Huadong on a consultancy basis in 1985, and it is no coincidence that the Chardonnay has a pronounced Australian character, with peachy, fruit-salad and oak flavours. If Chardonnay has an international face, this is it. Successive Australian wine-makers did the vinification in China from 1985 until the arrangement ended in 1990. The drinks multinational Hiram Walker now owns shares in Huadong and, with sound investment, the quality of the wine should continue to improve. A Chardonnay to serve at blind tastings.

CYPRUS

Total vineyard area: 60,000 acres
Area planted to Chardonnay: approximately 40 acres

Chardonnay only deserves a mention here, in the pressure-cooker of the Mediterranean, because of the pioneering work of Nearchos Roumbas, who runs the Department of Agriculture's Model Winery, just outside Limassol. So far, the experience Roumbas accumulated in France, Italy, Spain, Greece and Switzerland has been under-used by the four big companies which run the local wine industry, but things might change, even in Cyprus.

Two grapes – Mavro (for reds) and Xynisteri (for whites) – dominate the island's vineyards, but Roumbas has proved that you can grow Cabernet Sauvignon, Cabernet Franc, Mourvèdre, Grenache, Cinsault, Shiraz, Riesling, Sémillon and Chardonnay with some success. The experimental Chardonnay was planted in 1980, using vines from Champagne, and the first vintage was in 1984. The 1989 was made with 20 g of residual sugar and 14 per cent alcohol, but had lots of acidity too. When I tasted it in Limassol, it was round, sweet and fruity with good acidity. Not a world-beater, but a lot better than Xynisteri.

The 1990 was fermented out to dryness, though I have not tasted the result. Roumbas says that if the variety is planted high enough, and on north-facing slopes, it could produce interesting results in the future. He thinks it could be used to replace Mavro. All he has to do is persuade a few more people that he's right.

ENGLAND

Total vineyard area: 2,700 acres
Area planted to Chardonnay: 65 acres

It was Sir Guy Salisbury-Jones, the man credited with resur-
recting the English wine industry, who planted the first
experimental Chardonnay cuttings at Hambledon Vineyard,
Hampshire, in the early fifties. His enterprising lead, allegedly
inspired by a boozy dinner at Clos de Vougeot in Burgundy,
was followed in the seventies by Ian and Andrew Paget at
Chilsdown, William Ross at Barnsgate Manor and Gillian
Pearkes at Yearlstone in Devon.

Of the pioneers, only Pearkes has had any success with
Chardonnay. Low yields and a favourable microclimate have
helped her to get the grapes ripe – the principal hurdle facing
would-be Chardonnay producers in England and Wales.
Pearkes ferments her wine in Limousin oak, and the results are
good, if unspectacular.

The last five years have witnessed a revival of interest in
Chardonnay. Intrepid wine-makers have decided to give it
another chance, possibly encouraged by the warmer 1989 and
1990 vintages, bringing the area under vine to around 65 acres.
Nyetimber in Sussex, Wellow Vineyard in Hampshire, Denbies
in Surrey and Throwley Vineyard in Kent have all made sizeable plantings, with a view to making sparkling wines. The
initial results look promising, though at the time of writing
Wellow Vineyard is up for sale.

FRANCE

| Total vineyard area: 2.3 million acres
| Area planted to Chardonnay: 55,000 acres

France may no longer be the world's largest producer of Chardonnay – that particular gong is now in Californian hands – but it continues to produce the supreme examples of the grape. The wines of Chablis, Champagne and the Côte de Beaune have spawned imitations all over the world and, even if individual examples do not always live up to their lofty reputations, these are wine styles to which other non-French producers consistently aspire.

As Chardonnay's worldwide popularity has blossomed, so French plantings have increased in number. In 1969, for example, there were only 24,000 acres of Chardonnay. While many of these new vineyards have popped up in traditional Chardonnay areas, particularly Burgundy and Champagne, the grape has also appeared as far away as Corsica, Gascony, the Loire and the Ardèche. There are even a few (strictly illegal as far as *appellation contrôlée* is concerned) vines in Bordeaux. In most cases, these new Chardonnays are not allowed to aspire any higher than Vin de Pays status.

The majority of plantings are still divided between Champagne (20,700 acres) and the four Burgundian *départements*: Saône et Loire (11,115 acres), Rhône (250 acres), Côte d'Or (3,458 acres) and Yonne (7,410 acres), but there are now Chardonnay vineyards (whether authorized or not) in almost every French viticultural region. In some areas, such as the Midi, the Loire and the southern Rhône, it is used to add a bit of breed to local blends, but an increasing number of producers are now releasing varietal Chardonnays, many of them from some fairly unlikely sources.

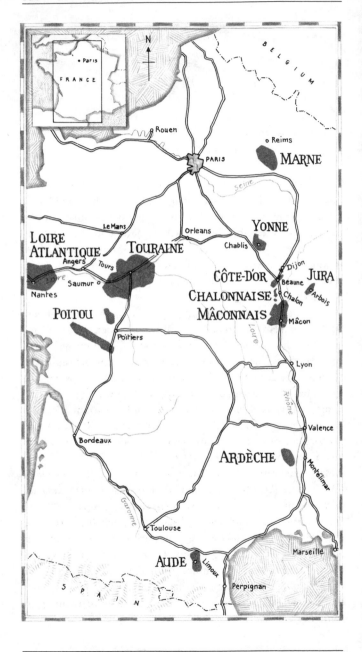

Burgundy

Burgundy produces all of the greatest and many of the worst Chardonnays in the world. This complicated, and often frustrating region, stretching from chilly Chablis to the warm slopes of the northern Beaujolais, is a mecca for Chardonnay lovers. Chablis, Meursault, Puligny-Montrachet, Corton-Charlemagne . . . the names are supremely evocative, even for people who have never tasted a drop of white Burgundy.

Chardonnay is a more consistent performer than its playing partner Pinot Noir, but the production of Burgundy's greatest vineyards is still alarmingly small. More than thirty times as much Chardonnay is produced in California as in the three great white wine villages of Meursault, Puligny-Montrachet and Chassagne-Montrachet.

Viticultural Burgundy can be divided into four main areas: the Yonne, where Chablis is produced; the Côte d'Or, which is divided into the Côte de Nuits and the Côte de Beaune; the Côte Chalonnaise; and the Mâconnais. (The Beaujolais is sometimes lumped in with the rest of the Burgundian *vignoble*, but this seems questionable to me.) In terms of total output, Burgundy is dominated by the Côte d'Or (35 per cent) and the Mâconnais (35 per cent), with the rest divided more or less equally between the other two areas. Chardonnay, of varying complexity, is produced in all four.

For the socially minded, Burgundy has its very own, carefully delineated class system. The aristocracy is represented by the Grands Crus (Blanchot, Bougros, Les Clos, Grenouilles, Preuses, Valmur, Vaudésir, Montrachet, Corton-Charlemagne, Bâtard-Montrachet, Bienvenues-Bâtard-Montrachet, Chevalier-Montrachet and Criots-Bâtard-Montrachet), which account for about 1 per cent of all white Burgundy.

Next come the professional classes, or Premiers Crus, the most important of which are to be found in the villages of Chablis, Beaune, Meursault, Puligny-Montrachet, Chassagne-Montrachet, Saint-Aubin, Auxey-Duresses and Rully. These represent roughly 14 per cent of total production. They are

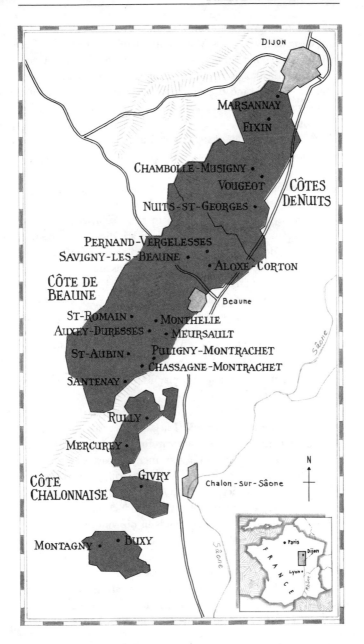

followed in the great chain of Burgundian being by white-collar village *appellations* such as Meursault, Chablis or Beaune. After that, there is a range of blue-collar regional *appellations* (Mâcon Villages or Beaujolais Blanc, for example). And last, and very definitely least, come the more common generic *appellations*: Bourgogne Blanc, Bourgogne Grand Ordinaire and Bourgogne Chardonnay.

This is a useful way of looking at Burgundy, but it provides no more than a sketch. To add colour and nuance, you have to consider the region in a little more detail. Burgundy's vineyards are divided into parcels, according to soil and microclimate. Some of these parcels are tiny – Le Montrachet, arguably the most famous white-wine vineyard in the world, covers fewer than 20 acres. These vineyards in turn are divided between a number of producers. Fifteen different growers or families own vines, side by side, in Le Montrachet, for instance.

The situation is further complicated by the French system of inheritance taxes. In the past, family properties were kept intact from one generation to the next by a simple expedient – if necessary, one heir bought out the others. Nowadays, families have to sell off precious vineyards just to pay the taxes; the price of land, particularly in Chablis and the Côte de Beaune, is so exorbitant that few can afford to pay it. This merely intensifies the proliferation of names.

In Burgundy, more than any other wine region, the question of who owns the vines is crucial. Burgundy is a marginal grape-growing climate which repays careful vineyard husbandry. Grapes that are grown only a few metres apart can produce totally different wines. Part of this is attributable to subtle differences in the structure of the soil, but viticulture is argu-ably even more important. Overproduction – a very Burgundian blight – begins and ends in the vineyard.

There are considerable differences between *appellations* – it is difficult to confuse a Rully with a Puligny-Montrachet – but within each *appellation*, from the loftiest Grand Cru to the most ordinary patch of Bourgogne Blanc, there are good, bad and mediocre producers. Unless you have tasted somebody's wine, you have no way of knowing how drinkable it will be. Sadly, the bad and mediocre often outnumber the good, making Burgundy one of the least reliable fine-wine regions. It may be impossible to make great wine from mediocre grapes, but it is all too easy to perform the opposite transformation. As one Australian wine-maker commented: 'The Burgundians grow the greatest grapes in the world; then they do everything they can to stuff them up.'

Cooperatives and *négociants* do not have a monopoly here; some of the worst white Burgundies of all are produced by individual domaines. The common wisdom holds that domaine-bottled Burgundies are generally better than the offerings from *négociants* and cooperatives, but this is not necessarily true. Certainly the increase in domaine-bottling over the last twenty years has reduced the power of the *négociants*. (Cooperatives, which are nearly all situated in the Côte Chalonnaise and the Mâconnais, have suffered less from the trend towards domaine-bottling.) But the best merchants have fought back. Many have bought vineyards of their own; others have moved to secure regular supplies of good grapes by setting up long-term contracts with individual growers. Another development has been the tendency to buy grapes rather than must or finished wine. This gives the good *négociant* more control over what he puts in bottle; less fastidious merchants, of whom there are many, apparently couldn't care less.

For all these improvements, however, the majority of Burgundy's best white wines are made by single domaines. I would place the merchants Louis Jadot and Joseph Drouhin on or near the same level as the finest individual growers, but a large business will never be able to pay the same attention to detail as a man working with a small quantity of wine, produced entirely from his own vines. On those rare occasions when soil, climate, grape variety and human endeavour combine in glorious harmony, domaine-bottled white Burgundy is beyond compare.

*

BURGUNDIAN APPELLATIONS

Chablis

The tasting room at Domaine de la Maladière, William Fèvre's imposing stone winery in the centre of Chablis, is lined with empty bottles. There are dozens of them, from every corner of the wine-making world: Chile, California, Mexico, New Zealand and Australia. The bottles have one thing in common. None is French, but every single label bears the word Chablis. My own particular favourite is California Chablis With a Twist of Lime, a wine that, like most generic 'Chablis', does not contain a single drop of Chardonnay, which is, of course, the only white grape permitted in the real stuff.

The image of Chablis has been damaged by association with thousands of lesser products. (According to Jean-Paul Droin, only six out of one hundred bottles of 'Chablis' are actually produced in Chablis itself.) A similar fate has been suffered by Champagne. But while the more powerful Champenois have had considerable success in preventing the abuse of their name, in Chablis no joy. Sad times in the Yonne? Well, yes and no. It would be easier to feel sorry for the Chablisiens if their wines were always exemplary, but two recent trends have set worrying qualitative precedents.

The first is vineyard expansion. Plantings in Chablis are increasing at an astonishing rate – something like 10 per cent per annum – and many of them are not in suitable parts of the *appellation*. Viticulturally, Chablis is borderline territory, closer to Champagne than to Burgundy. In other words, it is a place where grapes are threatened by frost and need the right exposure to ripen properly in all but the warmest years. Many of the new vineyards have a tendency to produce tart, green grapes that damage what reputation Chablis has left.

'The vineyard area may be elastic,' says William Fèvre, 'but quality isn't.' Ever one for the fray, Fèvre heads the local Syndicat de la Défense de l'Appellation Chablis, which advocates the restriction of the Chablis *appellation* to vineyards sited on (supposedly) the best friable Kimmeridgian clay and limestone soil. The opposite camp, which favours expansion in non-Kimmeridgian sites, is called La Fédération des Viticulteurs Chablisiens, and is led by Jean Durup of Domaine de l'Eglantière. Durup is one of the largest vineyard owners in the *appellation*, alongside Moreau, Domaine Laroche, William Fèvre and the Beaune-based *négociant* firm, Joseph Drouhin, but most of his vines are classified as Chablis or Petit Chablis. Perhaps this explains his position. Certainly, to date, Durup's team is winning the argument.

There is still considerable room for expansion – something like 2,500 acres of Chablis and 3,000 acres of Petit Chablis. Plantings of Petit Chablis are fairly small, but even here there is an ominous trend. Several local producers have proposed that the *appellation* Petit Chablis be replaced by the less pejorative Hautes Côtes de Chablis. In response, the governing Institut National des Appellations d'Origine has suggested doing away with Petit Chablis altogether, and rechristening it Chablis. This is not going to do wonders for the region's image.

The second alarming trend is rising yields. The region has just been blessed with three very-good-to-excellent vintages on the trot – an improvement on the post-war years when ten crops out of sixteen were destroyed by frost – and there has been a distressing tendency to push the crop to its limit. Some growers claim that it is difficult to restrain Nature, that in this case quantity is not detrimental to quality, but I remain unconvinced.

If poor Chablis and Petit Chablis are all too common (these are the two basic *appellations*, below the generally more lofty Premiers and Grands Crus) there are still an impressive number of producers, both growers and merchants, whose wines embody all that is best about Chablis – that crisp, complex, citrusy, minerally flavour that no other wine region can imitate. Viticulturally, Chablis is part of Burgundy, but it would be difficult, if not always impossible, to confuse a Chablis with a Meursault or a Mâcon.

There are subtle differences between the seven Grands Crus (Bougros, Vaudésir, Les Clos, Preuses, Grenouilles, Valmur and Blanchot) and the leading Premiers Crus (Monts de Milieu,

Montée de Tonnerre, Chapelot and Fourchaume), all of which are situated on the right bank of the Serein river on a steep south-west-facing slope above the village of Chablis.

Among the Grands Crus, Les Clos is the most structured, concentrated and age-worthy; Vaudésir and Valmur tend to be similar in style, but with a little less intensity than Les Clos; Preuses and Grenouilles are often the most forward and aromatic, while Bougros and Blanchot lean towards rusticity.

Keeping track of all the Premiers Crus is not easy. There are forty in total, though only a dozen or so of these appear regularly on labels (Fourchaume, Montée de Tonnerre, Monts de Milieu, Vaucoupin, Les Fourneaux, Beauroy, Côte de Léchet, Vaillons, Mélinots, Montmains, Vosgros, Butteaux, Chapelot and Forêts, or La Forest as it is sometimes known). Among the top Premiers Crus, it is Monts de Milieu and Montée de Tonnerre which come closest to the sheer class of Les Clos. Fourchaume is usually a little fuller in style.

There are several different styles of Chablis, with producers falling into one of three main camps: the oaked, the unoaked and the partially oaked. Traditionally, all Chablis was fermented in barrels, but with the development of new technology, and the not inconsiderable financial constraints of buying new oak, most have switched to vinifying their wines in stainless-steel or lined-concrete tanks.

The best of the tank commanders is Louis Michel, who makes clean, delightfully aromatic Chablis from a broad range of Grands and Premiers Crus. This camp also includes Jean Durup, Albert Pic and J. Moreau et Fils. In the well and truly oaked school of Chablis, the leading producer is William Fèvre, who owns some of the most impressive vineyards in the *appellation*.

Not many producers have embraced new oak as wholeheartedly as Fèvre. Several of the top names ferment all or part of their Grands and Premiers Crus in barrel, but use stainless steel for their lesser wines. At the big and toasty end of the scale, Jean-Paul Droin is a name to watch. The local cooperative, La Chablisienne, also makes a good range of wines, both oaked and unoaked, as do the *négociants* Laroche and Drouhin, and the two finest producers in the village, Vincent Dauvissat and Jean-Marie Raveneau.

> Best producers: Jean-Marie Brocard, La Chablisienne*,
> Vincent Dauvissat*, Jean-Paul Droin*, Joseph Drouhin*,
> Jean Durup, William Fèvre*, Jean-Pierre Grossot,
> Domaine Laroche*, Louis Michel*, Jean-Marie
> Raveneau*, Philippe Testut, Robert Vocoret

The Côte d'Or

Most Côte d'Or Chardonnay comes from the Côte de Beaune. On the more northerly Côte de Nuits, the grape is a much rarer beast – only the communes of Vougeot, Chambolle-Musigny, Nuits-Saint-Georges and Morey-Saint-Denis make white wine, and even here it is in pretty short supply. Despite appearances to the contrary, red wines outnumber whites on the Côte d'Or by roughly four bottles to one. Three-quarters of all the white wine produced in Burgundy's most prestigious region comes from just three world-famous villages on the Côte de Beaune: Meursault, Puligny-Montrachet and Chassagne-Montrachet. But there are other communes which are capable of producing first-class Chardonnay too. Aloxe-Corton and Pernand-Vergelesses, which share the Grand Cru Corton Charlemagne, are the salient examples, but lesser white-wine *appellations*, such as Saint-Romain, Saint-Aubin, Auxey-Duresses and Beaune are also worth a look.

Aloxe-Corton/Pernand-Vergelesses/Ladoix-Serrigny

The majestic Corton hill is one of the great sights of the Côte d'Or, a continuous vine-clad slope crowned with trees. This is the source of Corton Charlemagne, the only white Grand Cru north of Beaune. Situated at the northern limit of the Côte de Beaune, Corton Charlemagne is divided between the communes of Aloxe-Corton, Pernand-Vergelesses and Ladoix-Serrigny, although the majority of the *cru* is in Aloxe.

Named after the Holy Roman Emperor (who almost certainly owned a vineyard here) Corton Charlemagne is surpassed only by Le Montrachet and Chevalier-Montrachet at the summit of white Burgundy. At over 1,600 hectolitres, production is large – more than the entire village of Meursault – but prices are still astronomic.

There are small quantities of white wine produced in the three communes which are not entitled to Grand Cru status, the best of which, labelled Pernand Blanc, comes from Pernand-Vergelesses. On the Corton hill itself, the *appellation* laws are more complicated. Red vines that are situated in Corton-Charlemagne are sold as Corton, while white vines in Corton are labelled Corton-Charlemagne. Got that? Good, because it's not quite as simple as that. Wines produced in the vineyards called En Charlemagne (in Pernand), Les Pougets, Les Languettes, Les Renardes, Le Corton and Le Charlemagne (in Aloxe) and Le Rognet-Corton, Basses Mourottes and Hautes Marottes (in Ladoix) are all labelled Corton-Charlemagne, while those from the Grand Cru sites of Les Vergennes (in Ladoix), Les Perrières and Le Clos du Roi (both in Aloxe) are called Corton Blanc. To make things even less clear, the word 'Charlemagne' *tout court* is sometimes used.

Given the reputation and price of Corton-Charlemagne, it is not surprising that growers are replacing Pinot Noir with Chardonnay in vineyards which are more suited to red wines than whites. The best sites for Chardonnay are near the top of the south-east-facing slope, just below the Bois de Corton on stony limestone soil.

Its price notwithstanding, Corton-Charlemagne is the most consistent of Burgundy's white Grands Crus. When young, it is simultaneously the most concentrated but also the most closed of Chardonnays. One has a sense of a huge lion waiting to pounce. Of all white Burgundies, Corton-Charlemagne is the one which rewards patience. The two leading producers of Corton-Charlemagne, at least in terms of acreage, are Bonneau du Martray and the *négociant* Louis Latour. Latour's wines tend to be bigger and more oaky than those from Bonneau du Martray. Tiny quantities of exquisite Corton-Charlemagne are produced by Jean-François Coche-Dury in Meursault and the Nuits-Saint-Georges *négociant*, Joseph Faiveley.

Best producers: Bonneau du Martray*, Jean-François
   Coche-Dury*, Joseph Drouhin*, Joseph Faiveley*,
   Hospices de Beaune, Louis Jadot*, Louis Latour*,
   Domaine Rollin, Georges Roumier, Domaine
   Tollot-Beaut

Beaune

Nearly all the wine from this, the third largest commune on the
Côte d'Or, is red, but one exceptional white wine is produced
by the *négociant* Joseph Drouhin. This comes from the Premier
Cru Clos des Mouches, a 62-acre vineyard at the southern end
of the *appellation* bordering the village of Pommard, and is
somewhere between a Meursault and a Corton-Charlemagne in
style.

Best producers: Bouchard Père et Fils*, Joseph Drouhin*

Auxey-Duresses

Traditionally, the white wines of Auxey-Duresses were sold
(fraudulently) as Meursault or (legitimately) as Côte de Beaune
Villages, but in the last decade they have begun to emerge as
good, reasonably priced Chardonnays in their own right. Most
of the Chardonnay is planted on the Coteaux du Mont Melian,
where the soil is suitably shallow. Auxey-Duresses white wines
tend to be leaner than those from Meursault, their westerly
neighbour. As a result, the wines age surprisingly well.

Best producers: Gérard Creusefond, Jean-Pierre Diconne,
   Maison Leroy, Michel Prunier

Saint-Romain

Saint-Romain is situated behind Auxey-Duresses on the edge of
the Hautes Côtes de Beaune. The wines are influenced by their
altitude, and tend to be high in acidity. In cool vintages, they
are a little too austere, but the best-exposed chalky sites, such as
Le Jarron and Sous Roche, can produce excellent wines in
warmer years. There are no Premiers Crus vineyards.

Best producers: Henri et Gilles Buisson, Bernard Fèvre,
Jean Germain, Alain Gras, René Thévenin-Monthélie

Saint-Aubin

Of all the lesser *appellations* of the Côte de Beaune, Saint-Aubin
is consistently the most impressive. This small sleepy village has
two famous neighbours – Puligny-Montrachet and Chassagne-
Montrachet – and at least one local grower has vines in some
very prestigious Grand Cru sites near by. There are nineteen
Premiers Crus in Saint-Aubin, but no Grands Crus. For white
wines, the best-known are Le Charmois, En Remilly, Sous
Roche Dumay and La Chatenière. The most propitious sites
near the hamlet of Gamay produce wines that are remarkably
similar to good village-level Puligny-Montrachet. These are
some of the best value white Burgundies of all.

Best producers: Jean-Claude Bachelet, Marc Colin*, Henri
Prudhon, Roux Père et Fils, Gérard Thomas

Meursault

Meursault is the largest and most picturesque of the three great
white wine villages of the Côte de Beaune. The village's two
landmarks – the Hôtel de Ville, with its brightly coloured
snakeskin-style roof, and an imposing church spire – are both
visible from afar. Contrasted with Chassagne- or Puligny-
Montrachet, Meursault is a busy, sometimes bustling place – a
prosperous country town, not a sleepy Burgundian hamlet.

Despite the fact that it produces more white wine than its
two illustrious neighbours, some of which is truly brilliant,
Meursault has no Grands Crus. According to the grower
Bernard Michelot, the reason is simple enough: 'In the early
days of *appellation contrôlée*, no one was motivated enough to
ask.' Pierre Morey, wine-maker at Domaine Leflaive in
Puligny-Montrachet as well as a Meursault producer in his own
right, says that Meursault was discriminated against because of
small plantings of a productive hybrid called Ravat after the
Second World War.

Whatever the reason, for the time being Meursault can aspire no higher than its Premier Cru vineyards. Excluding the three Premiers Crus in the next door village of Blagny, which are sold as Meursault-Blagny Premier Cru, the most important are Les Gouttes d'Or, Les Bouchères, Le Porusot, Les Genevrières, Les Charmes and Les Perrières. Of these, the one that consistently produces wines of Grand Cru level is Les Perrières. The village also makes a small amount of red wine, mainly sold as Volnay-Santenots from vines on the north-eastern side of the village. The soil is heavier here than in the Premier Cru vineyards to the south of Meursault, and is more suited to red-wine production than white.

Volnay-Santenots notwithstanding, the village's finest Premiers Crus – Les Charmes, Les Genevrières and Les Perrières – are all situated mid-slope between Meursault and Puligny-Montrachet. These wines tend to sell at a premium, and are usually the most complex and full-flavoured of Meursault's white wines. Of the three, Les Genevrières is usually the most elegant, aromatic and racy, Les Charmes is richer and more structured, and Les Perrières the most intense and long-lived. As well as its Premiers Crus, Meursault has a complex network of *lieux-dits*, or vineyard-designated wines. These are not entitled to Premier Cru status, but the best of them are often a notch above basic village Meursault. The ones to look out for are Clos de la Barre, Le Tesson, Les Meix Chavaux, Le Limouzin and Les Narvaux.

Meursault is often richer and more buttery than Chassagne- and Puligny-Montrachet, but there are almost as many different styles as there are producers. The wines of Comtes Lafon, François Jobard and Bernard Michelot, to take three of the village's best-known growers, are utterly distinct.

Meursault has a large number of growers who bottle their own wine, as well as producing substantial quantities of *négociant* Burgundy. Inevitably perhaps, the variation in quality can be enormous. Tempted by high prices to increase their yields, many producers make wine, particularly at village level, which is dull and over-cropped. At its most seductive, however, Meursault is a glorious wine – packed with soft, rich flavours of

butter, hazelnuts and cinnamon. It is usually more forward than
the Grands and Premiers Crus of Chassagne- and Puligny-
Montrachet, but the top wines are perfectly capable of ageing
for at least a decade in bottle.

> Best producers: Robert Ampeau*, Bernard Bachelet, Jean-
> Pierre Boillot, Bernard Boisson-Vadot, Jean-François
> Coche-Dury*, Louis Jadot*, Patrick Javillier, François
> Jobard*, Labouré-Roi, Comtes Lafon*, Olivier Leflaive*,
> Joseph, Pierre et Thierry Matrot*, Bernard Michelot-
> Buisson*, Pierre Morey*, Jacques Prieur*, Guy Roulot*

Puligny-Montrachet

At first sight, Puligny-Montrachet feels less like a wine village
than Meursault or Chassagne-Montrachet. The most
celebrated white-wine commune of all is discreet about its
reputation. There is no more than a handful of signs quietly
indicating the whereabouts of world-famous names such as
Leflaive, Carillon, Sauzet and Clerc. Visitors are tolerated but
not encouraged.

Whatever the outward signs, this is the pinnacle of Chardonnay production. Puligny-Montrachet lets its wines do the talking. It has four out of a possible six white-wine Grands Crus
(two of them shared with Chassagne-Montrachet) and at least
half a dozen Premiers Crus (Les Perrières, Le Clavoillon, Les
Combettes, Les Referts, Les Pucelles and Le Cailleret) which
regularly turn out stunning wines.

Of the three great white-wine villages of the Côte d'Or,
Puligny-Montrachet is the one whose top wines consistently
display the most breed and elegance. There is a finely structured balance to a great Puligny-Montrachet which is unmis-
takable. It is a wine to sip and savour, a wine that can take five
years or more to approach its peak. To drink a Le Montrachet
too young is almost a crime.

The water-table is close to the surface in Puligny, with
two main consequences. Cellars are rare (because of the risk
of flooding), and yields, particularly in a year like 1988, can

be excessive. At village level, Puligny is less reliable than Chassagne, though generally a much better bet than Meursault, which produces nearly twice as much wine.

Unlike its two illustrious neighbours, Puligny is dominated by the presence of *négociants* – another reason for the comparative scarcity of those signs. There are far more growers who bottle their own wine in Meursault and Chassagne. Prominent merchants include Drouhin, Latour, Bouchard Père and Jadot, backed up by two more local names, Olivier Leflaive and Chartron et Trébuchet, whose premises are virtually next door to one another in the centre of Puligny.

Puligny's Grands and Premiers Crus are all situated to the north and west of the village. The Grands Crus are all lumped together, on the border with Chassagne-Montrachet, at the western limit of the commune. Montrachet and Bâtard-Montrachet have a foot in both villages, but Chevalier-Montrachet and Bienvenues-Bâtard-Montrachet belong to Puligny alone. All four are sited mid-slope in an especially favourable, sheltered microclimate. Generalizations are difficult, but Bâtard and Bienvenues tend to be the fullest wines of the quartet. Chevalier, second in the pecking order in my view, has more finesse and structure, while Le Montrachet combines the qualities of the other three Grands Crus to exquisite perfection.

The best Premiers Crus are to be found strung out along the Côte to the north-east at the same altitude as the Grands Crus. They are separated from lesser village-level vineyards by a thin ribbon of road, called the Sentier des Couches. The ones close to the Grands Crus (Le Cailleret, Les Pucelles) tend to be racier and more distinguished than those on the border with Meursault (Les Combettes, Les Referts and Champ Canet).

Best producers: Louis Carillon*, Jean-René Chartron*, Chartron et Trébuchet*, Henri Clerc*, Joseph Drouhin*, Louis Jadot*, Domaine Leflaive*, Olivier Leflaive*, Paul Pernot, Château de Puligny-Montrachet*, Étienne Sauzet*

Chassagne-Montrachet

'The best white wines in the world' reads the sign at the entrance to the quiet, almost somnolent village of Chassagne-Montrachet. Some might disagree with the boast, but there is no denying that, in André Ramonet and Jean-Noël Gagnard, Chassagne contains at least two of the finest Chardonnay producers on the planet.

For all that, Chassagne is not a white-wine community in the way that Meursault or Puligny-Montrachet are. One under-appreciated fact about Chassagne, the most southerly of the great white-wine communes of the Côte de Beaune, is that it produces more red wine than white. It is, nevertheless, Chassagne's white wines that have created the village's reputation. There may be a higher density of wine-making superstars in Meursault and Puligny, but the basic quality of Chassagne's white wines is superior to that of either of its neighbours. Basic Chassagne is a safer bet than village Meursault or Puligny.

Chassagne plays host to three Grands Crus (Le Montrachet, Bâtard-Montrachet and the minuscule Criots-Bâtard-Montrachet) and a solid, occasionally spectacular, line-up of Premiers Crus (the most exciting being Les Caillerets, Les Embrazées, Les Champs-Gain, Les Chaumées, Les Chenevottes, Les Ruchottes, La Maltroie and Les Vergers). At Premier Cru level, a designation which covers nearly half of the commune's vineyards, Chassagne's reds are often the equal of its whites.

Most of Chassagne's top Chardonnays come from the three Grands Crus, two of which (Le Montrachet and Bâtard-Montrachet) are shared, more or less equally, with neighbouring Puligny-Montrachet. (Chassagne sits behind Puligny on the far side of the Route Nationale 6.) At village and Premier Cru level, Chassagne wines tend to be fuller and more forward than those of Puligny, but with better balance than most Meursaults.

For the Grands Crus they have in common, the differences between Chassagne and Puligny are less marked. As a rule, the wines of Criots-Bâtard-Montrachet, which at 3.9 acres is the second smallest Grand Cru of the Côte d'Or (after La

Romanée), are lighter and more ethereal than either Le Montrachet or Bâtard-Montrachet (both of which are discussed in the Puligny-Montrachet introduction).

Domaine-bottling is popular in Chassagne. The bewildering number of related growers (particularly in the Gagnard, Delagrange, Ramonet and Morey families) makes distinguishing between them an enjoyable Burgundian game. As well as a list of excellent domaines, most of whose wines are cheaper than the top growths of Meursault and Puligny, two Beaune-based *négociants* have important toeholds in the commune. Joseph Drouhin vinifies and sells the wines of the Marquis de Laguiche estate, and Louis Jadot performs the same service for the Duc de Magenta.

Best producers: Jean-Marc Blain-Gagnard*, Marc Colin*, Michel Colin-Deléger*, Joseph Drouhin*, Richard Fontaine-Gagnard*, Jean-Noël Gagnard*, Louis Jadot*, Comtes Lafon*, Château de la Maltroye*, Bernard Morey*, Jean-Marc Morey*, Pierre Morey*, Michel Niellon, André Ramonet*, Domaine de la Romanée-Conti*

The Côte Chalonnaise

The Côte Chalonnaise, or Région de Mercurey as it is sometimes known, is an under-appreciated buffer zone between the Côte d'Or and the more southerly Mâconnais. It consists of five villages (Bouzeron, Rully, Mercurey, Givry and Montagny) stretched out along the D981 as it wends its way south. All five of these *appellations* produce Chardonnay, although in Bouzeron, where the local speciality is Aligoté, it has to be labelled Bourgogne, Côte Chalonnaise.

Red wines have the upper hand in the region, to the tune of 75 per cent, with Chardonnay restricted to less than 15 per cent of the land under vine. Nevertheless, the Côte Chalonnaise can be a good, comparatively inexpensive (by Burgundian standards) source of Chardonnay, even if much of the local production is siphoned off into Crémant de Bourgogne blends.

Rully and Montagny are the two most important Chardonnay villages, but there is also a small amount made in Givry and Mercurey. In fact, one of the top white wines in the area, Antonin Rodet's Château de Chamirey, is a Mercurey Blanc. Good Givry Blancs are made by Michel Derain, Veuve Steinmaier and Jean-Marc Joblot. Rully has a handful of good growers (Henri and Paul Jacqueson, Raymond Bêtes and Armand Monassier), even if the previously excellent Domaine de la Folie is struggling a little at the moment. Montagny, which tends to produce slightly more opulent wines than Rully, also has a few reliable names. The Cave des Vignerons de Buxy, Louis Latour and Bernard Michel are the pick of the bunch.

Unlike the Mâconnais, the region is not dominated by cooperatives, although the Cave des Vignerons de Buxy is an exemplary operation. Roughly 80 per cent of Côte Chalonnaise wine is made and sold by private growers and *négociants*. Some of these merchants are based in the Côte d'Or, but there are good local names, too, especially Antonin Rodet and Emile Chandesais. The best growers can produce decent, if rarely stunning Chardonnays. In style, they are closer to the Côte de Beaune than to Mâcon. For instance, there is much more barrel-fermentation here than in the Mâconnais, possibly because the wines fetch a higher price than most things produced around Mâcon. Nevertheless, the region has yet to fulfil its potential, at least as far as Chardonnay is concerned. Too many Côte Chalonnaise wines taste thin and unexciting to me. Lower yields and less easy recourse to chaptalization would improve the situation.

Best producers: Cave des Vignerons de Buxy, Émile Chandesais, Joseph Drouhin*, Joseph Faiveley, Domaine de la Folie*, Henri et Paul Jacqueson*, Louis Jadot*, Jean-Marc Joblot, Michel Juillot, Louis Latour*, Olivier Leflaive*, Antonin Rodet*, Veuve Steinmaier et Fils, Aubert and Pamela de Villaine*

*

Mâconnais

You'd expect an area which contains a village called Chardon-nay to be swimming in the stuff, and you'd be quite right too. Whereas the Côte Chalonnaise is dominated by Pinot Noir, in the Mâconnais it is Chardonnay, with more than two-thirds of the vineyard area, which has the upper hand. In an average year, the Mâconnais accounts for more than 40 per cent of all white Burgundy.

With the obvious exception of Pouilly-Fuissé, this is Burgundy's bargain basement: a large, cooperative-dominated region producing substantial quantities of more or less palat-able white wine. Too many vineyards are over-cropped, machine-picked and planted in the wrong place, but the best Mâcon whites are full, fruity and easy to drink. Outside Pouilly-Fuissé, oak ageing is unusual. A more common flavour is the grapefruity, almost spicy character of the local Chardonnay clone, called Chardonnay Musqué.

The majority of the wine is sold as Mâcon Blanc, Mâcon Supérieur or as more expensive Mâcon-Villages. There are forty-three villages entitled to the latter *appellation*, and these are allowed to use their own name – as in Mâcon-Prissé or Mâcon-Lugny, for example. Most of the best villages (Lugny, Viré, Clessé and Prissé) are to be found in the central and southern areas of the *appellation*, not far from the Beaujolais. In fact, top Beaujolais *négociants* like Georges Dubœuf and Louis Tête are also a very good source of Mâcon whites.

These villages notwithstanding, the leading *appellations* of the Mâconnais are Saint-Véran and, of course, Pouilly-Fuissé. Two other Pouilly satellites, Pouilly-Fuissé and Pouilly-Vinzelles, situated between Pouilly-Fuissé and the city of Mâcon, are also entitled to their own *appellations*. Both produce tiny quantities of wine which is rarely a patch on the best Saint-Vérans or Pouilly-Fuissés.

Saint-Véran was promoted to full *appellation* status in 1971, and covers the villages of Saint-Vérand (*sic*), Davayé, Prissé, Chasselas, Leynes and Chânes, as well as a few adjoining vineyards in the Beaujolais *cru* of Saint-Amour and the commune of Solutré. The vineyards are situated to the north and south of Pouilly-Fuissé, which neatly divides the *appellation* in half. Indeed, several of the leading producers of Saint-Véran (Château de Fuissé, Bernard Léger-Plumet, Roger Luquet, Thierry Guérin) are based in Pouilly-Fuissé. Saint-Véran is usually cheaper than its more glamorous neighbour, and can represent very good value for money.

Pouilly-Fuissé is more variable. A lot of what is produced (particularly by *négociants* and the cooperative in Chaintré) in the steep vineyards of Pouilly, Vergisson, Solutré, Fuissé and Chaintré fails to live up to the *appellation*'s inflated prices. Once again, high yields are to blame. Really good Pouilly-Fuissé from a producer like Château de Fuissé is something else altogether: a full-bodied blast of Chardonnay packed with rich, ripe fruit. Oak fermentation is widely practised (and at these prices, quite right too), giving the wines an extra dimension. Pouilly-Fuissé is not a wine to cellar for decades, although the best examples can survive for at least a decade in bottle.

Best producers: André Bonhomme, Jean-Michel Drouin, Georges Dubœuf, Domaine Lapierre, Domaine Ferret*, Château de Fuissé*, Henri Goyard*, Thierry Guérin, Louis Jadot*, Roger Lassarat, Bernard Léger-Plumet*, Producteurs de Lugny, Roger Luquet*, Gilles Noblet*, Cave de Prissé, Jean Thévenet*, Cave de Viré

White Burgundy vintages

1991. Spring frosts and an uneven flowering resulted in a small crop. Rain during harvest reduced levels of acidity and potential alcohol. The best wines will be elegant enough, but they are unlikely to be long-lived.

1990. Extremely dry summer weather was followed by as much as 40 mm of rain in the week before the harvest and this increased yields. The wines are ripe, high in alcohol, but with good balancing acidity. A vintage to enjoy now or to keep for another five to ten years.

1989. A very hot summer produced rich, opulent wines that are high in alcohol but generally lack acidity. Despite their undoubted appeal, these are big, aromatic, concentrated wines that will not age as well as the 1990s in most cases. Overripeness and botrytis were both features of the vintage.

1988. High yields, particularly in Puligny-Montrachet, were the scourge of this vintage. On the whole, the grapes were healthy, with good natural acidity, and produced crisp, elegant wines. Nevertheless, many of them lack depth and concentration of fruit. Lower yields might have solved the problem.

1987. Not a great year for white Burgundy. Rain and low temperatures during harvest yielded wines that are low in natural alcohol and high in malic acidity. The best producers made good, rather than spectacular wines, but even these will not age well.

1986. Probably the best vintage of the decade, particularly in Meursault, where yields were roughly half of what they were in Puligny and Chassagne. The best wines are classic white Burgundies: full-bodied, balanced and complex. Others are surprisingly dilute. My feeling is that, owing to good levels of acidity, they will age better than the more blowsy 1985s. Botrytis added complexity to the vintage.

1985. A smaller vintage than 1986, which generally produced more forward, aromatic wines. After a long, hot summer most of the grapes were left with good, rather than excessive potential alcohol, but low acidity. The best wines are superb, but the overall quality was patchy, particularly in the Mâconnais and Côte Chalonnaise. Another great year in Meursault.

1984. The least interesting vintage of the decade. A combination of rain and unripe grapes produced thin, lean wines of little appeal. The acidity may keep them alive for some time. A case for euthanasia?

1983. An early, atypical vintage. Yields were low, but most of the wines are hot, alcoholic and overripe, often with a pronounced botrytis character. Not a vintage to cellar.

1982. Like 1988 and 1990, a substantial crop. The wines are good, sometimes excellent, but lack a bit of depth and acidity. Most are smooth, harmonious and ready to drink. Producers who restricted yields were particularly successful.

ROBERT AMPEAU

6 rue du Cromin, 21190 Meursault

Chardonnay vineyard: 10 acres

Production of Chardonnay: 20,000 bottles

Labels: Robert Ampeau; Michel Ampeau

Quality: 🍇🍇🍇   Price: ★★★—★★★★★

Best vintages: 1978, 1982, 1989

Even by Burgundian standards, Robert Ampeau is an eccentric. A lively, opinionated fount of folklore and gossip, Ampeau believes that most white Burgundy is drunk too young. To make sure no one tastes his wines before they're ready, he squirrels them away in his cellar for as long as fifteen years before release. In 1990, he was selling the 1977s, 1980s and 1984s. The 1976s and 1978s were not yet on the market.

Ampeau makes six different Chardonnays: Bourgogne Blanc, Meursault, Meursault Charmes, Meursault Perrières, Meursault La Pièce sous Le Bois and Puligny-Montrachet Les Combettes. They are all vinified in up to 20 per cent new oak, and can be among the most interesting bottles in Meursault. Ampeau is particularly successful in off-vintages.

The quality of the wines is variable. Some are patently aged for far too long, and combine oxidation with hard, unyielding acidity. Most are made in a fairly rustic, heavy style that can seem slightly dirty at times. Others seem to have the gift of eternal life – Ampeau's 1979 Les Combettes and 1978 Perrières are particularly delicious. If you want to taste Burgundian Chardonnay with a bit of age, this is a good place to start.

*

JEAN-MARC BLAIN-GAGNARD

Rue de Santenay, 21190 Chassagne-Montrachet

Chardonnay vineyard: 8 acres

Production of Chardonnay: 20,000 bottles

Quality: 🍇🍇🍇🍇   Price: ★★★★/★★★★★

Best vintages: 1983, 1985, 1988, 1989, 1990

So many Gagnards, so little wine. Jean-Marc Blain's family comes from the Loire and before he met Claudine Gagnard he was destined to be a wine-maker in Sancerre. Instead, he married into the Gagnard clan in Chassagne-Montrachet and, like his brother-in-law Richard Fontaine, who lives next door, began to make wine in Burgundy instead.

Blain-Gagnard is a shy, freckle-faced man who produces more red wine than white. He and his wife took over half of grandfather Edmond Delagrange's vines in 1980; the old man continues to bottle a little bit of wine under his own label and still potters around the courtyard when visitors arrive. The Blain-Gagnards inherited some choice parcels in two Grands Crus: Bâtard-Montrachet and Criots-Bâtard-Montrachet; and four Premiers Crus: Caillerets, Morgeot, La Boudriotte and Clos Saint-Jean. Jean-Marc Blain also makes excellent village Chassagne-Montrachet.

All the wines are barrel-fermented, with a maximum of 20 per cent new oak. They stay on their *grosses lies* (with no settling before fermentation) until April, are racked twice and lightly filtered before bottling. Blain is a great believer in minimum intervention. His wines are complex, balanced Chardonnays that need between three and five years to show well. In 1990, his best wines were Caillerets, Criots-Bâtard-Montrachet and La Boudriotte. The Criots was particularly fine. Other producers make more concentrated Bâtard, but few can match Blain's elegant, racy Chassagne-Montrachet. The Loire's loss was definitely Burgundy's gain.

*

DOMAINE BONNEAU DU MARTRAY

Rue de Frétille, 21420 Pernand-Vergelesses

Chardonnay vineyard: 22 acres

Production of Chardonnay: 50,000 bottles

Quality: 🍇🍇🍇🍇   Price: ★★★★★

Best vintages: 1983, 1985, 1988, 1989

This historic domaine has the largest holdings in Corton-Charlemagne, totalling nearly one-third of the Grand Cru. In fact, according to Burgundy expert Anthony Hanson, it includes the very vineyards that belonged to the Emperor Charlemagne in the eighth century. Since the death of René Bonneau du Martray in 1969, it has been run from Paris by his nephew, Jean le Bault de la Morinière.

Opinions differ on who makes the best wine from Corton-Charlemagne. My own list would include Latour, Chartron et Trébuchet, Jadot, Dubreuil, Coche-Dury, Rapet and Delarche – but Bonneau du Martray is consistently there or thereabouts. For me, it falls just short of greatness.

Wine-maker Henri Bruchon likes to ferment his Corton-Charlemagne for six days in tank before transferring it to (one-third new) barrels. The wine is left on its fine lees for twelve to fifteen months. Yields are low here, and most of the vines were planted in the early fifties. There is also a one-hectare experimental plot, where Raymond Bernard of ONIVINS is looking at the development of five different clones.

Henri Bruchon is a reticent fellow, a yellow Gauloise permanently drooping from his bottom lip, and his wines are similarly undemonstrative when young. The 1987 will be ready after five years, but in more concentrated vintages the wines can take seven or eight years to approach maturity. They are high in natural alcohol – there was no chaptalization in 1988, 1989 or 1990 – but are balanced by acidity and depth of fruit. The 1990 and 1989 are both splendid wines.

*

BOUCHARD PÈRE ET FILS

Au Château, BP 70, 21202 Beaune

Chardonnay vineyard: 57 acres

Production of Chardonnay: 1 million bottles

Labels: Bouchard Père et Fils; Domaines du Château de Beaune

Quality: 🍇   Price: ★★★/★★★★★

Best vintages: 1986, 1989, 1990

Bouchard Père et Fils is among the oldest, most respected *négociant* houses in Beaune, with vineyards in some of Burgundy's plum white-wine locations. It is the largest landowner in Chevalier-Montrachet (with 5 acres), and the third largest in Montrachet (with 2.2 acres). It also has vines in Meursault Genevrières, Beaune Clos Saint-Landry and Corton-Charlemagne.

The potential at Bouchard Père et Fils is enormous, which makes the current quality of many of their white wines especially disappointing. This venerable company has gone through difficult times in the late eighties, and the problems seem to have affected the wine-making, too. Many of the 1989s, whether purchased (as grapes) or taken from the company's own vineyards (Domaines du Château de Beaune), are heavy, alcoholic and unstructured. The Corton-Charlemagne tastes distinctly ordinary; only the Chevalier-Montrachet is up to scratch.

Over the last two vintages, the Bouchards appear to have realized that they were slipping behind top *négociants* like Louis Jadot and Joseph Drouhin, and have invested in a large experimental wine-making programme. The results in 1990, according to one French critic, were extremely promising. I have not tasted the wines, but I hope he is right. Bouchard Père et Fils belongs in the front rank of Burgundian houses; for the time being, it is underperforming.

*

LOUIS CARILLON ET FILS

Rue Drouhin, 21190 Puligny-Montrachet

Chardonnay vineyard: 20 acres

Production of Chardonnay: 40,000 bottles

Quality: 🍇🍇🍇🍇🍇   Price: ★★★★/★★★★★

According to one source, the Carillon family have been making wine in Puligny-Montrachet (or Puligny as it was then) since the seventeenth century. It may be auto-suggestion, but to me, this solid, unruffled continuity is reflected in the wines. The Carillons are not usually listed among the village's superstars, but on current form they are producing some of the finest wines in Puligny-Montrachet.

The domaine has a good spread of Chardonnay vineyards, from straight Puligny-Montrachet, right up to a small parcel of Bienvenues-Bâtard-Montrachet. It has larger holdings in four Premiers Crus: Les Referts, Champ Canet, Les Combettes and Les Perrières.

All the Premiers and Grands Crus are barrel-fermented, in up to 15 per cent new oak, and spend eleven months on their lees; the Puligny-Montrachet is one-third tank-fermented but is entirely oak-aged. The taste of wood never seems aggressive on any of the wines, and the standard of wine-making is usually high, even in difficult years. Some barrels are sold to *négociants*, but the Carillons reserve the best wines for themselves.

The emphasis here is on racy, elegant wines with good acidity. The best of them, particularly in a vintage like 1988, can age for up to a decade. Excellent wines were produced in 1989 and 1990. In 1989, the stars were Les Referts and the Bienvenues-Bâtard; in 1990, Champ Canet and Les Perrières were my favourites. These are some of the most complex, minerally Chardonnays in Burgundy.

*

LA CHABLISIENNE

8 Boulevard Pasteur, 89800 Chablis

Chardonnay vineyard: 1,800 acres

Production of Chardonnay: 2 million bottles

Labels: La Chablisienne; Cave des Vignerons de Chablis;
Union des Viticulteurs de Chablis; Château Grenouille.
Wines may also appear under the names of individual
members of the cooperative, though this practice is
being phased out

Quality: 🍇🍇–🍇🍇🍇🍇   Price: ★★–★★★★

Best vintages: 1983, 1985, 1986, 1988, 1989, 1990

La Chablisienne is consistently one of France's best cooperatives. Set up in 1923, it has 260 members and produces a range
of twenty Chardonnays; the only Grand Cru missing from the
line-up is Valmur. The success of La Chablisienne owes much
to the canny managerial skills of its director, Jean-Michel
Tucki, who arrived in 1969 and has done much to establish the
cooperative's reputation.

The Chablisienne's oenologist, Nathalie Fèvre (no relation
to William at the Domaine de la Maladière), uses a combination of oak and/or vats, depending on the wine. The Petit
Chablis, Chablis and the lighter Premiers Crus (Fourchaumes
and Beauroy) see no oak; the other Premiers Crus and all the
Grands Crus are barrel-fermented, with up to 50 per cent new
oak on some wines. On certain cuvées, the oak is a little too
obvious, but in general it is applied judiciously.

Given the size of production at La Chablisienne – it accounts
for around 30 per cent of the *appellation* – the quality of the
wines is impressive. The Chablis Vieilles Vignes and basic
Chablis are benchmark styles: fresh, elegant and well-made. Of
the Premiers Crus, the most enjoyable are the Vauligneau and
the Côte de Léchet; the Grands Crus are even better, rich,
structured and lightly oaked. The cooperative's two top wines
are Les Preuses and Grenouilles, which is sold under the label
Château Grenouille.

CHARTRON ET TRÉBUCHET

13 Grande Rue, 21190 Puligny-Montrachet
Production of Chardonnay: 200,000 bottles
Labels: Chartron et Trébuchet; Dupard Aîné (France and Germany)
Quality: 🍇🍇🍇/🍇🍇🍇🍇   Price: ★★–★★★★★
Best vintages: 1985, 1988, 1989, 1990

Jean-René Chartron and Louis Trébuchet are an appealing double act. Chartron, vigneron and former mayor of Puligny-Montrachet, and Trébuchet, former managing director of Jaffelin and widely tipped to be the next mayor of Beaune, set up their *négociant* business in 1984 and have earned a reputation as producers of some first-rate white Burgundies. The firm also distributes the wines from Jean-René Chartron's own 20-acre domaine. The wines are made by the same oenologist, Michel Roucher, but, following the dictates of French law, the two installations are quite separate.

Chartron et Trébuchet sells a broad range of white wines from the Côte de Beaune and the Côte Chalonnaise, and like rival *négociant* Olivier Leflaive, whose offices are just round the corner, buys most of its production as grapes or must. Except for the Bourgogne Blanc, all the wines are vinified in oak; the proportion of new barrels varies from 10 to 40 per cent. Michel Roucher likes to control the fermentation of his wines. To this end, he uses selected yeasts and malolactic bacteria.

The resulting wines have lots of finesse, though some of the lesser *appellations* (Mercurey Blanc and Saint-Romain, for instance) can lack depth. The best wines here are the two Saint-Aubin Premiers Crus (Les Combes and La Chatenière), the range of Puligny-Montrachets (particularly Les Garennes and the two Grands Crus, Bâtard-Montrachet and Le Montrachet) and an explosive, unctuous Corton-Charlemagne. In 1990, there were few better examples of this exalted *appellation*.

CHÂTEAU DE LA MALTROYE

21190 Chassagne-Montrachet

Chardonnay vineyard: 20 acres

Production of Chardonnay: 55,000 bottles

Quality: 🍇–🍇🍇   Price: ★★–★★★★★

Best vintages: 1985, 1988, 1989, 1990

This beautiful and imposing château owns an impressive string of vineyards in Chassagne-Montrachet, including parcels of Bâtard-Montrachet and four Premiers Crus (La Romanée, the eponymous Clos de la Maltroye, Morgeot and Les Chenevottes). It also produces village Chassagne-Montrachet, Santenay Blanc and Bourgogne Blanc.

Slightly more white wine is made here than red, and it is the whites that have earned the domaine the greater number of plaudits. The emphasis is firmly on oak ageing – even the château's Aligoté gets a generous dollop of *fûts neufs* – whether in barrels or larger *foudres*. The owner, André Cornut, bottles his wines after ten to twelve months.

Despite a long list of awards, the wine-making is inconsistent in my view. In some cases, it seems excessively old-fashioned. The Morgeot Vigne Blanche and the white Clos de la Maltroye are both excellent – the former lean and nutty; the latter sweet, rich and aromatic – but there are disappointing wines, too. Many of the 1989s seem slightly dirty to me, with a peculiar, almost smoky aroma of damp straw. The 1990s, tasted in barrel, seemed cleaner, so perhaps the problem has been ironed out.

JEAN-RENÉ CHARTRON

13 Grande Rue, 21190 Puligny-Montrachet

Chardonnay vineyard: 20 acres

Production of Chardonnay: 60,000 bottles

Quality: 🍇🍇🍇🍇   Price: ★★★—★★★★★

Best vintages: 1985, 1988, 1989, 1990

The wines from Jean-René Chartron's domaine are vinified in exactly the same way as those that appear under the Chartron et Trébuchet label. The important difference, according to wine-maker Michel Roucher, is that he can control the vineyard and, just as important, the pressing of the grapes.

The domaine wines are more consistent than the *négociant* bottlings, though at the top end there is little to choose between the best *appellations*. Chartron owns Chardonnay vines in Puligny-Montrachet, three Premiers Crus (Les Folatières, Clos de la Pucelle and Clos du Cailleret), and Chevalier-Montrachet. The Chevalier is well made, if not quite in the top flight, but I have had some splendid bottles of Les Folatières and Clos de la Pucelle.

HENRI CLERC

Place des Marronniers, 21190 Puligny-Montrachet

Chardonnay vineyard: 34 acres

Production of Chardonnay: 80,000 bottles

Labels: Henri Clerc et Fils; Domaine de la Truffière

Quality: 🍇🍇🍇–🍇🍇🍇🍇   Price: ★★/★★★★★

Best vintages: 1982, 1985, 1986, 1988, 1989, 1990

By Burgundy's postage-stamp standards, this is a considerable domaine, with 66 acres planted in the Côte d'Or. Bernard Clerc owns vines in Vougeot and Beaune, but the majority of his holdings are in and around Puligny-Montrachet. Clerc's large headquarters, stuffed with antiques and knick-knacks, are a landmark in Puligny, situated as they are on the corner of the main square.

There are a number of wine-making peculiarities here. Clerc centrifuges his must before fermentation for a start. With the exception of the crisp, well-made Bourgogne Blanc, all the wines are barrel-fermented and spend eleven months on their lees. The Grands Crus (Bâtard-Montrachet, Chevalier-Montrachet and Bienvenues-Bâtard-Montrachet) get up to 80 per cent new oak; the Premiers Crus (Les Champs-Gain, Les Folatières, Les Combettes and Les Pucelles) around 35 per cent. At least one-quarter of Clerc's wines – and this is the second unusual point – do not go through malolactic fermentation. He puts this down to conditions in his cellar; it is certainly not done deliberately, but it does give the wines a bit of extra lift.

Clerc sells as much as one-third of his production to the *négoce*, but bottles the rest himself. The quality of the wines is variable. I preferred the 1990s to the 1989s by a considerable margin when I tasted at the domaine. Some bottlings have a curious almost Muscat-like flavour to them, but the top wines here can be very good indeed, with considerable elegance and structure. Clerc's three Grands Crus are all on the oaky side, although there is plenty of countervailing fruit and concentration. The star wines here are two Premiers Crus, Les Pucelles and Les Combettes.

JEAN-FRANÇOIS COCHE-DURY

9 Rue Charles-Giraud, 21190 Meursault

Chardonnay vineyard: 16 acres

Production of Chardonnay: 37,500 bottles

Quality: 🍇🍇🍇🍇🍇   Price: ★★★–★★★★★

Best vintages: 1985, 1986, 1989

Jean-François Coche-Dury, a tall, stooping figure with sad eyes, makes some of the finest wines in the Côte de Beaune, ergo the world. He has vineyards in a number of different *appellations* – from a precious acre leased in Corton-

Charlemagne, to a full range of Meursault village and Premiers Crus sites. The quality of Coche-Dury's Chardonnays, whether Bourgogne Blanc or Meursault Perrières, is exemplary.

The wines are all barrel-fermented, in up to 75 per cent new wood for the Corton-Charlemagne. The Meursault Perrières sees as much as 50 per cent *fûts neufs*, while the other wines never go above 20 per cent. Coche-Dury likes to keep his wines in barrel for as long as twenty-two months; one of his 1988s took thirteen months to finish its malolactic fermentation. He never filters his wines.

The wines produced at this domaine are naturally rich and concentrated – Coche-Dury works with low yields and did not chaptalize in 1988, 1989 or 1990 – but are always underpinned by ripe, balanced acidity. They drink well when young, but will happily age for at least ten years. All of Coche-Dury's white wines are outstanding, but the Meursault Perrières and the Corton-Charlemagne have what a sports commentator once called 'that little bit extra'. Readers who want to taste a cheaper Coche-Dury Chardonnay should buy his racy, elegant Bourgogne Blanc.

MARC COLIN

21190 Saint-Aubin-Gamay

Chardonnay vineyard: 16 acres

Production of Chardonnay: 20,000 bottles

Quality: 🍇🍇🍇🍇🍇   Price: ★★★–★★★★★

Best vintages: 1983, 1985, 1986, 1989

Marc Colin is one of the Côte de Beaune's most talented wine-makers. Tucked away as he is in the Saint-Aubin hamlet of Gamay, his reputation is less elevated than it deserves to be. Colin has the firm handshake and tanned, wiry frame of a passionate, hard-working vigneron. When I called to visit him early one morning, he had been out in the vines since daybreak. Fulfilment was written all over his face.

That same fulfilment is reflected in the wines. This domaine makes almost as much red as it does white, but rightly it is the whites which have attracted more attention. Colin produces nine Chardonnays in all: three Saint-Aubin Premiers Crus (Les Combes, En Remilly and La Chatenière); Puligny-Montrachet; Chassagne-Montrachet; Chassagne-Montrachet Les Champs Gain; Chassagne-Montrachet Les Caillerets; Puligny-Montrachet La Garenne; and Le Montrachet.

Fermentations are carried out at comparatively warm temperatures in a mixture of tank and barrel, usually starting in one and finishing in the other. The wines all go through malolactic fermentation and are left on their lees for up to eleven months before bottling.

Like several other leading producers in Burgundy, Colin preferred the structure of his 1990s to his 1989s; 1990 was certainly an extremely successful vintage at the domaine. The Saint-Aubin En Remilly has great fruit, elegance and length; the Caillerets is more complex, with notes of lemon, walnut and aniseed; and the Montrachet, from a 0.3-acre parcel of sixty-year-old vines, has all the concentration one expects from Burgundy's finest white-wine *appellation*. Fruit and restrained power are the hallmark of Colin's wines, from the Saint-Aubins right up to Le Montrachet.

MICHEL COLIN-DELÉGER

3 Impasse des Crêts, 21190 Chassagne-Montrachet

Chardonnay vineyard: 15 acres

Production of Chardonnay: 25,000 bottles

Labels: Michel Colin-Deléger; François Colin;
  Colin-Saint-Abdon

Quality: 🍇🍇🍇🍇   Price: ★★★/★★★★

Best vintages: 1982, 1983, 1985, 1986, 1989, 1990

Michel Colin is one of the most respected growers in Chassagne-Montrachet, producing elegant, well-defined white and red wines under a variety of labels. He owns Chardonnay vines in Chassagne-Montrachet and in no fewer than seven Premiers Crus: six in Chassagne (Les Chaumées, Les Vergers, Les Chenevottes, En Remilly, Morgeot and La Maltroie) and one (Les Demoiselles) in Puligny. Unlike his cousin Marc Colin, who also makes superb white wines, he has no Grand Cru vineyards.

Colin's Chassagne-Montrachet and Les Chaumées complete two-thirds of their fermentation in stainless steel, and are then transferred to barrel. His other wines are entirely (20 per cent new) oak-fermented. They always go through malolactic fermentation and are bottled after eleven months.

The six Premiers Crus are made to a very high standard. They are wines that take some time to show at their best, with firm, minerally flavours when young. My favourites are En Remilly, Morgeot and the fine, concentrated Les Demoiselles, produced from a tiny patch of fifty-year-old vines. This could easily be mistaken for one of its more patrician Grand Cru neighbours.

RENÉ & VINCENT DAUVISSAT

8 Rue Émile-Zola, 89800 Chablis

Chardonnay vineyard: 23 acres

Production of Chardonnay: 65,000 bottles

Quality: 🍇🍇🍇🍇🍇   Price: ★★★/★★★★

Best vintages: 1983, 1986, 1988, 1989, 1990

René Dauvissat and his son Vincent make concentrated, hand-crafted wines from two Grand Cru (Les Clos and Les Preuses) and three Premier Cru (La Forest, Les Séchet and Vaillons) sites. Their small domaine is one of the top three in the village, and has a long tradition of bottling its own wines, dating back to 1925.

René Dauvissat is one of the few growers who has never abandoned oak ageing, even in times of comparative penury. All five of his wines are fermented in tank, except for 15–20 per cent which is fermented in new oak. But, after malolactic fermentation, the wines are blended and then aged for up to ten months in barrel. Most of these are between two and five years old, although there are some *fûts* and *feuillettes* that have been at the domaine since the early sixties.

All the Dauvissats' wines are first-class. The Vaillons is usually the most open and aromatic; the other four take longer to come round. In most vintages, my favourite wine is the La Forest. The unfiltered 1989 and the 1990 (tasted in barrel) were both wonderful: ripe and honeyed, but with enough acidity to balance the weight of alcohol. This is Chablis at its most seductive: complex, refreshing and beautifully structured.

JEAN-PAUL DROIN

> 8 Boulevard de Ferrières, 89800 Chablis
>
> Chardonnay vineyard: 49 acres
>
> Production of Chardonnay: 70,000 bottles
>
> Labels: Jean-Paul Droin; Domaine Bertonière (bottled by Labouré-Roi)
>
> Quality: 🍷🍷🍷🍷   Price: ★★–★★★★
>
> Best vintages: 1983, 1986, 1988, 1989, 1990

There have been Droins making wine in Chablis since the mid seventeenth century. Jean-Paul Droin is a passionate young twelfth-generation vigneron who makes Chablis in a rich style reminiscent of the Côte de Beaune. He sells half of his production (covering the gamut of Petit Chablis, Chablis, five Grands Crus and seven Premiers Crus) to the *négociant* house of Labouré-Roi, but makes a total of fourteen wines in his own right.

Droin has been using oak barrels since the 1986 vintage. There have been a few disasters along the way, he concedes, particularly with his Fourchaume, but in the last two vintages he has produced some outstanding wines. Only occasionally (on the 1990 Blanchots, for example) does the oak get out of hand.

The Grands Crus (Valmur, Vaudésir, Grenouilles, Les Clos and Blanchot) are entirely fermented in new oak, with lees stirring and bottling after ten months. Two of the Premiers Crus (Vaillons and Montée de Tonnerre) are fermented in one- to four-year-old barrels, while the rest (Fourchaume, Montmains, Côtes de Léchet, Vaucoupin and Vosgros) are fermented in *cuve* but go through malolactic fermentation in oak, sometimes on the lees of one of the Grands Crus. Droin's Chablis and Petit Chablis are both oak-free zones, and prove that he can make wines in a fresh, aromatic style too.

Droin's Premiers and Grands Crus are big and buttery, with sweet vanillin and toffee flavours in ripe years like 1989 and 1990. The best of them (Montmains, Vosgros, Vaudésir and Grenouilles) can stand comparison with the top properties in Meursault, though there is a question mark against their longevity. In a blind tasting, I would probably not place them in Chablis.

JOSEPH DROUHIN

7 Rue d'Enfer, 21200 Beaune

Chardonnay vineyard: 113 acres

Production of Chardonnay: approximately 2 million bottles

Quality: 🍇🍇🍇–🍇🍇🍇🍇🍇   Price: ★★/★★★★★

Best vintages: 1985, 1988, 1989

This impressive family-owned *négociant* is based in the heart of old Beaune, a few yards away from the site of a former pagan temple on the intriguingly named rue d'Enfer. Robert Drouhin, the company's elegant, third-generation director, is one of Burgundy's great ambassadors, a steely-eyed defender of the region's wines. 'I do not make Chardonnay,' he told me defiantly. 'I make Meursault, Puligny-Montrachet and dozens of different wines.' His statement is somewhat undermined by the fact that the dreaded 'C' word appears on his basic Bourgogne Blanc La Forêt, but then Drouhin has never been a man to let tradition stand in the way of commercial considerations for too long.

Drouhin is certainly a house that has kept pace with the times. It has extensive, modern production facilities and, in Laurence Jobard, one of Burgundy's leading wine-makers. Drouhin's wines are consistently among the best, and most expensive, *négociant* bottlings, with the emphasis on clean, modern wines of considerable elegance and finesse. All the top Chablis and Côte d'Or wines are barrel-fermented, in up to one-third new wood, and in some cases spend as much as sixteen months in oak.

As well as buying (mainly) grapes from growers in the Côte d'Or, Mâconnais and Beaujolais regions, Drouhin has extensive plantings of its own in Chablis, the Côte d'Or and now Oregon. Outside Chablis, most of its Premiers and Grands Crus vineyards are planted with Pinot Noir, although the Beaune Clos des Mouches Blanc is a delicious curiosity. Since 1947, Drouhin has also made and marketed the wines of the Marquis de Laguiche, including that from the largest (5-acre) parcel of Montrachet.

Drouhin's white wines are better than its reds. The range of Chablis (especially the Grand Cru Les Clos) is strong, but there are good whites from other regions of Burgundy, too. The La Forêt, a blended wine from Chablis, the Côte d'Or and the Mâconnais, is fresh, fruity Chardonnay with some oak character, while further up the scale Drouhin makes excellent village-level wines from Chassagne-Montrachet, Rully and Saint-Aubin.

The pick of the firm's Chardonnays, pardon me, white Burgundies, are the Beaune Clos des Mouches, the Corton-Charlemagne and the Laguiche wines. The Montrachet is good, if overpriced. My advice is to buy the spicy, complex Laguiche Chassagne-Montrachet instead.

*

DOMAINE FERRET

71960 Fuissé

Chardonnay vineyard: 34 acres

Production of Chardonnay: 30,000 bottles

Quality: 🍇–🍇🍇🍇   Price: ★★★/★★★★

Best vintages: 1985, 1988, 1989

Now in her eighties, Jeanne Ferret still spends long hours pottering around her small, crowded cellar in Fuissé. A characterful woman of strong opinions, Ferret was one of the first producers to bottle her own wine, and did much to establish the name of Pouilly-Fuissé in the USA. She has been making the wines at Domaine Ferret since 1943 and insists on running the property to her own specifications. If you telephone to place an order, it is Mme Ferret who answers; if you come to taste, it is Mme Ferret who receives you. 'I'm like the Président de la République, monsieur; very much in demand.'

The quality of the wines at this famous domaine is variable, possibly because of its owner's refusal to share the workload. Most of the production is now sold off to *négociants*, although the best bottles can be superb.

The wines are released under two labels: Tête de Cru, the basic cuvée; and the modestly named Hors Classe. They start their fermentation in tanks, but finish it in oak. Mme Ferret dislikes a strong taste of oak in her wines, and racks them back into tank after malolactic fermentation, where they stay for up to eighteen months. She produced superb Hors Classe wines in 1990 and 1985, closer to a Puligny-Montrachet than a Pouilly-Fuissé, with elegance, breed and spicy concentration.

WILLIAM FÈVRE

14 Rue Jules-Rathier, 89800 Chablis

Chardonnay vineyard: 123 acres

Production of Chardonnay: 1 million bottles

Labels: Domaine de la Maladière; William Fèvre; Ancien
Domaine Auffray

Quality: 🍇🍇-🍇🍇🍇🍇   Price: ★—★★★★

Best vintages: 1986, 1988, 1989, 1990

President of the Syndicat de la Défense de l'Appellation de
Chablis and author of a pamphlet entitled *Les Vrais Chablis et les
autres*, William Fèvre is a passionate opponent of ersatz
Chablis. To make a point about California 'Chablee' and its ilk,
Fèvre once released a wine with Napa Vallée de France on the
label. He has also spoken out against the extension of plantings
in Chablis itself, a position which has brought him into conflict
with some local growers. Ever the maverick, Fèvre recently
announced that he intends to make Chardonnay (but not
Chablis) in Chile's Maipo Valley.

Fèvre has the largest holding of Chablis Grand Cru vineyards
(40 acres), as well as a further 83 acres of Premier Cru and
straight Chablis. He supplements his own sizeable production
(300,000 bottles) by buying grapes from other growers in the
appellation. The wines are sold under three different labels but,
to my knowledge, no distinction is made between the domaine
wines and wines from other vineyards.

Unlike most producers in Chablis, Fèvre uses a substantial
proportion of new oak in the ageing of his wines. He first
started to use barrel-fermentation with the 1984 vintage. Many
of the wines were light and oak gave them a little more weight,
according to Fèvre. He now barrel-ferments everything but his
Petit Chablis, using 25 per cent new oak on all his other cuvées.
The resulting wines are made in a clean, modern style that can
appear excessively oaky when young. With time, the oak settles
down. In general, I find them a little lacking in concentration,
although the best wines (Les Clos, Vaudésir and Montée de
Tonnerre) are excellent in good vintages.

DOMAINE DE LA FOLIE

71150 Chagny

Chardonnay vineyard: 35 acres

Production of Chardonnay: 50,000 bottles

Quality: 🍇   Price: ★★

Best vintages: 1984, 1986

Until comparatively recently, Domaine de la Folie was the best Chardonnay producer in Rully. The departure of wine-maker Xavier Noël-Bouton, amid bitter family feuding, has coincided with a precipitate decline in quality. Some feel that it was Noël-Bouton's handling of the 1987 and 1988 vintages which started the rot. If so, things have not improved since. The 1990s, which were entirely tank-fermented, are not a patch on some of the older barrel-aged wines. Clos Saint-Jacques, the domaine's top wine, comes from a superb vineyard site; it is a shame to see it going to waste.

DOMAINE FONTAINE-GAGNARD

Rue de Santenay, 21190 Chassagne-Montrachet

Chardonnay vineyard: 9 acres

Production of Chardonnay: 20,000 bottles

Quality: 🍇🍇   Price: ★★★★/★★★★★

Best vintages: 1986, 1989, 1990

Richard Fontaine was an air-force mechanic until he married Laurence Gagnard, daughter of Jacques Gagnard-Delagrange, in 1983. Richard Fontaine-Gagnard made the 1983 and 1984 vintages with his father-in-law, during which time the wines continued to appear under Laurence's name. But since 1985 he has been entirely responsible for the domaine. Like his brother-in-law, Jean-Marc Blain-Gagnard, his vines were inherited from Edmond Delagrange, Jacques's father.

Eight different Chardonnays are made at the domaine, from village Chassagne-Montrachet right up to Bâtard-Montrachet. All of the wines are barrel-fermented, with up to 35 per cent new oak, although the proportion will be reduced in the next few vintages. The wines stay on their lees for eleven months in barrel and all go through malolactic fermentation.

Fontaine-Gagnard is a shy, rather careful man and his wines reflect his personality: lean and slow to develop. The Chassagne-Montrachet is the most open and aromatic, with honeyed, appley fruit, but even so it takes a while to marry in bottle. Further up the scale, the wines are elegant and full of understated spicy, citrus and butterscotch complexity, always supported by crisp acidity.

The Premiers Crus Morgeot, Les Vergers and La Maltroie are consistently superb, though each needs at least five years to show well. The Bâtard-Montrachet, the richest and most muscular of Fontaine-Gagnard's wines, is a good example of the *appellation*.

CHÂTEAU DE FUISSÉ

71960 Fuissé

Chardonnay vineyard: 74 acres

Production of Chardonnay: 180,000 bottles (Château de Fuissé); 300,000 bottles (*négoce*)

Quality: 🍾🍾🍾 🍾🍾🍾🍾🍾   Price: ★★★ ★★★★★

Best vintages: 1982, 1983, 1985, 1986, 1988, 1989, 1990

Few would contest Jean-Jacques Vincent's standing as the leading grower in Pouilly-Fuissé. Some critics have put the wines of Jeanne Ferret on the same level, but the comparison seems far-fetched to me. In the Mâconnais, Château de Fuissé reigns supreme, producing Chardonnays of great depth and complexity. If only all Pouilly-Fuissés were as good.

Parts of the château – which, despite the odd suit of armour, has an attractive, almost Mediterranean feel to it – date back to the fifteenth century. The wine-making lineage is considerable, too. Jean-Jacques, who has been in charge since 1967, is the fourth generation of the Vincent family to run Château de Fuissé. Significantly, the estate was one of the first in the area to bottle its own production.

As well as producing Chardonnay from three different *appellations* (Pouilly-Fuissé, Saint-Véran and Mâcon), Vincent makes excellent Beaujolais and, since 1985, has run a profitable *négociant* business specializing in the white wines of the Mâconnais.

The Saint-Véran and Mâcon Blanc are both splendid unoaked Chardonnays with honeyed, grapefruity intensity. These are fermented at controlled temperature in stainless steel and, as a rule, do not go through malolactic fermentation.

The domaine's top wines, however, are its Pouilly-Fuissés – the area where the estate has its largest plantings (54 acres). Vincent makes three different cuvées: Jeunes Vignes Cuvée Première; Château Fuissé and Château Fuissé Vieilles Vignes. The last two wines are (20 per cent new) barrel-fermented and left on their lees for eight months; the Jeunes Vignes is sometimes aged in oak for a short period of time, usually on the lees of the Château wines. In 1989 and 1990 – both ripe vintages in the Mâconnais – Vincent also blocked the malolactic fermentation on his three Pouilly-Fuissés.

The style of wine-making here emphasizes aroma and richness of fruit. The wines often have a slight sweetness to them, and are always ripe and alcoholic. This is not to say that the wines cannot age. A fabulous 1978 Vieilles Vignes I tasted at the château still had plenty of life twelve years on. In most vintages, Vincent's Vieilles Vignes is his, and Pouilly-Fuissé's, best wine – full, creamy, oaky and concentrated. The price is high but, in this case, justifiably so.

JEAN-NOËL GAGNARD

Rue des Champs-Gain, 21190 Chassagne-Montrachet
Chardonnay vineyard: 11 acres

Production of Chardonnay: 28,000 bottles

Quality: 🍷🍷🍷🍷🍷   Price: ★★★★/★★★★★

Best vintages: 1982, 1983, 1985, 1986, 1988, 1989, 1990

Of all the Gagnards wielding pipettes in Chassagne-Montrachet, Jean-Noël Gagnard produces the best white wines. A charming, hospitable man, Gagnard appears untouched by success. His personality is in marked contrast to that of his brother, Jacques Gagnard-Delagrange, who refuses to receive journalists.

Gagnard owns vines in one Grand Cru (Bâtard-Montrachet), six Premiers Crus (Morgeot, Caillerets, Les Chenevottes, Les Champs-Gain, La Maltroie and Blanchot Dessus) and in Chassagne-Montrachet village. The basic Chassagne is vinified in *cuve* but aged in oak for six months; the rest of Gagnard's wines are (up to 25 per cent new) barrel-fermented. The Bâtard sees as much as 80 per cent new wood, although the wine is so rich that you hardly notice.

One of the best wines from this domaine is a blend of four Premiers Crus (Les Champs-Gain, La Maltroie, Les Chenevottes and Blanchot Dessus). The other two Premiers Crus are both superb, if a little less forward. But the jewel of this estate is the Bâtard, a powerful, brilliantly made Chardonnay with complex flavours of vanillin, cinnamon, toast and lemon and at least a decade up its sleeve. This is one of the finest examples of Grand Cru white Burgundy.

HENRI GOYARD

Domaine de Roally, 71260 Viré

Chardonnay vineyard: 7.4 acres

Production of Chardonnay: 25,000 bottles

Quality: 🍷🍷🍷/🍷🍷🍷🍷   Price: ★★

Best vintages: 1988, 1989, 1990

In a region dominated by mediocre, cooperative-produced wines, Henri Goyard stands out as a model of careful integrity. He makes two wines – a Mâcon-Viré and a Mâcon-Montbellet – both of which are clean and intensely concentrated. While some growers machine-harvest at yields of up to 160 hl/ha, Goyard hand-picks his grapes at no more than 50 hl/ha. Like Jean Thévenet, he likes to work with ripe grapes, and produces richly aromatic wines with a touch of residual sugar. He ferments at low temperatures in stainless steel, but uses natural yeasts to avoid making what he calls 'technical wines'. The Montbellet is consistently one of the best wines in the Mâconnais.

HENRI ET PAUL JACQUESON

Rue de Chèvrement, 71150 Rully

Chardonnay vineyard: 9 acres

Production of Chardonnay: 16,000 bottles

Quality: 🍇🍇/🍇🍇🍇   Price: ★★★

Best vintages: 1982, 1985, 1986, 1988, 1989

The Jacquesons (father Henri and son Paul) make some of the best wines, both red and white, in Rully. Henri Jacqueson was one of the first producers in the area to bottle his own wines and, though he has now officially retired, he continues to receive visitors, dispensing bucolic aphorisms as he goes.

The red Jacqueson wines are more concentrated than the two whites, but this is still a good source of comparatively inexpensive Chardonnay. The domaine intends to increase its production of Chardonnay over the next few years, with new plantings in three additional Premiers Crus: Raclot, Vauvry and La Pucelle.

The wines are two-thirds tank-fermented, although in 1991 the percentage of oak (all new and one-year-old) will be increased to 50 per cent. Henri Jacqueson says that temperature control (20–22 °C) in tank gives the wines more aroma. The Rully Premier Cru Grésigny was particularly good in 1990 and 1988. In 1989 it was a trifle blowsy. Whatever the vintage, this wine should be drunk within the first five years.

LOUIS JADOT

5 Rue Samuel-Legay, 21200 Beaune

Chardonnay vineyard: 10 acres (Jadot); 25 acres (Duc de Magenta)

Production of Chardonnay: 3.6 million bottles

Quality: 🍇🍇🍇–🍇🍇🍇🍇🍇   Price: ★★–★★★★★

Best vintages: 1983, 1985, 1986, 1988, 1989

A tasting with Jacques Lardière, the energetic, supremely gifted wine-maker at the *négociant* house of Louis Jadot, is one of life's most rewarding experiences. Lardière charges around the cellar collecting samples, thrusting them in front of you. 'Here, try this, and this, and this.' If Lardière had his way, he'd spend a week tasting wines with you. His passion and enthusiasm are reflected in the success that this, Burgundy's leading *négociant*, has enjoyed over the last decade. Lardière's talents are harnessed and complemented by the shrewd buying and marketing skills of managing director André Gagey and his son, Pierre-Henry.

Jadot are equally strong in red and white wines, although their red-vineyard holdings are the more extensive. As well as owning Chardonnay vines in Corton-Charlemagne, Chevalier-Montrachet Les Demoiselles and Puligny-Montrachet Les Folatières, Jadot vinify and market the wines of the Duc de Magenta estate in Chassagne-Montrachet. They also purchase grapes all over Burgundy, from Chablis to the Mâconnais.

Whether from bought-in fruit or its own production, Jadot made a string of excellent white wines in the eighties, with the same consistent quality stretching from the lowliest Bourgogne

Blanc (labelled Chardonnay) right up to Grand Cru level. Jadot is particularly impressive in lesser *appellations* like Saint-Aubin and Rully, but at its best in the great Chardonnay villages of the Côte de Beaune. The top wines – Bâtard-Montrachet, Morgeot, Les Perrières and Les Combettes – showed superb concentration in 1989 and 1990.

One interesting wine-making peculiarity at Jadot is that many of the white wines do not go through complete malolactic fermentation, as Jacques Lardière feels the wines age better without it. Most of the wines are barrel-fermented. The percentage of new oak and of malolactic fermentation varies from wine to wine. In a company this size, the individual attention that is given to each bottling is quite remarkable. If only all Burgundian *négociants* were as careful.

FRANÇOIS JOBARD

2 Rue de Leignon, 21190 Meursault

Chardonnay vineyard: 11 acres

Production of Chardonnay: 22,000 bottles

Quality: 🍇🍇🍇🍇🍇   Price: ★★★/★★★★

Best vintages: 1988, 1989, 1990

François Jobard, a lean, reticent fellow with chiselled features, makes a superb range of Meursault and Meursault Premiers Crus. His wines are austere and steely when young – the opposite of the lush exuberance of Comtes Lafon, the village's other leading domaine – but age brilliantly in bottle.

Jobard is a man who takes his time. Some of his wines stay on their lees in barrel for as long as two years. His cellars are extremely chilly, as my feet can testify, and it is this which retards their development in barrel. He disturbs his wines as little as possible: light *bâtonnage* in November and one racking is about all the excitement they get.

Jobard has vines in four Premier Cru sites – Charmes, Genevrières, Poruzot and Meursault Blagny – as well as in

Meursault Villages. The straight Meursault, the Charmes and the Genevrières are usually more forward than the Poruzot and Meursault Blagny, but none of them is a child prodigy. My own favourites are the Charmes and the Meursault Blagny.

All the Premiers Crus see at least 15 per cent new oak, though this is rarely apparent on the palate. Above all, the thing that distinguishes Jobard's subtle, demanding wines is their structure and balance. Only a handful of producers can match them for complexity.

DOMAINE DES COMTES LAFON

Clos de la Barre, 21190 Meursault

Chardonnay vineyard: 18 acres (24 acres from 1993)

Production of Chardonnay: 42,000 bottles

Quality: ♛♛♛♛♛   Price: ★★★★/★★★★★

Best vintages: 1982, 1985, 1988, 1989

A disappointed wine lover once said that to find a great white Burgundy you had to open at least a dozen expensive bottles. The frustration and, in a strange way, the joy of Burgundy is its very unpredictability. All too often, respectable names turn out very unrespectable wines. This domaine is the rule-proving exception, consistently producing Chardonnay of mind-boggling complexity. If you can find, never mind afford, a Lafon white Burgundy, you are in for a treat.

Dominique Lafon, the estate's highly talented young winemaker, fashions some of the richest, most intense white wines on the Côte de Beaune. The Lafon style is for powerful, hedonistic wines, the inverse of those made by François Jobard, the commune's other leading domaine.

Since 1984, when Dominique Lafon took over the domaine from his father René, the estate has reclaimed a number of vineyards that were previously farmed, *en métayage*, by other growers. So far, the Lafons have taken back 25 acres; the final six acres will be under their control from the 1993 vintage.

Many of these vines used to be in the hands of Pierre Morey. His, and our, only consolation is that they will not go to waste *chez* Lafon. An additional benefit is that there will be a bit more Lafon wine on the market. Just don't expect the prices to go down.

Eight Chardonnays are produced here: Meursault, Meursault Clos de la Barre, Meursault Les Charmes, Meursault Les Genevrières, Meursault Les Désirées, Meursault Les Perrières, Meursault Les Gouttes d'Or and Le Montrachet. All of them are first-rate. Apart from the 1983 vintage, when botrytis was a problem, the domaine was on top form in the eighties. The years 1988, 1989 and 1990 were all, in different ways, great, but the 1989 looks the pick of the bunch.

The wine-making emphasizes power and opulence, combined with elegance and definition. The grapes are picked ripe – in 1990 Dominique Lafon left some of his Chardonnay on the vine until 15 October – and yields can go as low as 25 hl/ha. All the wines are barrel-fermented in at least 20 per cent new oak. The wines are vinified in a temperature-controlled room (12–20 °C), and are transferred after the first six months to the Lafons' cool, peaceful cellar. The wines remain on their lees for as long as two years; rackings are gentle and there is no filtration.

Choosing between these wines is difficult. The 5-acre monopole Clos de la Barre, which stretches downhill from the front of the cellar, is village Meursault of rare breed and concentration. Among the Premiers Crus my favourites are Les Charmes and Les Perrières – the first elegant and structured; the second richer and more intense. Les Genevrières is also superb. But the finest wine of the lot is Le Montrachet. The 1989 ranks as one of the greatest white wines I have ever tasted. It has length, depth and beautiful balance. You could drink it young (provided your bank manager agrees to the second mortgage), but it will be even better in ten years' time. White Burgundy does not get any better than this.

*

DOMAINE LAROCHE

L'Obédiencerie, 89800 Chablis

Chardonnay vineyard: 250 acres

Production of Chardonnay: 600,000 bottles from own vineyards; 1.9 million bottles as a *négociant*

Labels: Domaine Laroche; Bacheroy-Josselin

Quality: 🍇🍇–🍇🍇🍇🍇   Price: ★★–★★★★★

Best vintages: 1982, 1983, 1985, 1986, 1989

With 15 acres of Grands Crus and 67 acres of Premiers Crus, Domaine Laroche has some of the most important vineyard holdings in Chablis. Until 1989, it owned the Château de Puligny-Montrachet, but sold the domaine to the bank Crédit Foncier in order to concentrate on Chablis. The firm also sells a large amount of Chardonnay, from sources as diverse as Corsica, the Loire and Pouilly-Fuissé, under its *négociant* labels.

Domaine Laroche is run by the slim, urbane Michel Laroche, the founder's great-grandson. He has presided over important developments within the company, introducing three Vin de Pays Chardonnays (from the Loire, the Pays d'Oc and Corsica) in 1984 and a partially oak-fermented Michel Laroche Réserve Personnelle, which blends Chardonnays from five different Burgundian sources.

Despite these innovations and a flourishing *négociant* business in the Côte de Beaune and the Mâconnais, the heart of Domaine Laroche remains in Chablis. In 1989 and 1990, it produced a string of excellent, nuanced wines, from the basic, unoaked Chablis Saint-Martin to some top-notch Grands Crus.

Since 1980, Laroche has used new barrels on some of its Premiers and Grands Crus, though Michel Laroche does not like the flavour of new oak to be too strong. The percentage never goes above 30 per cent, and Laroche still ferments most of its wines in tank. The best Laroche wines are those from its own vineyards, particularly Fourchaume, Blanchot and Les Clos.

LOUIS LATOUR

18 Rue des Tonnelliers, 21200 Beaune

Chardonnay vineyard: 25 acres (Burgundy); Ardèche vines all under contract

Production of Chardonnay: 1.4 million bottles (Burgundy); 1 million bottles (Ardèche)

Quality: 🍾🍾–🍾🍾🍾🍾🍾   Price: ★★–★★★★★

Best vintages: 1982, 1983, 1986, 1989, 1990

Louis Latour is one of Burgundy's more controversial figures. His decision to set up an operation producing Chardonnay in the southern French region of the Ardèche, and to use his own name on the label, set traditionalists clucking in Beaune. But Latour's brave gamble has paid off: the Ardèche wine, produced from Chardonnay grown by 150 local producers, has gone from strength to strength over the last decade as the age of the vines has increased. The wine, a Vin de Pays des Coteaux de l'Ardèche, is stainless-steel-fermented, and has nice weight, full fruit and reasonable acidity. In 1989, Latour also made 3,000 bottles of an oak-fermented Grand Ardèche, but this is less interesting than the basic Ardèche wine.

Despite its success in the south of France, Louis Latour is fundamentally a Burgundian *négociant*, and a very good one at that. Latour is better known for its white wines than its reds, justifiably so in my opinion. Latour owns a small parcel in Chevalier-Montrachet and a more substantial 23.5 acres in Corton-Charlemagne – the company has a cobwebbed ageing cellar in nearby Aloxe-Corton.

Latour's Corton-Charlemagne is well made, with a high percentage of new oak. In 1989 and 1990, it was extremely impressive with rich, complex layers of flavour. The Latour bottling might not have the elegance and breed of those from Coche-Dury or Louis Jadot, but it is still a complex wine which shows well when young but ages gracefully, too.

The quality of Latour's other white Burgundies is usually high. Three further Grands Crus (Chevalier-Montrachet,

Bâtard-Montrachet and Montrachet) are all top-notch; the more basic village and regional wines are reliably drinkable, if a little short of sparkle. Two interesting Latour curiosities are the white Beaune Les Grèves and lean, sculpted Meursault Blagny. Both wines are well worth seeking out.

DOMAINE LEFLAIVE

21190 Puligny-Montrachet

Chardonnay vineyard: 54 acres

Production of Chardonnay: 114,000 bottles

Quality: 🍾🍾🍾–🍾🍾🍾🍾🍾   Price: ★★★–★★★★★

Best vintages: 1985, 1986, 1989

Domaine Leflaive is the most famous name in the Côte de Beaune. It has extensive holdings in some of Puligny-Montrachet's best sites, and is capable of producing truly brilliant white Burgundies. When they are on form, Domaine Leflaive's Chardonnays are among the most sublime in the world. The wines can be closed and difficult to judge when young, but often develop beautifully with age.

The large pile of New World Chardonnays in the corner of the tasting room is testament to the near-mythical status the domaine enjoys among overseas wine-makers. Other producers come here on bended knee.

Great domaines deserve to be judged by the highest standards, and in recent vintages there have been a few disappointments at Domaine Leflaive. A combination of young vines and excessive yields have compromised the quality of some of the wines. The standard of the 1985s and 1986s was high – the domaine produced superb Clavoillons, Chevalier- and Bâtard-Montrachets in both vintages – but I have found certain 1987s and 1988s rather ordinary. In both years, the basic Puligny-Montrachet seemed lean and insipid; the 1987 Clavoillon was a very poor wine: bitter and over-chaptalized. Only the 1988

Pucelles lived up to the domaine's exalted reputation – and prices.

In 1989, admittedly a much better vintage, the wines were more consistent, though the Puligny-Montrachet again lacked depth. The Bâtard-Montrachet, on the other hand, was a triumph: toasty, citrusy and elegant, with near-perfect balance. With Pierre Morey as wine-maker, the domaine should regain its position at the peak of Burgundian Chardonnay. High yields should not be allowed to stand in the way of quality.

OLIVIER LEFLAIVE FRÈRES

Place du Monument, 21190 Puligny-Montrachet

Chardonnay vineyard: 15 acres

Production of Chardonnay: 480,000 bottles

Quality: 🍇🍇🍇–🍇🍇🍇🍇🍇   Price: ★★/★★★★★

Best vintages: 1985, 1986, 1989, 1990

With a surname like Leflaive, selling wine in Burgundy is never going to be a problem. And so it has proved for Olivier Leflaive, a musician and theatrical impresario turned *négociant*. As well as directing his extremely successful wine business, Olivier (in conjunction with his cousin, Anne-Claude) has now taken over the running of the family domaine from his uncle, Vincent.

Olivier Leflaive Frères was set up in 1985 and has rapidly established itself as one of the finest *négociants* in Burgundy. Appropriately, Leflaive specializes in white wines from the Côte de Beaune and Côte Chalonnaise: 20 per cent of the wine sold comes from the commune of Puligny-Montrachet. In the last few years, Leflaive has strengthened his hand by buying vines in Puligny, Chassagne and Meursault.

Leflaive has been well served by two excellent wine-makers: Jean-Marc Boillot and, since 1989, Franck Grux. The Chardonnay style that has evolved is of clean, crisp, modern wines with some oak and, at the top end, considerable depth and complexity. In most cases, they are wines to drink young.

The firm's benchmark wine is its Bourgogne Blanc, an equal blend of oak- and tank-fermented Chardonnay. Leflaive's selections from the Côte Chalonnaise are consistently good – look out for the Montagny, the Mercurey Blanc and the Rully Premier Cru Rabourcé. So are many of the wines from lesser Côte de Beaune villages like Saint-Romain, Saint-Aubin and Pernand-Vergelesses. The basic Meursault and Puligny wines were also first-class in 1989 and 1990. And at Premier Cru and Grand Cru level, the Pucelles, Bâtard and Bienvenues-Bâtard-Montrachet can be every bit as good as the wines from Domaine Leflaive.

DOMAINE LÉGER-PLUMET

Les Gerbeaux, 71960 Solutré-Pouilly

Chardonnay vineyard: 20 acres

Production of Chardonnay: 50,000 bottles

Labels: Clos du Chalet; Les Chailloux; Les Cornillauds

Quality: 🍇🍇🍇🍇   Price: ★★★

Best vintages: 1985, 1989, 1990

Bernard Léger-Plumet, a pharmacologist by training, took over the running of this domaine when his father-in-law, Henri Plumet, died in 1983. He still manages to juggle two careers; his surgery is in a downstairs room, looking out on to the vines. His double life raises a few eyebrows: 'It's hard for wine-makers to accept a doctor and hard for doctors to accept a wine-maker.'

Whatever his standing among the local vignerons, Léger-Plumet has turned the domaine into one of the leading properties in Pouilly-Fuissé. (Until his arrival, most of the wine was sold off in bulk to *négociants*.) Léger-Plumet's taste is for elegant, minerally, long-lived wines: he is one of the few producers in Burgundy who does not allow his wines to go through malolactic fermentation.

He makes three excellent Chardonnays: a Saint-Véran (Les

Cornillauds) and two Pouilly-Fuissés – Les Chailloux and Clos du Chalet, the latter from a fifty-four-year-old walled vineyard. All three spend some time in (up to 25 per cent new) oak, but they never seem heavy or oversplintered. These are wines for people who want finesse in their Pouilly-Fuissé.

ROGER LUQUET

71960 Fuissé

Chardonnay vineyard: 30 acres

Production of Chardonnay: 100,000 bottles

Labels: Clos du Bourg; Clos de Condemine; Les Grandes Bruyères; Mâcon-Fuissé; Pouilly-Fuissé

Quality: 🍇🍇🍇   Price: ★★

Best vintages: 1983, 1985, 1986, 1989

The emphasis at Roger Luquet's modern domaine is on fruity wines for early drinking. Until recently, and this in response to public pressure, Luquet would not allow an oak barrel past his front door. Nowadays, he uses 5–10 per cent barrel-ageing on his Pouilly-Fuissé, but you sense he does it with a degree of reluctance.

A fourth-generation wine-maker who was among the first in Pouilly-Fuissé to bottle his own production, Luquet produces Chardonnay under five labels: Saint-Véran (Les Grandes Bruyères), Pouilly-Fuissé, Clos du Bourg (a walled vineyard surrounding the precarious, jerry-built church in Fuissé), Mâcon Blanc (called Clos de Condemine) and Mâcon-Fuissé. All of Luquet's wines are pure, fresh, aromatic expressions of the grape, but the Saint-Véran is particularly good value for money. The Clos du Bourg can age for up to five years in good vintages.

*

DOMAINE MATROT

12 Rue du Martray, 21190 Meursault

Chardonnay vineyard: 34 acres

Production of Chardonnay: 48,000 bottles

Labels: Pierre Matrot; Joseph Matrot; Thierry Matrot

Quality: 🍇🍇🍇🍇   Price: ★★–★★★★★

Best vintages: 1982, 1985, 1986, 1988, 1989, 1990

Thierry Matrot is one of the most appealing growers in Burgundy. A funny, intelligent cove with a taste for outlandish modern art, he epitomizes the younger generation of winemakers in Meursault: thoughtful, cosmopolitan and open to new ideas, but with a strong sense of tradition. An hour tasting with Matrot is an hour well spent.

Matrot makes seven Chardonnays (Bourgogne Blanc, Meursault, Meursault Blagny, Meursault Les Charmes, Meursault Les Perrières, Puligny Les Chalumeaux and Puligny Les Combettes) under three different labels: Joseph Matrot (his grandfather), Pierre Matrot (his father) and, since 1989, Thierry Matrot. He has been in charge of the domaine since 1983 and, although the name on the label may vary according to who owns the vines, all of the wines are stamped by his personality.

New oak is used sparingly here. Matrot believes that the flavour of new oak is killing white Burgundy and never uses more than 10 per cent on his wines. The Bourgogne Blanc is entirely tank-fermented; the forward, buttery Meursault sees only old wood. The 1989s at Domaine Matrot were rich and alcoholic. My feeling is that they will be ready long before the better-balanced 1990s, or 1988s. The wines here are consistently interesting, reflecting nuances of *terroir* rather than levels of barrel toast. My favourites are the Meursault and the Meursault Charmes.

*

LOUIS MICHEL

9 Boulevard de Ferrières, 89800 Chablis

Chardonnay vineyard: 49 acres

Production of Chardonnay: 150,000 bottles

Labels: Louis Michel; Domaine de la Tour Vaubourg

Quality: 🍇🍇🍇🍇   Price: ★★—★★★★

Best vintages: 1983, 1986, 1988, 1989, 1990

Jean-Loup and Louis Michel make some of the cleanest, freshest wines in Chablis. In the great oak-versus-stainless-steel debate, the Michels are firmly in the latter camp. They make nine wines, mainly from Grand Cru and Premier Cru vineyards, and not one goes anywhere near an oak barrel.

The Louis Michel style has only emerged in the last twenty years. Until 1970, all of his wines were made in old oak. By 1980, the estate had switched entirely to stainless steel. The wines are fermented at 18–20 °C, using dry yeasts, and have fresh, crisp fruit when young.

The best wines (Les Clos, Montmains, Montée de Tonnerre) will age for up to eight years. Otherwise, they should be consumed in the first five years. Michel's bottlings amply reflect their vineyard origins and are a premium example of Chardonnay in its purest, unadorned form.

BERNARD MICHELOT

31 Rue de la Velle, 21190 Meursault

Chardonnay vineyard: 49 acres

Production of Chardonnay: 100,000 bottles

Labels: Bernard Michelot; Geneviève Michelot; Chantal Michelot; Odile Michelot

Quality: 🍇🍇🍇/🍇🍇🍇🍇   Price: ★★★★/★★★★★

Best vintages: 1982, 1985, 1986, 1987, 1989, 1990

Bernard Michelot is one of the most dynamic figures in Burgundy: a small, barrel-chested vigneron with strong blue eyes and the energy of five men. In a region which is sometimes accused of being inhospitable, Michelot stands out as someone who always finds time to show visitors around. For twenty years, he was president of the local *syndicat*, and did much to restore the reputation of Meursault.

Michelot makes a total of thirteen Chardonnays, which may appear under any one of four names – those of his three daughters or of Michelot himself.

Michelot's wines are often considered oaky; for many years he has advocated the use of up to 25 per cent new barrels. He is characteristically unrepentant. 'Lots of people criticized me for using new oak,' he says, 'but now they've got more than I have.'

Michelot leaves his wines on their lees for twelve months and always produces some of the fullest, most approachable wines in Meursault. The oak seems a little intrusive in vintages like 1984 and 1987, but works well in riper years like 1989 and 1990. In my experience, the wines do not age particularly well. Michelot's best wines are consistently his Meursault Perrières and Meursault Charmes, but he makes very drinkable, commercial wines throughout the commune, from Bourgogne Blanc to Premier Cru level. He now shares the wine-making with his son-in-law, Jean-François Mestre.

BERNARD MOREY

2 Rue du Nord, 21190 Chassagne-Montrachet

Chardonnay vineyard: 11 acres

Production of Chardonnay: 25,000 bottles

Quality: 🍇🍇   Price: ★★★★/★★★★★

Best vintages: 1983, 1985, 1988, 1989

One of Albert Morey's two sons, Bernard has been making wine under his own label since 1981. Albert kept half an acre of Bâtard-Montrachet, which he bottles under his own name, but otherwise divided his vines between Bernard and his younger brother, Jean-Marc.

Bernard has slightly more Chardonnay than Jean-Marc. He makes wine from four Premiers Crus in Chassagne-Montrachet (Les Baudines, Morgeot, Caillerets and Les Embrazées) as well as village-level Chassagne and Saint-Aubin. The wines are fermented in (25 per cent new) oak, and are some of the most attractive in the commune. Bottling takes place after twelve months.

The 1990s and the 1988s were particularly successful here. In both vintages, Morey's best wine was his elegant, flavoursome Morgeot. These are wines to drink relatively young; even the Caillerets should be drunk within five to six years. Bernard Morey's red wines are also excellent.

JEAN-MARC MOREY

3 Rue Principale, 21190 Chassagne-Montrachet

Chardonnay vineyard: 10 acres

Production of Chardonnay: 20,000 bottles

Quality: 🍇🍇🍇🍇   Price: ★★★★/★★★★★

Best vintages: 1983, 1985, 1988, 1989

It should come as no great surprise that Jean-Marc Morey's Chardonnays bear a certain resemblance to those of his brother, Bernard. In some instances, the wines come from the same vineyard and are made, side by side in the same cellar, following the precepts of their father, Albert Morey. In both cases, vinification is identical, with 25 per cent new oak.

There are, however, subtle differences between the two domaines, not least in terms of the vineyards owned. Like Bernard, Jean-Marc has a parcel of vines in Caillerets, but he also makes wine from three other Premiers Crus (Les Champs-Gain, Les Chaumées and Les Chenevottes) where Bernard is not represented. Perhaps this explains my slight preference for Jean-Marc's wines. His basic Chassagne is one of the best, with full, spicy complexity and lots of finesse. Even better are Les Chaumées, rich and packed with fruit, and the more restrained, minerally Les Champs-Gain. These are Chardonnays of considerable breed.

PIERRE MOREY

9 Rue du Comte-Lafon, 21690 Meursault

Chardonnay vineyard: 20 acres

Production of Chardonnay: 20,000 bottles

Quality: 🍇🍇🍇🍇   Price: ★★★—★★★★★

Best vintages: 1986, 1989, 1990

As well as making the wine at Domaine Leflaive, Pierre Morey has his own vineyards in Meursault and Puligny-Montrachet. Under the system of *métayage*, whereby a grower leases vines from their owner, Morey has had to return some of his to the Domaine des Comtes Lafon. It was this, as much as anything, which encouraged him to take the job with the Leflaives. Alas, 1990 was the last vintage of Charmes and, from 1991, Morey will produce no more Montrachet. The only consolation is that the vines are going to a good home.

Pierre Morey is a brilliant wine-maker. He has done much to restore the slightly tarnished reputation of Domaine Leflaive, and the wines released under his own name are excellent, too. In style, Morey's wines are somewhere between the lush hedonism of Lafon and the lean asceticism of Jobard. He uses up to 50 per cent new oak on his Premiers and Grands Crus, but less for his village wines. Morey makes a Bourgogne Blanc that is better than most Meursault, and a nutty, intense bottling from the *lieu-dit* of Les Tessons that could easily pass for a Premier Cru. His best wine, excluding the soon-to-be-lost Montrachet and Bâtard-Montrachet, is the rich, balanced Perrières. The 1989 and 1990 vintages saw some outstanding wines produced at this domaine.

GILLES NOBLET

Domaine de La Collonge, 71960 Fuissé

Chardonnay vineyard: 20 acres

Production of Chardonnay: 30,000 bottles

Quality: 🍇🍇🍇   Price: ★★

Best vintages: 1983, 1985, 1988, 1989, 1990

Gilles Noblet is definitely a name to watch in Pouilly-Fuissé. Young, talented and enthusiastic, he has been bottling his own wines since 1978. Roughly 25 per cent of what he makes is still sold to local *négociants*; the remainder is released under three labels: Pouilly-Fuissé, Pouilly-Loché and Mâcon-Fuissé.

Noblet vinifies all three wines in a combination of (up to 10 per cent new) barrels and *foudres*. The wines stay on their lees until the end of March and are bottled a month later. As a rule, they do not seem overly marked by oak fermentation. Noblet produces ripe, alcoholic Chardonnay that is best drunk in the first five years. His most complete wine is his Pouilly-Fuissé, which combines zesty acidity and full honey and grapefruit flavours.

DOMAINE JACQUES PRIEUR

2 Rue des Santenots, 21190 Meursault

Chardonnay vineyard: 12 acres

Production of Chardonnay: 29,000 bottles

Quality: 🍇🍇–🍇🍇🍇🍇   Price: ★★★–★★★★★

Best vintage: 1990

This domaine has some of the most impressive holdings in the Côte d'Or, from Clos de Vougeot to a sizeable parcel in Le Montrachet. If producers were judged by vineyard sites alone, then Prieur would be among the top names. Unfortunately, owning great vines is not enough, and for much of the eighties,

Prieur did not live up to its billing. The wines were dull and frequently failed to reflect their lofty *appellations*.

Things appear to be on the up, however. In June 1988, the Mercurey-based *négociant* Antonin Rodet and four other investors purchased 50 per cent of the domaine and Bertrand Devillard, Rodet's dynamic managing director, is now co-manager at Prieur, too. Rodet itself is now part-owned by the Champagne house Laurent Perrier. Devillard has big plans for the domaine, and appears to work well with Martin Prieur, Jacques's grandson, who took over the wine-making in 1988.

For white wines, the difference between the 1989 and 1990 vintages is flagrant. While the former lack complexity, the latter have good balance and depth. The oak is cleaner and better integrated and the wines have rediscovered some length and elegance. The domaine's basic Meursault (Clos de Mazeray) is well made, but its star wines are the two Premiers Crus (Meursault Les Perrières and Puligny-Montrachet Les Combettes) and the Chevalier-Montrachet. The Montrachet remains a slight disappointment. It is early days, but Prieur seems to be on the way to regaining some of its former lustre. A name to watch.

CHÂTEAU DE PULIGNY-MONTRACHET

Rue de But, 21190 Puligny-Montrachet

Chardonnay vineyard: 27 acres

Production of Chardonnay: 50,000 bottles

Quality: 🍇🍇–🍇🍇🍇   Price: ★★–★★★★★

Best vintages: 1989, 1990

The Château de Puligny-Montrachet is one of four French properties owned by the financial group, Crédit Foncier. The purchase of this domaine, from Chablis *négociant* Laroche in 1989, was the firm's first venture outside Bordeaux. Crédit Foncier clearly has big plans for its Burgundian operation. The cellars and offices have been given a complete refit and now resemble the sort of thing one encounters regularly in California or Australia, but rarely on the Côte d'Or.

Under a succession of previous owners, the Château produced uninteresting wines, but now there are signs of a revival. Crédit Foncier have purchased vines in Meursault Perrières, Meursault Poruzot, Puligny La Garenne and Puligny Les Chalumeaux, and director Claude Schneider's long-term aim is to make 75 per cent of his wine from Premier and Grand Cru vineyards. For the time being, most of the domaine's Chardonnay is situated in less prestigious sites: Monthélie, Côte de Nuits Villages, Bourgogne Blanc (sold as Clos du Château), Saint-Romain, Puligny-Montrachet and Saint-Aubin. The best of these is the Clos du Château.

The vinification is extremely careful here. Wines begin their fermentation at controlled temperature in stainless steel and are then transferred to one-third new barrels. Some of the results are almost too clean and polished, but the 1990 Meursault Perrières and Meursault Poruzot fully demonstrate this domaine's potential.

DOMAINE RAMONET

21190 Chassagne-Montrachet

Chardonnay vineyard: 22 acres

Production of Chardonnay: 40,000 bottles

Labels: Ramonet; Ramonet-Prudhon

Quality: 🍇🍇🍇🍇🍇   Price: ★★★★/★★★★★

Best vintages: 1985, 1986, 1988, 1989, 1990

The Ramonets (father André and sons Noël and Jean-Claude) are great wine connoisseurs. As well as producing what many (this writer included) consider the greatest Chardonnay in the world, they have a cellar packed with goodies from other wine regions. These treasures are readily and generously shared with friends and visitors alike. It is not unusual to find half of Chassagne-Montrachet *chez* Ramonet tasting a line-up of old clarets.

The evening I visited, a mouth-watering vertical of Château Pétrus was on offer.

The Ramonets are, above all, great vignerons. That is, they know how to get the best from their vines. Yields are kept very low (27 hl/ha in some cases), and vineyards are allowed to rest for up to eight years before replanting. They are fortunate to have some superb parcels to work with. There are three Grands Crus (Bâtard-Montrachet, Bienvenues-Bâtard-Montrachet and Le Montrachet), five Premiers Crus (Les Ruchottes, Les Caillerets, Les Vergers, Morgeot and Les Chaumées), some Chassagne-Montrachet and (from 1990) a bit of Saint-Aubin.

Other producers have an equally valuable list of vineyards, of course, yet make uninteresting wines. Here there is a sense of someone taking the gifts of nature and allowing them full expression. Tasting a Ramonet Grand Cru is a sensual, life-enhancing experience. The only thing it will damage is your wallet.

All the domaine's wines are vinified in barrel, with up to 50 per cent new oak and very little in the way of temperature control. 'We really bash them about to start with,' says Noël. The Premiers Crus stay in oak for as long as fifteen months; the Grands Crus for twenty-one months. *Bâtonnage* (lees stirring) is usually done twice, between the alcoholic and malolactic fermentations. They are racked twice, fined with bentonite and casein and given a light filtration before bottling.

Two barrels in the corner of the cellar represent the Ramonets' entire production of Le Montrachet, the wine at the summit of white Burgundy. This is the sort of thing Chardonnay drinkers dream about. The 1990 and 1989 were both close to perfection, the former more reticent, the latter rich and complex. Both wines are loaded with flavours – mint, toffee, cinnamon, hazelnut, liquorice, apple and lemon to name but a few – and tasting them, one is left groping for superlatives. The lush, powerful Bâtard-Montrachet and crisp, aromatic Bienvenues-Bâtard-Montrachet are frequently just as good.

Of the Premiers Crus, Les Ruchottes is the most forward, and should be drunk within five years. The other four need a little more time. With wines like these, we can afford to wait.

If you want to taste a Ramonet wine, but can't afford a Premier or Grand Cru, the Saint-Aubin and village Chassagne-Montrachet are your best bet. These are like scaled-down versions of the top wines, but even here the class shines through. If even these are beyond your pocket, the Ramonets are generous providers of samples to the tasting room in the centre of the village.

JEAN-MARIE RAVENEAU

9 Rue Chichée, 89800 Chablis

Chardonnay vineyard: 17 acres

Production of Chardonnay: 45,000 bottles

Labels: Jean-Marie Raveneau; François Raveneau (until the 1989 vintage)

Quality: 🍇🍇🍇🍇🍇   Price: ★★★★/★★★★★

Best vintages: 1985, 1986, 1989, 1990

From a small, unassuming house on the outskirts of Chablis, Jean-Marie Raveneau produces the finest wines of the *appellation*. Other Chablis, even those of Vincent Dauvissat, simply cannot match the intensity of Raveneau's bottlings. His vineyards are divided between three Grands Crus (Blanchot, Les Clos and Valmur) and four Premiers Crus (Montée de Tonnerre, Vaillons, Butteaux and Chapelot). Raveneau does not make basic Chablis or Petit Chablis, though if he did the results would undoubtedly be outstanding.

Jean-Marie Raveneau ferments his wines in a combination of stainless steel, new and not-so-new oak. There are few hard-and-fast rules here, and Raveneau likes nothing more than a difficult vintage to test his wine-making skills. He considers his 1984s a personal triumph, and when you taste the 1984 Valmur, you can but agree with him. In most but not all cases, Raveneau leaves his wines in tank for six months and then ages them in oak for a further twelve months. The wines are fined, but never filtered.

All seven Raveneau wines are extremely fine examples of Chardonnay, displaying the lean, subtle structure of great Chablis fleshed out with lots of minerally fruit. The 1990 Blanchot was so rich that, when young, it almost had a New World intensity about it. If I had to pick just one Raveneau Chablis – and the task is an invidious one – then it would be Les Clos. This vineyard produced brilliant wine in 1989 and 1990. Both wines should be approaching their best sometime after the turn of the century.

ANTONIN RODET

71640 Mercurey

Chardonnay vineyard: 200 acres (owned or co-owned)

Production of Chardonnay: 1.8 million bottles

Quality: ♛♛♛–♛♛♛♛   Price: ★★–★★★★★

Best vintages: 1985, 1986, 1989, 1990

'Why should I make wine in Chile or the Ardèche, when there are so many unexploited vineyards in the Côte Chalonnaise?' says Bertrand Devillard, managing director of Antonin Rodet. Devillard, a charming, urbane Burgundian, is committed to the wines of his own region in general, and to those of the Côte Chalonnaise in particular.

Devillard's high standards are reflected in the wines. This Mercurey-based *négociant* sells vast quantities of white Burgundy, from Chablis to the Mâconnais. The quality is always reliable, sometimes excellent. It is also proprietor or co-proprietor of four domaines – Château de Rully, Château de Chamirey, Jacques Prieur and Château de Mercurey – and sells the Mercurey wines through its Duvergey-Taboreau subsidiary.

For the time being, Antonin Rodet is at its most impressive outside the Côte de Beaune, although Domaine Prieur has hitched up its wine-making socks lately. This should help Devillard realize his ambition to establish his company in the front rank of Burgundian merchants, alongside the likes of Louis Jadot and Joseph Drouhin. The Champagne house Laurent Perrier bought 66 per cent of Rodet in May 1991, a move which Devillard says will help the company to grow in importance.

Many of the Rodet bottlings represent extremely good value. Its Bourgogne Vieilles Vignes is full, fruity unoaked Chardonnay with lots of varietal flavour. Even better are the two domaine wines from the Côte Chalonnaise: the partially oak-fermented Château de Rully is one of the best two or three wines in the *appellation*; and the more complex, structured Château de Chamirey, Mercurey Blanc is consistently excellent. In 1990, this was the finest Chardonnay produced in the Côte Chalonnaise.

DOMAINE DE LA ROMANÉE-CONTI

Vosne-Romanée, 21700 Nuits-Saint-Georges

Chardonnay vineyard: 1.7 acres

Production of Chardonnay: 2,700 bottles

Quality: 🍇🍇🍇🍇🍇   Price: ★★★★★

Best vintages: 1985, 1989

As well as making some of the finest (and most expensive) red Burgundies, the legendary Domaine de la Romanée-Conti also makes brilliant Montrachet. This white wine, produced in tiny quantities, has few equals. Among the handful of growers with vines in Le Montrachet, only Marc Colin, the Ramonets and the Lafons can match its incredible concentration of flavours.

The production is tiny, smaller even than the six hundred or so cases of La Romanée-Conti. According to one source, importers have to buy fifty cases of the domaine's red wines to secure a single case of DRC Montrachet. The price is correspondingly stratospheric. Bottles are scarce, and I have tasted this marvellous wine only once. The 1985 was quintessential Montrachet – elegant and racy with a rich, nutty complexity that seemed to transcend mere wine-making. Would that DRC's only white wine were available in larger quantities.

GUY ROULOT

1 Rue Charles-Giraud, 21190 Meursault

Chardonnay vineyard: 20 acres

Production of Chardonnay: 40,000 bottles

Quality: 🍾🍾🍾🍾   Price: ★★—★★★★★

Best vintages: 1986, 1989, 1990

The untimely death of Guy Roulot in 1982 engendered a difficult few years for this excellent domaine. The wines were made first by the American Ted Lemon, now at Château Woltner in California, and then by Franck Grux, Roulot's nephew, who went to work for *négociant* Olivier Leflaive. Since 1989, the wine-making has been handled by Roulot's son, Jean-Marc. Despite the rapid succession of oenologists, the domaine has continued to produce first-class wines, a tribute to the talents of all three men.

Jean-Marc Roulot is a professional actor who still performs in Paris when time allows. These days, the opportunities are rare, as he has brought a good deal of enthusiasm to the running of the family domaine, reducing vineyard yields and experimenting with new fining agents. He has been well served by the 1989 and 1990 vintages, both of which show the domaine on top form.

Eight different Chardonnays are made here, and all of them are very fine. The Bourgogne Blanc is rich and long in the mouth; the five Meursault village wines (from the *lieux-dits* of Les Tillets, Les Meix Chavaux, Les Luchets, Les Tessons and Les Vireuils) are as good as many domaines' Premiers Crus; and the two Roulot Premiers Crus, Charmes and Perrières, are among the most ripe, concentrated wines in the commune. The Perrières is consistently the domaine's best wine.

The Roulot style produces wines that show well when young

but can age for five to eight years. They spend up to twelve months in 20–35 per cent new oak, depending on the wine, and have a lovely toffee'd, buttery richness on the palate. These are supple, charming wines that never, at any point of their development, seem austere.

ÉTIENNE SAUZET

21190 Puligny-Montrachet

Chardonnay vineyard: 25 acres (17 acres from 1991)

Production of Chardonnay: 75,000 bottles (48,000 from 1991)

Quality: 🍇🍇🍇🍇🍇   Price: ★★★—★★★★★

Best vintages: 1982, 1985, 1986, 1988, 1989

It was the late Étienne Sauzet who single-handedly created the reputation of this property. Since his death in 1975, the domaine has been run by his grandson-in-law, Gérard Boudot, who continues to produce superb white Burgundies.

The domaine is going through a difficult spell. It lost eight acres of vineyard in 1990 when Colette, Étienne Sauzet's daughter, divided the estate among her three children: Jean-Marc Boillot, Jeanine Boillot-Boudot and Henri Boillot. Jean-Marc Boillot decided to take his share of the domaine and make the wine under his own name. So, from 1991, there will be no more Puligny La Truffière at Étienne Sauzet. Production of the four other Premiers Crus (Les Combettes, Champ Canet, Les Referts and Les Perrières), two village wines (Puligny and Chassagne), and Bourgogne Blanc will be cut by one-third. But the two Grands Crus, Bâtard-Montrachet and Bienvenues-Bâtard-Montrachet, will remain intact. Praise the Lord.

Whatever Jean-Marc Boillot's considerable talents as a wine-maker, the loss of one-third of this great domaine is a considerable blow. Gérard Boudot produces some of the most concentrated, finely structured Chardonnays of all and from 1991 there will be fewer bottles to go round. The 1989 vintage yielded a string of brilliant wines; and the more forward 1990s looked equally good in barrel.

The top wines here see as much as 35–50 per cent new oak, but have enough depth and fruit to cope with the experience. They stay in barrel for as long as eighteen months, and are built to last. My favourite Sauzet wines are Les Perrières, Les Combettes and, of course, the two Grands Crus. The Bienvenues-Bâtard-Montrachet, made from a tiny patch of fifty-year-old vines, is a truly sublime bottle of Chardonnay.

JEAN THÉVENET

Domaine de La Bon Gran, 71260 Clessé

Chardonnay vineyard: 37 acres

Production of Chardonnay: 80,000 bottles

Labels: Domaine de La Bon Gran; Domaine Gillet;
Château de Besseuil

Quality: 🍇🍇🍇🍇   Price: ★★★–★★★★★

Best vintages: 1983, 1989, 1990

Jean Thévenet is one of the Mâconnais's great characters, a fascinating, garrulous eccentric who produces some very unusual wines. Thévenet took over from his father full-time in 1972, and has turned his domaine into one of the most interesting in Burgundy.

Thévenet is a strange mixture of traditionalist and iconoclast. He practises organic methods of viticulture and keeps yields below 40 hl/ha. Thévenet likes to pick his Chardonnay over-ripe, or '*levrouté*', preferably with some botrytis. As a result, his wines are usually full-bodied and often show a bit of residual sugar. They ferment naturally, sometimes for as long as two years, in a combination of tanks and old oak *foudres*.

In 1983, Thévenet made a late-harvest botrytis-affected Chardonnay for the first time, an experiment that raised hackles in the Mâconnais. He rightly counted it a success, and has since released a Cuvée Botrytis in 1989 and 1990. The 1983 and the

1989 are both great sweet wines: peachy, complex and botrytis-intense.

In most vintages, Thévenet releases a Cuvée Levroutée, which is medium-dry, and a 'dry' wine, which also has a bit of sweetness to it. He has three different sources: the Château de Besseuil in Clessé, the Domaine Émilian Gillet in Viré and Clessé, and the Domaine de La Bon Gran in Clessé. La Bon Gran is consistently the most interesting of the three. Even the 'dry' Bon Gran can have up to 30 per cent botrytis: the 1989 Mâcon Clessé, one of a series of great wines produced in this vintage, was rich, concentrated and well balanced.

Thévenet is scornful of prevailing production methods. High yields, chemicals, early picking and excessive chaptalization, he believes, are cheapening the reputation of the Mâconnais. Thévenet's own wines are the most expensive in the area, but when you taste something like the 1971 Bon Gran Mâcon Clessé the prices seem fully justified.

AUBERT DE VILLAINE

71150 Bouzeron

Chardonnay vineyard: 10 acres

Production of Chardonnay: 20,000 bottles

Quality: 👿👿👿   Price: ★/★★

Best vintages: 1988, 1989, 1990

Aubert de Villaine is best known as the co-owner of the Domaine de la Romanée-Conti, but this quiet, faintly donnish wine-maker has a second, less glamorous property in Bouzeron, a small village in the Côte Chalonnaise. De Villaine and his American wife, Pamela, make a Bourgogne Blanc, a Bourgogne Rouge and a Bourgogne Aligoté. The *appellations* are humble, but the wines are extremely patrician.

The Bourgogne Blanc, called Les Clous, is one of the best basic Burgundian Chardonnays. De Villaine planted the vineyard in 1973 and restricts his yields to 50 hectolitres per hectare – a lesson for less exigent growers. The wine is one-third barrel-fermented and is bottled after eight to ten months. Les Clous has plenty of weight and minerally richness on the palate, but never seems fat or overripe. It is one of Burgundy's great bargains.

Champagne

There may be the odd patch of homespun vines around Rouen or Rennes, but Champagne, situated 150 km to the east of Paris, gets the nod as France's most northerly *appellation*. A place where, in most vintages, grapes struggle to ripen fully – as anyone who has ever tasted a thinly acidic non-sparkling Coteaux Champenois will appreciate – Champagne nevertheless produces the world's finest sparkling wines. The Champagne method, by which wine undergoes a secondary fermentation in bottle and is left in contact with its lees, transforms tart, barely drinkable base wines into what can be some of the most complex beverages of all. The word 'can' is important, for too often Champagne is an overpriced, overhyped disappointment.

Chardonnay is a vital ingredient in Champagne. It is planted in each of the region's five *départements* (Marne, Aisne, Seine-et-Marne, Aube and Haute Marne) and accounts for just over 27 per cent of total plantings. Nearly all of the Chardonnay in Champagne is concentrated in the Marne *département*, which has 19,369 out of the current 20,681 acres of the grape. Outside the Marne, Chardonnay is a comparative nonentity; there are 303 acres in the Aisne, 407 acres in the Aube and tiny quantities in the Haute Marne and Seine-et-Marne.

In terms of vineyard area alone, Chardonnay is the least important of Champagne's three grape varieties. Pinot Noir (35 per cent) and Pinot Meunier (38 per cent) are both more substantial presences. Consequently, its contribution to non-vintage blends is often exaggerated, just as that of Pinot Meunier, generally the least patrician of the trio, is under-played.

Most Champagne is a blend of these three varieties. The character of each was described thus by one well-known pro-ducer: 'Pinot Meunier is like a child, with lots of youthful fruit, Chardonnay is more feminine, with grace and sophistication, while Pinot Noir tends to be the most masculine of our three varieties.' Sexist perhaps, but the comparison is a valid one. Chardonnay is usually the most acidic and latest-ripening of the three grapes, and is used to add breed and elegance to both vintage and non-vintage blends.

Since the Second World War, the overall style of Champagne has shifted towards blends with a higher propor-tion of Chardonnay. This has resulted in a proliferation over the last decade of all-Chardonnay, Blanc de Blancs blends. Chardonnay has existed in Champagne, under the pseudonym of Épinette, for at least two hundred years, but it was not until the 1920s that the first commercially available Blanc de Blancs was released. For many years, Blanc de Blancs Champagnes were dismissed as insubstantial by many producers, but more recently the style has become increasingly popular.

These days, houses which do not release a Blanc de Blancs are the exception rather than the rule. As the number of brands has increased, so the quality of Blanc de Blancs Champagne has declined. Instead of being restricted to years, like 1982 or 1985, when the Chardonnay was exceptional, Blancs de Blancs is now produced as a matter of course. The best houses and growers (listed below) continue to produce wines of exceptional finesse, but much that styles itself Blanc de Blancs is unworthy of the name. Where growers' Champagnes are concerned, it pays to be especially prudent. While it is more reliable than Pinot Noir, Chardonnay is still an inconsistent performer in Champagne, so grapes drawn from different areas are more likely to produce a balanced wine. In years such as 1982, 1985, 1989 and 1990, there is less to worry about.

Vineyard location is the key to quality. As André Carré of Mumm puts it: 'Champagne is a question of *crus* as much as one of grape varieties.' The best Chardonnay comes from the Côte des Blancs, a croissant-shaped row of hills which runs south-east of Épernay from Chouilly to Vertus. This is one of five major viticultural districts in the *appellation*, the other four being the Montagne de Reims, the Vallée de la Marne, the Aube and the Côte de Sézanne.

The best villages of the Côte des Blancs are its Grands Crus – Avize, Cramant, Le Mesnil-sur-Oger, Chouilly, Oger and Oiry – most of whose vineyards are given over entirely to Chardonnay. These are part of a network of seventeen Grands Crus and forty-one Premiers Crus, all of which are located in the Marne *département*. As a rule, the Grands and Premiers Crus of the Montagne de Reims and the Vallée de la Marne are planted predominantly with red grapes (Pinot Meunier and Pinot Noir), although good Chardonnay is produced in the villages of Bouzy, Ambonnay and Verzenay. The Chardonnays from these areas tend to be richer and more forward than those from the Côte des Blancs, which often have a citrusy note to them. In terms of soil structure, there are only minor variations between the three areas. All three benefit from the region's well-drained chalk subsoil, which can be as deep as 300 metres in places, but there is a higher percentage of clay in the Côte des Blancs.

There are also plantings of Chardonnay in the Côte de Sézanne, situated to the south-west of the Côte des Blancs, and in the more southerly Aube, which is virtually a semi-detached region of Burgundy. Though small, the Côte de Sézanne is a good alternative source of Chardonnay. The Aube, which has more in common with Chablis than the Marne Valley, pro-duces a fruitier style of Chardonnay that is ideal for young blends. Inexpensive Blanc de Blancs wines often contain a high percentage of Aube grapes. Blanc de Blancs Champagne comes in various shapes and sizes, from rich and creamy to elegant and austere. Everything depends on house style. Krug's Clos du Mesnil, which is aged in oak, is quite a contrast with Tait-tinger's lean Comtes de Champagne. As a general rule of thumb, though, Blanc de Blancs Champagnes do not have the body and character of Pinot Noir-based blends. (It is not true, as some have asserted, that Blanc de Blancs wines necessarily age better than other blends. Some do; some don't.) As Henri Krug once said, they are sonatas rather than full-blown symphonies. Nevertheless, at their most complex, they make music of celestial harmony.

> Best Champagne houses: Ayala, Billecart-Salmon, Charbaut*, Deutz, Charles Heidsieck, Henriot, Jacquesson, Krug*, Mumm, Bruno Paillard, Joseph Perrier, Pol Roger*, Louis Roederer, Ruinart*, Salon*, Taittinger*

> Best Champagne growers: Bonnaire-Boquemont (Cramant), Pierre Gimmonet et Fils (Cramant), Launois Père et Fils (Le Mesnil-sur-Oger), Lilbert Fils (Cramant), Pierre Peters (Le Mesnil-sur-Oger), Jacques Selosse (Avize), Sugot-Feneuil (Cramant)

A. CHARBAUT ET FILS

> 17 Avenue de Champagne, 51206 Épernay
>
> Chardonnay vineyard: 50 acres
>
> Production of Chardonnay: not released
>
> Labels: Crémant; Blanc de Blancs; Certificate
>
> Quality: 🍾🍾🍾/🍾🍾🍾🍾   Price: ★★★★/★★★★★
>
> Best vintages: 1979, 1981, 1985

Charbaut is a comparative parvenu among Champagne houses. This medium-sized family firm was founded just after the war by André Charbaut, who worked for many years as commercial director of Champagne Ducoin and was one of the Champagne region's great characters. In its initial phase, the house only sold wines from its own 140 acres in the Marne Valley (Mareuil-sur-Ay, Bisseuil and Avenay), but it has expanded considerably since then and now produces more than 1.8 million bottles, under a variety of *sous-marques* as well as its own label.

Charbaut moved from Mareuil-sur-Ay into new premises on

Épernay's avenue de Champagne in the early eighties – the town's equivalent of Park Lane or Fifth Avenue – able at last to brush shoulders with the likes of Pol Roger and Perrier-Jouët. Some of the firm's wines are certainly in the top flight – its Certificate Rosé is excellent, but its three Blanc de Blancs are even better, in my view.

Charbaut's fifty acres of Chardonnay are all situated in the Marne Valley and tend to produce wines with more body and depth of flavour than those on the more prestigious Côte des Blancs. René Charbaut, the son of the founder, considers these wines too rich to be bottled on their own and blends them with the production of bought-in grapes from Avize, Vertus, Mesnil-sur-Oger, Grauves and Bergères-les-Vertus.

The lightest Charbaut Blanc de Blancs is its charming Crémant; the non-vintage Blanc de Blancs has a little more depth and concentration; but the house's best wine is its superb vintage Certificate Blanc de Blancs. The current vintage (1985) is typically firm in character, with a yeasty, almost earthy depth that is closer to a Blanc de Noirs than a Blanc de Blancs. It certainly has the structure to age for at least a decade.

KRUG (CLOS DU MESNIL)

5 Rue Coquebert, 51000 Reims

Chardonnay vineyard: 4.5 acres

Production of Chardonnay: 17,642 bottles (1982)

Quality: 🍾🍾🍾🍾🍾   Price: ★★★★★

Best vintages: 1979, 1981, 1982

Clos du Mesnil may well be the most expensive Chardonnay in the world. This delicious, ludicrously priced wine comes from a small walled vineyard that the Krug family has owned at Le Mesnil-sur-Oger, on the Côte des Blancs, since 1971.

The vines are situated in the heart of the village and originally belonged to the local Benedictine monastery. When the Krug brothers – Henri and Rémi – took over this historic vineyard, much of it was badly in need of replanting. The first Clos du Mesnil, therefore, was not made until 1979 and has been followed by releases in 1981 and (the current) 1982.

If you can afford it, this is one of the world's great wines, with finesse, elegance and more concentration than any other Blanc de Blancs. Like all Krug's wines, the base cuvée is fermented in old oak barrels; Krug is one of the few houses to continue this ancient practice.

Krug wines are never cheap, but they are also rarely disappointing. Less opulent Krug *aficionados* should stick to the cheaper, non-vintage Grande Cuvée, which contains roughly 35 per cent of Chardonnay.

POL ROGER

1 Rue Henri-Lelarge, PO Box 199, 51206 Épernay

Chardonnay vineyard: 74 acres

Production of Chardonnay: not released

Quality: 🍇🍇🍇🍇   Price: ★★★★★

Best vintages: 1975, 1979, 1982, 1985

In a market increasingly dominated by large international groupings, Pol Roger remains one of the few independent Champagne houses. Christian de Billy, the firm's small, rosy-cheeked chairman, says it will remain so while he is in charge: 'I have enough money to retire without selling my firm. I don't want to move to Switzerland or Bermuda.'

De Billy and his elegant, gentlemanly cousin Christian Pol Roger are a highly appealing duo, consistently producing some of the best wines in the region. They have nearly two hundred acres of vines, mainly around Épernay in the Marne Valley, as well as plantings in Cramant, on the Côte des Blancs; accordingly, they buy in around 55 per cent of their needs.

Pol Roger is sometimes described as a Pinot Noir house, a reference to the depth and structure of its vintage blend and two prestige cuvées, Réserve Spéciale 'PR' and Cuvée Winston

Churchill (a tribute to the great man's unstinting consumption of Pol Roger Champagne). Nevertheless, Pol Roger's blends have included a greater percentage of Chardonnay in the last decade.

The house also releases an outstanding Blanc de Blancs (labelled, with a nod to the New World, Blanc de Chardonnay). The wine was first produced in 1959, though naturally the word Chardonnay did not make an appearance until more recent times. In style, it is often heavier than the company's non-vintage blend, which accounts for 75 per cent of its sales, but still displays the elegance and finesse of the best Blanc de Blancs.

Pol Roger's Blanc de Chardonnay is always a vintage wine, and is usually aged for five to six years before release. It is produced almost exclusively from Champagne's best vineyards (the Grand Cru villages of Cramant, Avize, Oger and Mesnil), and the class is richly apparent in the wine. Of the two most recent vintages, I am particularly fond of the 1982. Winston Churchill, I am convinced, would have enjoyed it too.

RUINART

4 Rue des Crayères, 51100 Reims

Chardonnay vineyard: approximately 20 acres

Production of Chardonnay: 120,000 bottles

Quality: 🍇🍇🍇🍇🍇   Price: ★★★★★

Best vintages: 1975, 1982, 1983

Ruinart, which makes a big fuss about being the oldest Champagne house, has managed to retain its individualism despite being swallowed up by the giant Moët & Chandon group in 1963. For some reason, however, the image of this splendid producer has lagged some way behind the quality of its wines. An underpromoted Champagne house, now there's a rarity.

Ruinart specializes in Chardonnay – even its aromatic,

eminently reliable non-vintage blend has at least 35 per cent. Ruinart draws on the vineyard resources of the Moët group as well as buying Chardonnay on the open market. Its flagship wine is the vintage Dom Ruinart Blanc de Blancs, which combines fruit from the Côte des Blancs with a more unusual 15 per cent from the Montagne de Reims.

The Blanc de Blancs, like all Ruinart's vintage wines, is aged for six to eight years before release. This is a wine of considerable complexity, with delicious, aromatic concentration; the Montagne de Reims grapes add a bit of extra body and depth. Dom Ruinart has been made in most recent vintages (1979, 1981, 1982, 1983, 1985 and 1986). Of the two current releases, the 1983 is leaner than the full, creamy 1982, but both are superb wines.

SALON

PO Box 3, Le Mesnil-sur-Oger, 51190 Avize

Chardonnay vineyard: 2 acres

Production of Chardonnay: 60,000 bottles

Quality: 🍇🍇🍇🍇   Price: ★★★★★

Best vintages: 1973, 1976, 1982

Salon must be the only Champagne house to produce just one wine: its superlative vintage Blanc de Blancs. This small operation on the Côte des Blancs was founded by Eugène Aimé Salon, who made a fortune as a Parisian furrier before returning to his native region at the turn of the century. Captivated by the wines of Le Mesnil-sur-Oger, he started to make his own Champagne, initially for friends, but soon on a more commercial basis. By the late 1920s, Salon was the house wine at Maxim's in Paris. Never was a wine more appositely named.

From the outset, Eugène Aimé Salon chose to specialize in Chardonnay. Salon le Mesnil was the first commercially available Blanc de Blancs, and since its initial vintage in 1911, it has drawn all its grapes (from a combination of its own vineyard and local growers) from the Grand Cru village of Le Mesnil-sur-Oger.

Salon le Mesnil is made exclusively in vintage years – approximately one harvest in three – and is usually aged for at least seven years before release. Like Krug, that other star of Le Mesnil-sur-Oger, Salon uses wood in the maturation of its base wine, but does not allow it to go through malolactic fermentation. The resulting cuvée is one of the most complex Blanc de Blancs in Champagne. The 1982 is an incredible wine, with a fine mousse, rich nutty fruit and great length.

The house is now owned by the highly respected firm of Laurent Perrier, which happily incorporates Salon's grapes into its own wines in non-vintage years.

TAITTINGER

9 Place Saint-Nicaise, 51061 Reims

Chardonnay vineyard: 300 acres

Production of Chardonnay: 500,000 bottles

Quality: 🍇🍇🍇🍇🍇   Price: ★★★★★

Best vintages: 1982, 1983, 1985

As a young First World War cavalry officer, Pierre Taittinger was billeted in the eighteenth-century Château de la Marquetterie at Pierry, south-west of Reims. He liked the place so much that, as the advertisement goes, he subsequently bought it in 1932. The château came with a sizeable vineyard which Taittinger supplemented with the purchase of the established Champagne house of Fourneaux. Over the years, Champagne Taittinger has acquired comparatively large plantings of nearly six hundred acres in the Côte des Blancs, the Montagne de Reims and the Aube – a godsend in these times of rapidly increasing grape prices.

Today, this impressive, family-owned business is run by Pierre's son, Claude: historian, regional spokesman and judo black belt. Claude has inherited his father's taste for elegant

Champagnes with a high proportion of Chardonnay. In fact, Taittinger's top Cuvée de Prestige, called Comtes de Champagne after the thirteenth-century crusader who allegedly brought a cutting of Chardonnay back from the Middle East, is a varietal Blanc de Blancs.

Comtes de Champagne is only made in good vintages, using grapes from top villages on the Côte des Blancs. First made in 1952, the initial vintage was launched five years later. The wine is usually aged for five to six years before release, but is certainly capable of further development in bottle. Of the top Blanc de Blancs, Comtes de Champagne is consistently among the most austere. Recent releases have been extremely fine – and correspondingly expensive.

Jura

Situated midway between Beaune and Geneva, the Jura is one of France's least-appreciated viticultural regions. The wines of this scenic, unspoilt area are characterized by their subtle, understated flavours, and tasters accustomed to the structure and fruit flavours of New World Chardonnays may find them difficult to appreciate at first.

Chardonnay (also known locally as Gamay Blanc or Melon d'Arbois) is the principal white grape here. It is produced under four separate *appellations*: Côtes du Jura, Arbois, L'Étoile and the sparkling Côtes du Jura Mousseux. (Arbois and L'Étoile are both sub-areas of the all-encompassing Côtes du Jura classification.) Except in the case of sparkling wine, where Pinot Blanc and Pinot Noir are used, Chardonnay is frequently blended with Savagnin, the region's second most important white variety. The two grapes are ideal confrères: Savagnin gives Chardonnay a bit of extra backbone and increases its ageing potential. The greater the percentage of Savagnin, the more structured and spicy the wine.

Excluding sparkling wine, which is produced mainly in L'Étoile and Côtes du Jura, there are two main styles of Chardonnay. The first emphasizes fruity, youthful aromas, while the second is marked by a lengthy period of controlled oxidation in barrel. This can impart something of the sherry-like character of the region's famous Vins Jaunes, which are made entirely from Savagnin. The best exponent of the former style is Domaines Rollet; in the nuttier, almost tangy camp, the top names are Domaine de la Pinte and Château d'Arlay.

Best producers: Château d'Arlay*, Jean-François Bourdy, Fruitière Vinicole d'Arbois, Domaine de la Pinte, Domaines Rollet

CHÂTEAU D'ARLAY

39140 Blettcrans, Jura

Chardonnay vineyard: 15 acres

Production of Chardonnay: 25,000 bottles

Quality: 🍇🍇🍇/🍇🍇🍇🍇   Price: ★★

Best vintages: 1986, 1988

Château d'Arlay, which has been run for more than thirty years by Comte Renaud de Laguiche, brother of the Burgundian Marquis of the same name, is one of the oldest properties in the Jura. It is situated outside the best-known white-wine *appellations* of the region (L'Étoile and Château-Chalon) in the catch-all Côtes du Jura, but consistently produces some of the most interesting Jura Chardonnays.

By Jura standards, Renaud de Laguiche is a modernist. He is experimenting with new trellising methods and small Burgundian barrels for his Chardonnay. The wine is fermented in tank, goes through malolactic, and is aged principally in large old oak containers. Unlike many producers, de Laguiche regularly tops up his wine in barrel. (To do this, he uses Savagnin, the other important local white grape, which ends up accounting for around 7 per cent of the blend.) As a result of this topping-up, they have less of the nutty, oxidized flavour of many Jura white wines, but their character is still quite marked.

The Chardonnay is aged in oak for at least two years – a minimum for good Jura wines, according to de Laguiche – and is very much an old-fashioned kind of wine. For lovers of sweet, ripe California Chardonnay, a wine like this, with its subtle shadings of flavour, is difficult to comprehend. It is worth persevering, though. Jura whites may be an acquired taste, but they make wonderful accompaniments to food.

Limoux

Limoux's location to the south-west of the ancient Cathar stronghold of Carcassonne would suggest a warm climate, but the average temperature here is much lower than you'd expect, particularly in areas such as Saint-Hilaire, Saint-Polycarpe and the Haute Vallée de l'Aude. Perhaps this explains Limoux's reputation as a producer of sparkling wines. Blanquette de Limoux, according to the locals, has a much longer history than Champagne.

The main grape in Blanquette is the local Mauzac, but since 1975 Chardonnay and Chenin Blanc (up to a maximum of 30 per cent) have also been permitted, in order to spice up the blend. Chardonnay now covers roughly one-sixth of the *appellation*'s 7,500 acres.

In 1990, a second sparkling-wine *appellation*, called Crémant de Limoux, got the nod from the Institut National des Appellations d'Origine. This has to have at least 30 per cent Chardonnay and/or Chenin Blanc, but no more than 20 per cent of each. At least one producer has ignored the rules and released an unannounced varietal sparkling Chardonnay.

The local cooperative, which dominates the *appellation* to the

tune of 60 per cent of its production, has also been experiment-
ing with still Chardonnay, sold as Vin de Pays d'Oc or Vin de
Pays de la Haute Vallée de l'Aude, since 1976. Most of its
Chardonnay is made in stainless steel, but its toasty, barrel-
fermented wines are also promising, if ludicrously expensive.
Other palatable Chardonnays are made by Domaine de
Martinolles, Jean-Pierre Robert, Jacques Astruc, Gino Buoro,
Gérard Averseng and Eric Vialade.

Loire

Chardonnay's rise to prominence in the Loire Valley is comparatively recent – the Cave du Haut Poitou did not make its
first Chardonnay until 1967, and plantings of the variety in
Anjou, Touraine and Saumur were scarce until the early
eighties – but, as it has done elsewhere, the grape has gained
rapidly in stature. There are currently more than 2,000 acres of
Chardonnay in the Loire, and the figure is increasing at a
considerable rate of knots.

Despite its popularity with growers, varietal Chardonnays
are not permitted in any of the Loire's still-wine *appellation
contrôlée* areas. Saumur Blanc, Touraine Blanc and Anjou Blanc
are allowed to add up to 20 per cent, but that's as far as it goes.
Producers such as Domaine de Bablut and Domaine des Hauts
de Sanziers both sell their Chardonnays as Vins de Pays du
Jardin de la France.

For sparkling wines, the regulations are a little more lenient.
Saumur Mousseux is restricted to 20 per cent, but for Crémant
de Loire, a producer can use as much Chardonnay as he or she
likes. Nevertheless, with the exception of the Cave du Haut
Poitou's Diane de Poitiers brand, no one, to my knowledge, has
produced a varietal sparkling Chardonnay in the Loire. According to Alain Seydoux of Gratien & Meyer, this is because 'Loire
Chardonnay doesn't ripen properly'.

For still wines, Chardonnay is permitted, either as blending material or as a varietal, in a number of VDQS areas, namely Haut Poitou, where the local cooperative has had considerable commercial success with the grape in Cheverny and Valençay. Chardonnay also pops up in Orléans, under the *nom de cépage* of Auvernat Blanc, although the wine has to be labelled Orléanais Blanc.

Even as a VDQS or Vin de Pays, Chardonnay commands a premium. In the Pays Nantais, Louis Métaireau has expressed concern that growers are ripping out Muscadet vines and replacing them with Chardonnay. In theory at least, producers are not allowed to blend the two varieties. This is one of the drawbacks of increasing Chardonnay production. We can probably survive with a little less Muscadet, but what happens when growers start pulling out old Chenin Blanc vineyards to make way for Chardonnay?

So far, Chardonnay has underperformed in the Loire. It tends to be fresh, fruity, floral and unoaked, with a good lick of acidity, but even the best examples lack concentration and complexity. In most cases, this is because the vines are still young, so expect improvements over the next decade.

> Best producers: Domaine de Bablut (Anjou), Berger Frères (Montlouis), Cave du Haut Poitou (Haut Poitou), Domaine des Hauts de Sanziers (Saumur), Daniel Montigny (Orléans), Domaine Petit Château (Vallet), Château de la Ragotière (Muscadet)

Other Regions

Alsace

Chardonnay's role in Alsace is confined to a walk-on part as an authorized grape in sparkling Crémant d'Alsace blends. Since 1976, when Crémant was dignified with its own *appellation contrôlée*, Chardonnay, Riesling, Pinot Blanc, Pinot Noir, Pinot Gris and Auxerrois can be legally combined in any number of permutations. To my knowledge, there are no varietal sparkling Chardonnays in Alsace. Kuentz-Bas made an extremely good, all-Chardonnay Crémant in 1982 and 1983, but stopped making the wine because they couldn't sell it at a viable price. The only still Chardonnay I have encountered is a variable effort from the *négociant* Emile Boeckel, which he has been making since the mid-seventies. (Strictly speaking, this is illegal, as any non-sparkling Alsace Chardonnay should be labelled Pinot Blanc, Klevner or Clevner.) Forthcoming releases from top growers Olivier Humbrecht and Marc Kreydenweiss sound a good deal more exciting.

Corsica

The Île de Beauté, as Corsica is justly known, is a new port of call for Chardonnay. The grape is not permitted in any of the island's *appellation* wines (Patrimonio, Ajaccio and Vin de Corse), being confined to Vin de Pays de l'Île de Beauté status. Nearly all of the Chardonnay is planted on the eastern coastal plain between Bastia and Ghisonaccia. Most of the wine is made by cooperatives, although Skalli, the Languedoc-based merchants also make two good Corsican Chardonnays at their Samuletto and Diana estates. In 1991, they planted a further 173 acres of the grape, so expect an increase in production by the middle of the decade. The top cooperatives are Aléria and (especially) the Union des Vignerons Associés du Levant, or UVAL, both of which make clean, unoaked modern-style Chardonnays.

Coteaux du Lyonnais

The grapes grown here, in the hills to the south-west of Lyon, reflect the area's proximity to Beaujolais. Most of the wine is red Gamay, but there is a little white, too, made from a blend of Chardonnay and Aligoté, although at least one grower (François Descôtes) makes a varietal Chardonnay. Most of the Chardonnay is planted in the southern part of the *appellation*, close to Côte Rôtie, where it tends to produce forward, full-flavoured wines.

Midi

The Midi contains some of France's most exciting new Chardonnay producers: the Australian-owned Domaine de la Baume near Béziers, the innovative *négociant* Robert Skalli in Sète, and the peripatetic Englishman Hugh Ryman. With the exception of Blanquette and Crémant de Limoux, Chardonnay is not permitted for *appellation contrôlée* production in the Midi, so all three sell their Chardonnays as Vin de Pays d'Oc, the catch-all denomination which covers the whole of the Languedoc-Roussillon area. In one sense, this is to their advantage, enabling all three to blend grapes from different sources, in the cooler climate of Limoux or much warmer Carcassonne. Of these three producers, Domaine de la Baume uses the least oak in its rather lean, grapefruity Chardonnay. The Ryman Chardonnay is a much lusher, vanillin and tropical-fruit affair. Skalli releases two Chardonnays: one fruity and clean; the other (called Collection) oaky and more complex.

Provence

Jacques Réynaud, the impish owner of Château Rayas in Châteauneuf du Pape claims to use (illegal) Chardonnay in his white wine. Not far away, in the village of Cairanne, one of the leading growers also adds a little illicit Chardonnay to his white blends. All over Provence, rashes of Chardonnay are breaking out. Not all of it is cloak-and-dagger stuff, either. Near Nice, in the tiny *appellation* of Bellet, Chardonnay has been authorized since the mid-fifties, although the principal grape is the local Rolle. Chardonnay also pops up in the Coteaux d'Aix-en-Provence, where it is sold as Vin de Pays des Bouches-du-Rhône, the Coteaux de Pierrevert (sold as Vin de Pays des Alpes-de-Haute-Provence) and the Côtes du Lubéron.

Savoie

Savoie does not produce the world's most exciting Chardonnays, but this large, mountainous region, with its scattered vineyards, plays host to sizeable, well-established plantings of the grape, alongside more interesting local varieties such as Jacquère, Molette, Mondeuse and Roussette. Chardonnay can be sold (unblended, if so desired) under both of the area's two main designations: AC Vin de Savoie and VDQS Vin du Bugey. Confusingly, Chardonnay is also sold as Roussette de Savoie or Roussette du Bugey. The Chardonnays produced in both Savoie and Bugey tend to be light and aromatic; they are best drunk young. The best Chardonnays come from Bugey and from the Savoie villages of Jongieux, Lucey, Billième and Saint-Jean-de-Chivetin. The top two Chardonnay producers, Eugène Morin and André Miraillet, both make Vin du Bugey.

GERMANY

Total vineyard area: 230,000 acres
Area planted to Chardonnay: approximately 50 acres

Not, it must be said, a country in the Chardonnay vanguard. The German authorities have not encouraged the importation of French vines, and it's easy to see why. What's the point of making yet another Chardonnay, when you can produce some of the finest Rieslings in the world? Chardonnay is not a permitted grape variety for quality wine production in any of Germany's eleven viticultural regions. Any plantings are either illegal or experimental (strictly speaking, for the purpose of viticultural research). Even experimental vineyards must not exceed 900 vines. Nevertheless, against formidable bureaucratic odds, a handful of German wine-makers are producing creditable Chardonnays in Baden, the Mosel, Rheinhessen, Rheinpfalz and Rheingau.

The first known plantings this century were at Schloss Reinhartshausen's Erbach estate in the Rheingau. These three acres were hidden away on a patch of land on the Mariannenau Island. From 1981 to 1985, the estate coyly blended its Chardonnay with Weissburgunder (Pinot Blanc) from the same vineyard. The first varietal wine was produced in the following year. By 1987, experiments with oak maturation were under way and successive vintages have produced adequate, if unspectacular, wines.

Dr Reinhard Muth at Weingut Rappenhof in the Rheinhessen has also been making Chardonnay since 1986. He made three *barriques* in 1986 and four in 1987. The 1987 was less oaky than the 1986, a trend which continued in 1988, when the wine was light, aromatic and fruity, with only a touch of oak ageing. It has something of the Muscatty quality often found in Mâcon Chardonnays. Not wildly exciting, but drinkable, none the less.

Muth and Schloss Reinhartshausen both have permission to cultivate Chardonnay on an experimental basis, and so include the word Chardonnay on their labels; others are more circumspect, calling their precious Chardonnay Weissburgunder or Auxerrois. How much longer can the German authorities hold out against the tide of Chardonnay? There are rumours that the maverick Baden region is about to give the grape official recognition. Here comes the flood?

HUNGARY

| Total vineyard area: 375,000 acres
| Area planted to Chardonnay: approximately 2,500 acres

Of all the former Eastern Bloc countries, Hungary may well have the greatest potential as far as Chardonnay is concerned. There have been plantings here since the early seventies, even if the resulting wines have suffered from lack of investment in modern technology. The industry, based on a system of state farms and semi-private companies, or Kombinats, is beginning to attract foreign investment and this could have a massive impact on the quality of its Chardonnay over the next decade. So far, the most exciting development is the arrival of Bordeaux-based oenologist Hugh Ryman as consultant at the Gyongyos-Domoszloi state farm in the Matra Hills.

The best Chardonnay vineyards are situated in Tokay (in tiny quantities), the Matra Hills and around Lake Balaton. The biggest plantings, however, are in the Pannonian Plain. To date, most Hungarian Chardonnay has been unoaked, but the two best producers, Csopak-Taja and Balatonbolar, have now started to experiment with oak ageing. A country to watch as a source of inexpensive Chardonnay.

INDIA

Total vineyard area: approximately 500 acres
Area planted to Chardonnay: 50 acres

Wine has been produced in India since the time of the Pharaohs, although most of the country's vineyards (including some planted by the British, of all people, in Kashmir and Baramati) were wiped out by the vine pest phylloxera. Today the only Indian wine of any repute (and the only source of Chardonnay) is Omar Khayyam, a Champagne-method sparkler named after the famous Persian philosopher-poet.

Omar Khayyam was the dream of Indian shipping and hotel magnate Sam Chougule, realized with technical advice from Champagne house Piper-Heidsieck. The vineyards (a mixture of Ugni Blanc and Chardonnay) are situated at 700 metres on the slopes of the Sahyadri mountains in the state of Maharashtra. The vines are planted in volcanic sand and are ungrafted.

As sparkling wines go, Omar Khayyam is pleasant enough, with good fruit and a slight earthiness reminiscent of Cava. The current blend is half Ugni Blanc and half Chardonnay. Encouraged by its success, Champagne India (as the company is called outside Europe) is experimenting with an unoaked still Chardonnay. The result should be interesting.

ISRAEL

| Total vineyard area: 5,550 acres |
| Area planted to Chardonnay: 125 acres |

Good kosher wine used to be a contradiction in terms, but with the emergence in the last decade of Golan Heights Winery (whose products appear under three different labels – Yarden, Gamla and Golan) orthodox Jews can at last drink Israeli products with something approaching enjoyment.

Golan Heights is the only decent winery in Israel; it is also the only Chardonnay producer of any size, with 106 acres under vine. As its name suggests, the key to Golan Heights' success is the altitude of its vineyards: 2,000 to 3,500 feet in the case of Chardonnay. These cool growing conditions, allied with well-drained volcanic soil, are producing wines that are very different in character to those grown in the oppressive heat of Israel's traditional lowland vineyards.

When the original vines were planted by eight kibbutzim, in 1977, they had to clear away 250 tanks destroyed in the Yom Kippur war. Chardonnay was not among the original varieties. The winery produced its first wines in 1981, but Chardonnay did not follow until five years later.

The wine has been improving ever since, and the 1990 is the most complex yet – 80 per cent barrel-fermented, with six months on its lees and full malolactic. The best barrels are bottled as Yarden Chardonnay; Golan is used as a second label. Golan Heights' Jewish-American wine-maker Jim Klein also produces a predominantly Chardonnay *méthode Champenoise* Yarden sparkling wine.

ITALY

Total vineyard area: 2.7 million acres

Estimated area planted to Chardonnay by region: 2,000 acres (Trentino-Alto Adige); 1,500 acres (Friuli-Venezia Giulia); 1,000 acres (Veneto); 750 acres (Lombardy); 700 acres (Piedmont); 500 acres (Emilia-Romagna); 370 acres (Tuscany); 150 acres (Puglia); 100 acres (Umbria)

In a country where style and fashion are paramount – even the policemen look as if they're about to prance down a catwalk – Chardonnay's increasing prominence should come as no great surprise. As Chardonnay's star (and price) has risen in the New World, so Italian wineries from Puglia to Piedmont have been inspired to produce their own versions of the world's trendiest grape. Fashion isn't the only reason for Chardonnay's growing popularity – when you taste Trebbiano, Italy's leading white variety, you can see why producers are anxious to plant something else.

Chardonnay is less of a parvenu in Italy than it might appear. The grape has been grown, albeit in small quantities, since the late eighteenth century, when the Medici ordered cuttings of what was almost certainly Chardonnay (Pineau de Bourgogne) from France. Chardonnay has been an established grape variety in the Alto Adige (Südtirol) region for over a century, under the name Gelber Weissburgunder. According to leading producer Alois Lageder, a local Chardonnay was presented at a wine fair in Vienna at the turn of the century.

In recognition of its historic presence in the area, Chardonnay was granted DOC (Denominazione di Origine Controllata) status in the Alto Adige in 1985. So far the only regions to give the grape official DOC recognition are Trentino and the Alto Adige, although it is also permitted in Franciacorta and

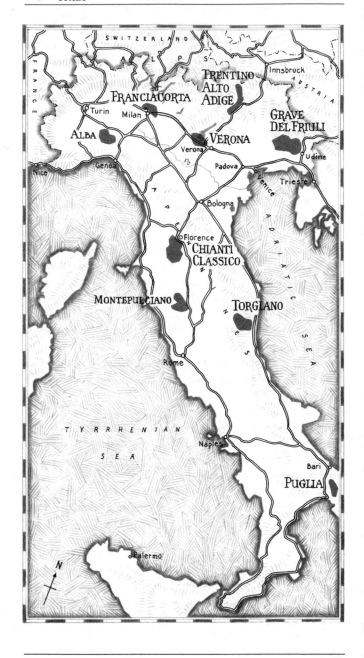

Pomino. Most Italian Chardonnay is sold as Vino da Tavola, although there have been attempts in Tuscany to incorporate it into a new classification called Predicato.

There is a good deal of confusion (some of it wilful) in Italy between Pinot Bianco and Chardonnay. The two grapes were registered independently, as part of a government vine census, in 1978, but for many growers the temptation to rechristen Pinot Bianco as Chardonnay has been too great. This tendency is particularly prevalent in the north-east. In regions where Chardonnay is a more recent arrival, such as Tuscany and Piedmont, bona fide cuttings have been installed.

Chardonnay is produced in all of Italy's major wine-making regions, although the largest plantings by far are in the north-east (Trentino, Alto Adige, Friuli-Venezia Giulia and Veneto). To date, most of the more interesting examples have come from northern and central Italy, but decent Chardonnay has also emerged in Puglia, of all places.

Chardonnay is produced in a host of different styles in Italy: from unoaked (Capezzana, Torrebianco, Terre Rosse), to oak-aged (Gaja, Lungarotti), to barrel-fermented (Pio Cesare, Avignonesi, Felsina Berardenga, Gravner). Some wineries (Isole e Olena, Capezzana) have experimented with more than one Chardonnay style; others (Lageder, Tiefenbrunner, Jermann) produce a series of different wines.

Chardonnay is also increasingly used for sparkling wine. Some of the best producers (such as Ferrari and Ca'del Bosco) blend it with Pinot Nero (Pinot Noir) in Champagne-style blends; others have adopted Chardonnay as a way of adding complexity to dullish local varieties. Now that the name of the grape is gaining recognition, more producers are making sparkling Chardonnays. Good, inexpensive *spumanti* are made by Viticoltori dell'Acquese (Piedmont) and Carpené Malvolti (Friuli-Venezia Giulia).

It may be too early to talk of a single indigenous Italian Chardonnay style, but over the last decade a number of impressive wines have emerged, drawing inspiration from France and the New World. In many instances, it is red-wine producers (Gaja, Pio Cesare, Isole e Olena and Avignonesi, among others) who have led the way, although white-wine specialists like Lageder, Jermann and Gravner have also come up with some first-rate wines. Outside the north-east, white-wine-making is still relatively recent in fine-wine areas such as Tuscany and Piedmont.

One interesting phenomenon is the blending of Chardonnay with other white varieties, such as Gewürztraminer and Sauvignon Blanc (Tenuta Caparzo), Trebbiano (Zenato) or just Sauvignon Blanc (Torrebianco). As producers develop greater experience of the grape, the quality of Italian Chardonnay will improve further. In several cases it is already very high. My only concern is the ludicrous prices of some of the wines.

> Best producers: Antinori (T), Avignonesi* (T), Borgo Conventi (F-V G), Ca' del Bosco* (L), Caparzo (T), Capezzana (T), Cavit (T-AA), Fattoria di Ama (T), Felsina Berardenga* (T), Frescobaldi (T), Gaja* (Pd), Gravner* (F-V G), Isole e Olena* (T), Jermann* (F-V G), Lageder* (T-AA), Lungarotti (U), Maculan (V), Pio Cesare* (Pd), Pojer e Sandri (T-AA), Puiatti (F-V G), Ruffino* (T), Tenute Torrebianco* (Pg), Terre Rosse (E-R), Tiefenbrunner (T-AA), Zenato (V)

AVIGNONESI

> Via di Gracciano nel Corso 91, 53045 Montepulciano
> Chardonnay vineyard: 35 acres
> Production of Chardonnay: 60,000 bottles
> Quality: 🍇🍇🍇🍇   Price: ★★★
> Best vintages: 1986, 1987, 1989

Avignonesi is the creation of three brothers – Ettore, Alberto and Leonardo Falvo – and makes an excellent range, both red and white, of Tuscan and not-so-Tuscan wines. Despite the Avignonesi family's historical roots in the area – the Palazzo Avignonesi in Montepulciano dates back to the sixteenth century – it did not get involved in wine until the 1970s, when Ettore Falvo, the wine-maker, married into the clan.

The first wines were made comparatively recently, in 1978, but the estate has already established an outstanding reputation. The Vino Nobile di Montepulciano is top-notch, but Avignonesi has also earned praise as an innovative producer of Vini da Tavola: I Grifi, a blend of Prugnolo Gentile and Cabernet Franc; and especially its oak-fermented Chardonnay, Il Marzocco.

The company owns three separate estates – Le Capezzine, La Selva and I Poggetti – but gets all of its Chardonnay from La Selva, a vineyard of sandy/clay soil near Cortona. The vines were grafted on to parcels of Trebbiano and Grechetto in 1984, yielding their first crop in 1985. It was not until 1986, however, that the wine got into its stride.

Il Marzocco is a rich, oaky wine that is vinified in new French oak and goes through full malolactic fermentation. Ettore Falvo uses pre-fermentation skin contact to extract more aroma, and the wine sometimes has a slightly bitter character. Il Marzocco is aged in barrel for five to six months before bottling. Incontrovertibly a wine that will age well, it has crisp, citrus flavours beneath the oak. Even so, the flavour of new barrels takes a year or two to mellow. The 1989 appeared to be made in a more restrained style than the buttery 1988, and was well up to the standard of the 1987. After only a handful of vintages, Il Marzocco is already recognized as one of Italy's finest Chardonnays.

Until 1989, Avignonesi also produced a second, unoaked Chardonnay, called Terre di Cortona, but this has now been discontinued.

CA' DEL BOSCO

Via Case Sparse 11, 25030 Erbusco, Brescia

Chardonnay vineyard: 17 acres

Production of Chardonnay: 50,000 bottles

Labels: Ca' del Bosco; Crémant (60 per cent Chardonnay);
   Franciacorta Bianco (65 per cent)
Quality: ♔♔♔/♔♔♔♔   Price: ★★★★★
Best vintages: 1985, 1988, 1990

Ca' del Bosco (literally, 'the house in the woods') is a polished,
state-of-the-art winery near Brescia, in the Franciacorta hills of
Lombardy. It is heavily influenced by the amusing, oversized
personality of its owner and creator, Maurizio Zanella. A self-
confessed Francophile and former student drop-out, Zanella
was banished from Milan to Ca' del Bosco at the age of seventeen by his father, a wealthy transport executive. After a subsequent trip to France, Zanella told his father that they should
plant vines around the family country home. Zanella senior
reluctantly agreed to finance the venture.

That was in 1967. Twenty-five years later Zanella junior has
turned Ca' del Bosco into one of Italy's foremost wineries. The
wines do not always match the hype, but then few wines could.
Zanella produces an impressive range of French-style wines –
'Maurizio Zanella' is a blend of Bordeaux grapes; Pinero is
made with Pinot Noir – and two DOC Franciacorta blends,
one white, the other red.

The winery's speciality, though, is sparkling wines. Zanella
even has a retired Champenois called (no pun intended) André
Dubois to help him in the cellar. All four of its *spumanti* contain
some Chardonnay, the most marked being the Crémant, which
has 60 per cent.

The Chardonnay at Ca' del Bosco was planted between 1978
and 1986. Since 1983, Zanella has produced a barrel-fermented
Chardonnay in addition to his sparkling wines. The Ca' del
Bosco Chardonnays tend to reflect their owner's girth: big and
chunky with pronounced oak flavours, closer to the New World
than France. Of recent vintages, the 1990 (tasted as a barrel
sample) was a more complete wine than the slightly clumsy
1989.

*

FELSINA BERARDENGA

Strada Chiantigiana 55484, 53019 Castelnuovo Berardenga
Chardonnay vineyard: 10 acres
Production of Chardonnay: 15,000 bottles
Quality: 🍇🍇🍇   Price: ★★★★
Best vintage: 1988

Giuseppe Mazzocolin and his consultant oenologist, Franco Bernabei, make some of the most structured, long-lived reds in the Chianti Classico district. Since 1987, they have been working the same magic with Chardonnay. In only three vintages, I Sistri has established itself in the front rank of Tuscan Chardonnays, rubbing shoulders with the wines of Isole e Olena, Castello di Ama and Avignonesi.

Mazzocolin grafted ten acres of Chardonnay on to old Sangiovese and Canaiolo vines in 1984. The first crop was in 1987, and the wine was fermented entirely in new French oak; unfortunately so, according to Mazzocolin. Like Paolo de Marchi at Isole, he has since reduced the percentage of new barrels, and now uses a combination of new, one-year-old and two-year-old Tronçais oak.

The 1988 I Sistri was a fuller and more complex wine, in which the oak was better integrated. It is a very Burgundian style, with subtle, rich fruit and good acidity. It was kept on its fine lees for eight months, where Mazzocolin subjected it to regular *bâtonnage*, or lees stirring. In common with the other I Sistri Chardonnays, it underwent full malolactic fermentation. The 1989 is more aromatic than the 1988: a light, early-drinking Chardonnay with lemony fruit and less oak. So far, 1988 is the star vintage.

Ever open to new ideas, Mazzocolin has also been playing around with a late-harvested Chardonnay, to be made in the style of a Vin Santo. The results have yet to see the light of day.

*

ANGELO GAJA

Via Torino 36, 12050 Barbaresco

Chardonnay vineyard: 26 acres

Production of Chardonnay: 22,500 bottles

Labels: Gaia e Rey; Rossj-Bas

Quality: 🍇🍇🍇🍇🍇   Price: ★★★★★

Best vintages: 1984, 1985, 1988

Angelo Gaja is probably the most famous Italian wine-maker in the world, a frequenter of international conferences and a self-publicist of considerable energy. Gaja is known for his garish cardigans and the excellence (and formidable price) of his wines. He is an innovative producer – he pioneered the use of new *barriques* for Barbaresco, and planted Piedmont's first Chardonnay, Sauvignon Blanc and Cabernet Sauvignon vines – and rarely makes a bad wine.

Gaja first thought of planting Chardonnay in the late sixties, when he realized that his soils were not sandy enough for Arneis, a subtle, almost liquoricey local white variety. He experimented with a few rows of Chardonnay, making small batches of wine throughout the following decade. The ten-acre Gaia e Rey vineyard was planted in Treiso in 1979, and the first vintage was released in 1983. Rossj-Bas, a second eight-acre vineyard 500 metres away in Barbaresco, was planted in 1984; the first vintage was 1988. Never a man to rest on his laurels, Gaja planted a third eight-acre Chardonnay vineyard in Serralunga d'Alba in 1990.

Angelo Gaja ferments his two Chardonnays at low temperatures in stainless steel for up to four weeks. Both are then aged in new French barrels (Allier, Tronçais and Vosges) for four to five months. After malolactic fermentation, they are transferred back to stainless steel and kept at 2 °C for settling. The wines are not filtered.

The main difference between the two vineyards is the age of the vines. The Gaia e Rey vineyard is also higher, at 400 metres, than the Rossj-Bas vineyard (280 metres). The Gaia e Rey Chardonnay is the richer of the two, producing nutty, wonderfully complex, though far from overblown, wines in 1984, 1985 and 1988. The 1984, which I last tasted in 1990, has aged gracefully. The 1989 Rossj-Bas is a subtler, lightly toasted Chardonnay with lemon and apple fruit and great length. Gaja insists that red wines are more important to him than his Chardonnays, but these are two of the finest examples in Italy.

GRAVNER

Via Lenzuolo Bianco 9, 34070 Oslavia (GO)

Chardonnay vineyard: 5 acres

Production of Chardonnay: 9,000 bottles

Quality: 🍇🍇🍇🍇🍇   Price: ★★★★★

Best vintages: 1982, 1985, 1988, 1989

Josko Gravner makes some of the most subtle, flavoursome white wines in Italy, with particular emphasis on Riesling, Ribolla Gialla, Sauvignon and Chardonnay. The grape has only recently gained official DOC recognition in Friuli-Venezia Giulia, but some of Gravner's plantings in Collio (and, according to gossip, Yugoslavia) are nearly twenty years old.

Gravner's experience with the variety shows – while many Italian Chardonnays still seem clumsy and over-oaked, his wines are subtle and concentrated with balanced acidity and good ageing potential. Only Angelo Gaja's Chardonnays can match Gravner's success with the grape.

The Chardonnay is 70 per cent French barrel-fermented, two-thirds of which is new oak. Selected yeasts are used to start the fermentation, but otherwise Gravner believes in minimal intervention. There is no temperature control and malolactic fermentation may or may not ensue. The barrel-fermented portion of the wine is aged on its lees for over a year and usually goes through malolactic of its own accord. The wine is released after eighteen months and is usually well worth the wait. My only complaint concerns Gravner's astronomical prices.

ISOLE E OLENA

50021 Barberino Val d'Elsa, Florence Provincia

Chardonnay vineyard: 7.5 acres

Production of Chardonnay: 8,000 bottles

Quality: 🍇🍇🍇 Price: ★★★

Best vintages: 1988, 1989

Paolo de Marchi, the young fresh-faced owner of Isole e Olena, makes one of the finest Chardonnays in Tuscany, as well as producing a Chianti Classico, a Vin Santo, an experimental Syrah and a varietal Sangiovese Super Tuscan (Cepparello) of a high order. Paolo de Marchi took over from his father in 1976, and his talents have transformed the estate.

Chardonnay is a comparative newcomer at Isole, and the style is still evolving at what is essentially a red-wine cellar. De Marchi grafted 2.5 acres of Trebbiano and Canaiolo over to Chardonnay in 1985; he planted a further 5 acres in 1989. His first attempt at Chardonnay, in 1986, was blended with Trebbiano and sold off as a Tuscan white wine. De Marchi had no experience of white-wine vinification, so in 1987 he made two separate Chardonnays: one oaked, the other unoaked. He decided against the latter because 'the style of Chardonnay we get in Tuscany is ripe and full-bodied, rather than crisp and acid'.

The 1988 Chardonnay, entirely fermented in new oak, was impressive in its youth, but has not aged well. The 1989, which has higher natural acidity, is a more complete wine. The new oak has been reduced to 50 per cent (the rest is matured in one-year-old barrels) and lees contact has been extended to twelve months. The wine has delicious balance, combining French oak and subtle fruit. The 1990 is more concentrated. After a very dry summer, yields were low, and the resulting wine took six months to complete its alcoholic fermentation. It has come out at a massive 14 per cent alcohol, and may yet produce an interesting, if atypical, wine.

JERMANN

Via Montefortino 17, 34070 Villanova di Farra d'Isonzo, Gorizia

Chardonnay vineyard: 15 acres

Production of Chardonnay: 35,000 bottles

Labels: Jermann; Where The Dreams Have No End

Quality: 🍇🍇🍇🍇   Price: ★★★—★★★★★

Best vintages: 1983, 1985, 1988, 1990

There have been Jermanns in Friuli since the end of the last century, but it is the modern ideas of Silvio Jermann, still in his mid-thirties, which have transformed this winery from a producer of dull, oxidized whites into one of Italy's most exciting names. Silvio's views did not initially find favour with his father; after a difference of opinion, he went to work for a Canadian brewery before returning to take over from Jermann senior in the late seventies.

Jermann produced his first Chardonnay in 1980 and has followed a consistent wine-making path ever since: low-temperature fermentation in stainless steel, with a small percentage of the grapes vinified in contact with their skins to enhance varietal aromas. The wine does not go through malolactic and has intense grapefruit and apricot flavours backed up by crisp acidity – Chardonnay in its purest form.

Since 1988, Jermann has produced a second Chardonnay, also a Vino da Tavola, called Where The Dreams Have No End. To be accurate, the wine is not a varietal Chardonnay; 20 per cent of the blend is made from local white varieties, but what's 20 per cent between friends? The title, incidentally, is a tribute to the rock band U2, an indication of how things have changed *chez* Jermann. Where The Dreams Have No End is barrel-fermented and spends a year on its lees – Jermann sometimes blends two vintages to produce a more complex wine. The result is fine, if ludicrously expensive. Prices, unlike dreams, have their limits.

ALOIS LAGEDER

Drususallee 235, 39100 Bozen

Chardonnay vineyard: 10 acres

Production: 180,000 bottles

Labels: Alois Lageder; Buchholz; Erlerhof; Löwengang

Quality: 🍇🍇–🍇🍇🍇🍇🍇   Price: ★★–★★★★

Best vintages: 1985, 1988

Alois Lageder, young, willowy and handsome is the leading producer in the Südtirol, or Alto Adige. The Lageders have been making wine here since 1855, when the region was still part of the Austro-Hungarian Empire: the area still feels markedly un-Italian. The current Alois (the fourth in a row) is the great-grandson of the founder, and has done much to extend the firm's renown. He was one of the first to see the potential of white wines in the Südtirol, and switched the emphasis of his winery away from more traditional reds.

White wines now account for 70 per cent of Lageder's wines; the average in the area is 30 per cent. He has been equally revolutionary in the vineyards, experimenting with new trellising systems, reducing yields and introducing a system of '*crus*' or single-vineyard wines.

Alois and his oenologist Louis von Dellemann make four different Chardonnays, all from the Südtirol. Only one, the oak-fermented Löwengang Chardonnay, comes from Lageder's own vineyards; the others are made with grapes bought from local farmers.

Lageder's unoaked Chardonnays have a lovely, crisp, peachy

character to them. The basic Chardonnay is a benchmark example of the grape in its unadorned form. The Buchholz Chardonnay, which comes from a single vineyard with older vines and higher elevation, is also fermented in stainless steel, with 30 per cent of the wine going through malolactic fermentation. It has the same level of ripeness, but a little more acidity and structure. In 1989 Lageder introduced a third unoaked single-vineyard Chardonnay, called Erlerhof. When I tasted it in April 1991, it seemed closed and a little bitter on the finish.

The best Lageder Chardonnay – and one of Italy's supreme examples – is Löwengang, a wine inspired by Robert Mondavi. The first vintage was in 1983, made with 100 per cent new Tronçais oak and full malolactic fermentation. The wine spends up to eleven months on its lees and, even in lesser years, displays creamy, toasty oak, underpinned by spicy, citrusy fruit. The best recent vintages were 1985 and 1988.

PIO CESARE

Via Cesare Balbo 6, 12051 Alba

Chardonnay vineyard: 3.7 acres

Production of Chardonnay: 6,000 bottles

Label: Piodilei

Quality: 🍇🍇🍇🍇/🍇🍇🍇🍇🍇   Price: ★★★★★

Best vintages: 1985, 1988

Pio Cesare is one of a number of top Italian red-wine producers who have turned their hands adroitly to Chardonnay in recent years: Angelo Gaja, Isole e Olena, Ruffino and Avignonesi are other names which spring to mind. Pio Cesare is best known for its Barolo, although it has arguably been even more successful with Chardonnay. For many, Pio Cesare vies with its Piedmontese neighbour, Angelo Gaja, as the finest exponent of the grape in Italy.

Pio Cesare is a family-owned *négociant* business, which has been based in Alba since 1881: Pio Boffa, the current managing director, is a fourth-generation wine-maker. It was Boffa who decided to plant Chardonnay on the site of an old Nebbiolo vineyard in Treiso in 1980. He conceived the wine in a certain style, and has stuck to it ever since.

Boffa likes to make full-bodied Chardonnays with good ageing potential. He harvests late so that his Chardonnay, called Piodilei, has enough power to cope with oak ageing. The grapes are destemmed, left in stainless-steel tanks for eighteen hours of skin contact, and then pressed. The juice is fined and then racked into 100 per cent new French barrels. The wine is left on its fermentation lees until December, when it is racked and put back into barrel for another three to five months. The approach is a careful one, mixing Burgundian techniques with more modern winery know-how.

Pio Boffa usually ages Piodilei for a year in bottle before release. The wine is often closed in its youth, but ages well, even in ripe years like 1988 and 1985. The 1987 and 1989s were lighter and more spicy, but still possessed the structure and elegance which distinguishes Piodilei. The sticky thumbprint of new oak, which mars some Italian Chardonnays, is not as evident as one would imagine. In fact, the only sad thing about this wonderful Chardonnay is that production is limited to around 6,000 bottles, with no increase in prospect.

RUFFINO

Via Corsica 12, 25123 Brescia

Chardonnay vineyard: La Pietra (37 acres); Castelvecchio del Libaio (85 acres)

Production of Chardonnay: 87,000 bottles (La Pietra); 690,000 bottles (Libaio)

Labels: Cabreo 'Vigneto La Pietra'; Libaio

Quality: 🍇🍇–🍇🍇🍇🍇   Price: ★★–★★★★

Best vintages: 1986, 1988

Ambrogio Folonari, the tall, urbane managing director of the well-known Tuscan house of Ruffino, is the man behind the Predicato concept, which has sought (unsuccessfully) to give Chardonnay and other untraditional wines semi-official recognition in the area. There are four Predicato designations and the one that applies to Chardonnay and Pinot Bianco (frequently confused in Italy), blended with up to 20 per cent Riesling, Müller-Thurgau or Pinot Grigio, is called Predicato del Muschio.

The concept remains a rather vague one, at least as far as the consumer is concerned, but it is fitting none the less that the leading Predicato white is Ruffino's own Cabreo, Vigneto La Pietra. This comes from the firm's vineyards at Panzano in the Chianti commune of Greve. The wine (a varietal Chardonnay) was first produced in 1983 and is a medium-bodied, flavoursome wine with some oak influence that can age for up to five years.

For La Pietra, the alcoholic fermentation is carried out in stainless steel, but the wine is aged for six months in Allier oak, where it undergoes malolactic fermentation. The sawdusty character has been refined since the initial vintage – the 1986 was especially fine, with lush, sweet fruit – but I still find the wine overpriced.

Ruffino also produce larger quantities of an unoaked Vino da Tavola Chardonnay called Libaio. This time the Chardonnay (blended with 10 per cent Sauvignon Blanc) comes from the Castelvecchio estate near Siena. Yields are higher and vines younger here, and the resulting wine is light, fresh and pleasant on the palate. It is entirely fermented (at controlled temperatures) in stainless-steel tanks.

TENUTE TORREBIANCO

70055 Minervino Murge, Bari
Chardonnay vineyard: 110 acres
Production of Chardonnay: 180,000 bottles

Labels: Preludio No. 1; Cantico di Torrebianco
Quality: 🍇🍇/🍇🍇🍇   Price: ★★/★★★
Best vintage: 1990

Puglia is an unlikely stamping-ground for Chardonnay, but the Torrebianco estate, hidden away in the heel of Italy, is producing some of the country's most interesting unoaked whites. The estate belongs to the Piedmont-based sparkling-wine producer, Gancia, and is situated at 200 metres above sea level on calcareous tufa soil. In what is still a warm climate, irrigation enables Gancia to grow Chardonnay, Sauvignon Blanc, Riesling, Chenin Blanc, Sylvaner, Pinot Gris, Pinot Noir and Picolit with varying degrees of success.

Chardonnay is the dominant variety, and so far it has produced the estate's best wines. Preludio No. 1 (an unoaked blend of 90 per cent Chardonnay and 10 per cent Sauvignon Blanc, for acidity and lift) was first produced in 1987, and has improved with every vintage. No wine was released in 1989, but the 1990 is the best yet, packed with crisp, refreshing green-apple and melon fruit. Preludio Number Two, to avoid confusion, is a blend of Sauvignon Blanc and Pinot Bianco.

With the 1988 vintage, Gancia also introduced a more expensive, oak-aged Chardonnay, this time without Sauvignon Blanc, called Cantico di Torrebianco. The 1988 was toffee'd if a little short on subtlety, but I expect better things in future. An estate to watch.

JAPAN

Total vineyard area: 65,000 acres
Area planted to Chardonnay: approximately 100 acres

Most Japanese 'wine' is made in the same way as its dreaded British (not to be confused with English) equivalent – with grape concentrate and water. But as interest in foreign, especially French, wine has grown, so a few determined Japanese wineries have been encouraged to have a go themselves. The greatest obstacle to quality-wine production is the strong likelihood of heavy rainfall just before harvest, but a few interesting wines, made from French varieties, have begun to emerge. The leading Chardonnay producer is Kobe, based in the town of the same name, to the west of Osaka. The wine is made in a crisp, fresh modern style and has some, but not much, varietal character. Other producers, including Suntory, are also experimenting with Chardonnay.

MEXICO

| Total vineyard area: 150,000 acres |
| Area planted to Chardonnay: approximately 250 acres |

The first vines were brought to Mexico by the Conquistadors, making this the oldest wine-producing country in the Americas. Has the wine industry developed much since? Well, to the consumer, Mexican wine might appear to be marooned in the sixteenth century but, in fact, there is a great deal of potential here, particularly in the northerly Baja California. Until recently most of the grapes grown in Mexico were picked as raisins or distilled and used to make brandy, but foreign investment by companies like Domecq and Seagram has produced some perfectly palatable wines.

Vinifera varieties were planted in small quantities at the end of the last century, and it is just possible that Chardonnay was among them. However, most of the Chardonnay in Mexico was planted in the last ten years. All of it is planted in the Calafia and Guadalupe Valleys in Baja California. Drinkable examples are made by Casa Pedro Domecq, Casa Madero, La Cetto and Caves de San Juan.

NEW ZEALAND

Total vineyard area: 13,432 acres
Area planted to Chardonnay: 2,146 acres

'Ladies and gentlemen, we are about to land in Auckland. Please put your watches back thirty years.' In wine-making terms, the stereotype could not be further from the truth. New Zealand wines, particularly its white wines, are among the most excitingly vibrant in the world. Sauvignon Blanc is the grape that has done the most to establish New Zealand on the international scene, but Chardonnay could rival and even overtake it in the long run. There are now at least half a dozen producers fashioning Chardonnays that are just as good as anything from California or Australia.

The rise of Chardonnay has been meteoric. It was first planted in the 1920s, but until the late seventies the wine was seen as little more than a generic, although decent, oak-aged examples had been made by McWilliams and Nobilo's. Quantities were limited and the vines often disease-ridden but, as new improved plantings matured, wine-makers began to experiment with the variety.

The first experimental barrel-fermented Chardonnay was produced by John Hancock at Delegat's, in 1982, and it was from this moment that a recognizable New Zealand style, or set of styles, began to emerge.

Subsequent modifications have concentrated on levels of barrel toast and malolactic fermentation in the winery, and on emphasizing regional characteristics in the vineyard. Chardonnay has increasingly been used for sparkling wine, and has even been made, at Hunter's, Millton, Dry River and Rongopai, as a late-harvest, botrytized wine.

Chardonnay is grown in all of New Zealand's wine-making

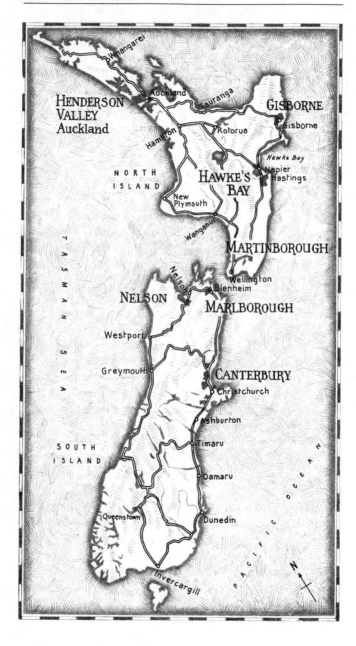

regions, from Northland to Central Otago, but the main areas of production are Hawke's Bay, Gisborne and Marlborough – with Marlborough, first planted in 1973, now the largest of them all. Chardonnay is now New Zealand's second most-planted variety after Müller-Thurgau, and the signs are that the area under vine will continue to increase. If Chardonnay ever loses its fascination, a lot of grape growers could find themselves cleaning windows for a living.

Most of today's New Zealand Chardonnays are aged, rather than fermented, in oak, but there is a growing number of wineries using full barrel-fermentation and lees contact to produce rich, complex wines. Te Mata, Martinborough and Villa Maria all produce excellent wines in this style, with partial malolactic fermentation. Only Kumeu River, to date, has used full malolactic. Other wineries prefer to avoid it altogether. In fact, faced with dramatically increased Chardonnay production and a declining demand, many producers have opted for an unoaked, low-price style. Most of these wines are unexceptional but the best (such as Nobilo's) could give a good Mâcon Blanc a run for its money.

To a certain extent, wine-making techniques have obscured regional Chardonnay styles, but there are still broad differences between the major grape-growing areas. It is important not to overstress the point. As the New Zealand wine writer Bob Campbell points out, there is a world of difference between Collards' Rothesay Chardonnay and the wine produced by Michael Brajkovich at Kumeu River, yet both are made from Auckland grapes.

As a rule, though, North Island Chardonnays (Auckland, Gisborne, Hawke's Bay and Wairapara) tend to be fuller and more tropical in flavour than the flintier, citrusy, lighter-bodied wines produced in the South Island. Most of the richer, barrel-fermented wines come from Hawke's Bay or Gisborne; those produced in Marlborough, with crisp, refreshing acidity and some barrel-fermentation, arguably represent a more interesting, indigenous cool-climate style.

*

Best producers: Babich*, Brookfields, Cloudy Bay*,
   Collards*, Coopers Creek, Corbans*, Delegat's, Dry
   River, Grove Hill, Hunter's*, Kumeu River*,
   Martinborough*, Matua Valley, Millton Vineyards,
   Montana*, Morton Estate*, Nautilus, Neudorf, Nobilo*,
   Palliser, St Helena, Te Mata Estate*, Vavasour, Vidal,
   Villa Maria*, Waipara Springs*

BABICH

Babich Road, Henderson, Auckland 8

Chardonnay vineyard: 17 acres

Production of Chardonnay: 110,000 bottles

Labels: Hawke's Bay Chardonnay; Stopbank Chardonnay;
   Irongate Chardonnay

Quality: 🍇🍇🍇/🍇🍇🍇🍇   Price: ★★/★★★

Best vintages: 1987, 1989

This sizeable Henderson Valley winery was founded by
Dalmatian emigrant Josip Babich in 1919 and is still very much
a family-owned operation. Babich's two sons, Joe and Peter, are
in charge now, but the winery continues to make excellent,
value-for-money wines, even if the styles on offer have changed
a bit since the early days, when Josip Babich produced, among
other things, a Palomino 'sherry'.

Babich makes three varietal Chardonnays, as well as a Sémil-
lon/Chardonnay blend. It owns Chardonnay vines in Henderson and a half share in the top-notch Irongate Vineyard in
Hawke's Bay. Babich also buys in fruit from Gisborne,
Marlborough, Auckland and Hawke's Bay growers.

The basic Hawke's Bay Chardonnay is a good, plump, oak-
aged wine intended for early consumption. More complex are
the two barrel-fermented, single-vineyard wines: Stopbank and
Irongate. The vineyard contrast is interesting – Irongate is
grown on stony river silt, whereas Stopbank comes from richer

soils – and the wines are very different in character. The Irongate is the more restrained with minerally, structured, almost austere flavours that take some time to develop their full potential; Stopbank is fruitier and less demanding. Irongate does not usually go through malolactic fermentation, whereas a percentage of Stopbank does. In good vintages, Irongate is one of New Zealand's leading Chardonnays.

CLOUDY BAY

PO Box 376, Jacksons Road, Blenheim

Chardonnay vineyard: 25 acres

Production of Chardonnay: 150,000 bottles

Quality: 🍇🍇🍇🍇/🍇🍇🍇🍇🍇   Price: ★★★

Best vintages: 1987, 1989, 1990

'Every bit as good as its reputation' ran the advertisement in a New Zealand magazine. For an operation that released its first wine in 1985 to be talking about 'reputation' might sound a trifle presumptuous, but in the space of only half a dozen vintages, Cloudy Bay has established an incredible worldwide following. Its success is a combination of several factors: packaging, the canny marketing skills of founder David Hohnen, who also runs Cape Mentelle in Western Australia, and the wine-making brilliance of Hohnen and fellow Australian Kevin Judd.

The wine that has earned Cloudy Bay superstar status is its Sauvignon Blanc, but there are many – David Hohnen included – who prefer the structure and complexity of the Chardonnay. The relationship between the two wines is symbiotic. The Chardonnay is usually released with at least a year's bottle age, a luxury which Hohnen ascribes to the popularity of the Sauvignon Blanc.

Cloudy Bay's Chardonnay is produced from the winery's free-draining gravel and stony silt vineyards in the South Island's Wairau Valley, and from local contract growers. So far,

Hohnen has only planted 75 out of 125 acres, so there is room for expansion. The trend over the past few vintages has been to use more of the winery's own fruit, as plantings come on stream. Unusually for a great Chardonnay, Cloudy Bay picks by machine, not by hand.

The style of Cloudy Bay's Chardonnay emphasizes its cool climate origins. The wine can be full-bodied (the 1989 had 14.5 per cent alcohol), but never tastes heavy, with deliciously crisp acidity and peach and melon fruit. The 1987 was still fresh four years later. Kevin Judd starts the fermentation of his Chardonnay in stainless steel, but (for some of the wine) finishes it in French oak barrels. The barrel-fermented portion (which can be as much as 50 per cent) stays on its lees for twelve months. Depending on the vintage, a variable amount of the wine goes through malolactic. All the wine is aged in oak.

In 1990, David Hohnen sold the majority of his equity in Cloudy Bay to the Champagne house Veuve Clicquot, though he remains very much in charge. It sounds impossible, but the move might increase its reputation even further. Cloudy Bay mania in France? Now there's a thought.

COLLARDS

303 Lincoln Road, Henderson, Auckland 8

Chardonnay vineyard: 29 acres in Auckland, Gisborne, Hawke's Bay and Marlborough

Production of Chardonnay: 54,000 bottles

Labels: Rothesay Vineyard; Gisborne; Hawke's Bay; Marlborough

Quality: 🍇🍇🍇🍇   Price: ★★/★★★

Best vintages: 1986, 1987, 1989

The Collard family – father Lionel, and his two sons Bruce and Geoffrey – are New Zealand's outstanding Chardonnay producers. Several companies turn out one, maybe two outstanding

Chardonnays, but the Collards make an impressive, award-winning quartet, drawing grapes from all four of New Zealand's major viticultural areas. The biggest parcel (10 acres) is the much-praised Rothesay vineyard in the Waikoukou Valley, but Collards also have Chardonnay planted in Gisborne (Witters Vineyard), Hawke's Bay (Yates Vineyard) and Marlborough (The Corners Vineyard).

Too often vineyard labels are little more than a marketing conceit, but not here. All four reflect considerable climatic differences. Each wine is made with flexibility, in order to maximize individual vineyard and regional characteristics. Fermentation may be entirely in French oak, or partially in oak, depending on the wine. In most vintages, all four Chardonnays go through malolactic fermentation and are given prolonged lees contact.

Collard Chardonnays rarely seem heavy-handed or over-oaked. The three North Island Chardonnays are generally fuller and riper than the Marlborough wine, with powerful, mouth-filling flavours of melon and peach, but never taste blowsy or sweet. The Marlborough Chardonnay tends to be greener and more herbaceous in style. All four wines are among the best examples of the variety in New Zealand.

CORBANS/COOKS/STONELEIGH

Great North Road, Henderson, Auckland 8

Chardonnay vineyard: 130 acres

Production of Chardonnay: 600,000 bottles

Labels: Corbans Private Bin Chardonnay; Longridge
    Chardonnay; Stoneleigh Chardonnay; Cooks
    Winemaker's Reserve Chardonnay

Quality: 🍇–🍇🍇🍇🍇   Price: ★★/★★★

Best vintages: 1986, 1987, 1989

The recent history of Corbans, New Zealand's second largest wine group, has been one of mergers and takeovers. In a series of interlocking moves during the eighties, worthy of a corporate soap opera, Corbans took over Cooks, which had itself joined forces with McWilliams three years earlier. Corbans is now owned by Brierley Investments, who decided to set up a joint-venture in Blenheim with bow-tied Australian entrepreneur Wolf Blass, in 1990. The following year – wouldn't you know it? – Wolf Blass was bought out by another Australian company, Mildara.

The group has extensive vineyards (420 acres) in Hawke's Bay and Marlborough and makes Chardonnay under a number of different labels, buying in about 75 per cent of its fruit. The Stoneleigh and Corbans Private Bin Chardonnays come from the South Island, whereas the Cooks and Longridge Chardonnays are both made with Hawke's Bay fruit.

All four wines are barrel-fermented, but there are marked differences of style between them. The Stoneleigh Chardonnay is usually the lightest in body and spends the least time on its lees; the Longridge Chardonnay is less distinguished in my view; and the two remaining wines, Cooks Winemaker's Reserve and Corbans Private Bin, are full and ripe with good lees character. The Corbans wine, which undergoes partial malolactic fermentation, gets my vote as the company's top Chardonnay, combining citrus and stone-fruit flavours with balanced acidity and subtle oak.

The company's house style, overseen by chief wine-maker Kerry Hitchcock, is to leave a little bit of residual sugar in its Chardonnays and all these wines give a slight impression of sweetness.

HUNTER'S

PO Box 839, Blenheim
Chardonnay vineyard: 25 acres
Production of Chardonnay: 48,000 bottles
Quality: 🍇🍇🍇/🍇🍇🍇🍇   Price: ★★★
Best vintages: 1987, 1989

Jane Hunter took over the running of this Marlborough estate from her late husband, Ernie, in 1987. As a former head viticulturist at Montana, she was well suited to the role, and the renown of Hunter's wines – in particular its Sauvignon Blanc – has increased under her stewardship.

Hunter's Chardonnay (40 per cent of which is barrel-fermented) is a similarly intense wine, with the emphasis firmly on crisp, fragrant cool-climate fruit. The wine does not go through malolactic fermentation, and shows firm, citrusy acidity and the imprint of eight months barrel-ageing. One-tenth of the wine is left in contact with its lees, but this is far from being a rich, buttery Chardonnay. It has the elegance to age for three to six years.

In 1987, Hunter's also produced a serendipitous botrytis Chardonnay, one of the few examples of this style. The vines, in what is usually a sparkling-wine vineyard in Rongapai, were 100 per cent affected. The wine is long, concentrated and very sweet, with a honey-and-peach botrytis character so intense that you forget you're tasting Chardonnay. Production, at 400 bottles, was tiny.

KUMEU RIVER WINES

2 Highway 16, Kumeu

Chardonnay vineyard: 11 acres

Production of Chardonnay: 35,000 bottles

Labels: Kumeu River; Brajkovich; San Marino Vineyards (in New Zealand)

Quality: 🍇🍇🍇🍇   Price: ★★★/★★★★

Best vintages: 1987, 1989

Michael Brajkovich, New Zealand's first Master of Wine, is one of the country's most cosmopolitan wine-makers. Educated at Roseworthy winemaking college in Australia, Brajkovich has worked for the Moueix family in Bordeaux and seems to spend half his life travelling through the world's vineyards. For someone who is still in his early thirties, Brajkovich's expertise and knowledge are deeply impressive. He has pioneered new trellising methods in New Zealand and makes an extremely interesting (and sometimes controversial) range of red and white wines.

The winery, sited in a West Auckland suburb, was bought by Michael's Yugoslav father, Mate, in 1944, but has really come to prominence since Brajkovich junior took over the wine-making.

Since 1987, Kumeu River has bought all of its fruit locally (80 per cent of it from its own vineyards). This is a mixed blessing – no Chardonnay was made in 1988, because of hurricane damage. Even in good years, the wines can lack balance and ageing potential. The 1987 was rich and butterscotchy when young, but faded after two years in bottle. The 1989 was superb when tasted in mid-1991, winning a Trophy at *Wine* magazine's prestigious International Challenge.

Brajkovich likes to pick his Chardonnay very ripe. Vinification is carried out in stainless steel and oak, using wild yeasts, with the proportion of oak varying from year to year. All of the Chardonnay is oak-aged for between five and nine months, and usually goes through malolactic fermentation. Brajkovich's use of malolactic has been criticized by other wine-makers, but it is a style which appeals unashamedly to the wine consumer. The wines are best drunk young.

MARTINBOROUGH

PO Box 85, Princess Street, Martinborough

Chardonnay vineyard: 12 acres

Production of Chardonnay: 42,000 bottles

Quality: ♔♔♔/♔♔♔♔   Price: ★★★

Best vintages: 1988, 1989

Martinborough is the star winery in the tiny viticultural district of Wairarapa, at the southern end of the North Island. The climate here is cool and dry and has encouraged local growers, comparisons with Burgundy in hand, to specialize in Pinot Noir and Chardonnay. Martinborough produces superb, award-winning examples of both grapes, with intense, well-defined flavours, as well as a good range of lesser white wines: Riesling, Müller-Thurgau, Gewürztraminer and Sauvignon Blanc.

The winery was established in 1980 and planted its first Chardonnay in the same year. The vineyard is sited on alluvial loam soils over alluvial gravel and has excellent drainage. New vines have been installed recently and, by 1993, the winery will reach a production ceiling of 120,000 bottles (42,000 of Chardonnay).

Don't shout about it in front of an All Black but, in common with several other leading names in New Zealand, the wines at Martinborough are made by an Australian. Larry McKenna trained at Roseworthy, then worked at Delegat's winery for six years, before he joined Martinborough in 1986.

McKenna's Chardonnays have won almost as much praise as his superb Pinots. The 1988 won the top prize at the Air New Zealand Wine Awards in 1989. The secret? McKenna vinifies his wine in barrel, but only puts between 20 and 50 per cent of it through malolactic fermentation, in order to retain a better balance of acidity. The wine remains in barrel for up to ten months, and the Martinborough style is characterized by a luscious, buttery texture and sweet, oaky fruit. Martinborough Chardonnays are at their best two to three years after bottling. My only complaint is that the alcohol can be too powerful for the fruit in vintages like 1989.

MONTANA

171 Pilkington Road, Glen Innes, Auckland

Chardonnay vineyard: 600 acres

Production of Chardonnay: 1.2 million bottles

Labels: Gisborne Chardonnay; Marlborough Chardonnay;
Show Reserve (formerly Private Bin Chardonnay)

Quality: 🍇🍇–🍇🍇🍇🍇   Price: ★★/★★★

Best vintages: 1985, 1987, 1988, 1989

Montana is the largest producer in New Zealand by some dis-
tance, controlling something in the region of 45 per cent of the
country's wine production. It is New Zealand's good fortune to
have such a dynamic, well-respected company running the
show. Montana makes vast amounts of commercial, well-made
wine and can also take the credit for developing the potential of
Marlborough as a quality grape-growing region. At the last
count over half of its 2,400 acres of vines were planted in the
South Island. It has further vineyards in Gisborne and Hawke's
Bay and wineries in four different sites, though its headquarters
are in Auckland. Truly, a massive operation.

Montana's most famous wine, certainly as far as export
markets are concerned, is its asparagusy Sauvignon Blanc, but it
also produces a good range of Chardonnays and two excellent
Pinot Noir/Chardonnay sparkling wines, Lindauer and
Marlborough Cuvée, the second of which is the result of a
felicitous joint-venture with Champagne house Deutz. Montana Chardonnays appear under the Penfolds New Zealand and
single vineyard Kaituna Hills labels, too.

The company's most appealing Chardonnay is its crisp, fruity
Gisborne wine, though I have also had good bottles of the more
complex barrel-fermented Show Reserve from Marlborough,
which has improved dramatically since 1986. The basic Montana Marlborough Chardonnay, which is stainless-steel fermented but aged in French and American oak, is drinkable in a
straightforward, seemingly off-dry, style. These are good, if not
great, Chardonnays.

MORTON ESTATE

State Highway 2, Aongatete via Katikati,
  Bay of Plenty

Chardonnay vineyard: 75 acres

Production of Chardonnay: 240,000 bottles

Labels: Yellow Label; White Label; Black Label

Quality: 🍇🍇–🍇🍇🍇🍇🍇   Price: ★★/★★★

Best vintages: 1986, 1987, 1989

Morton Estate's attractive, Cape-style building is the only winery in the lush, isolated Bay of Plenty. Morton Estate has a small, local planting of Pinot Noir, but sources the majority of its fruit from the more southerly Hawke's Bay and Gisborne areas. Morton has substantial vineyard holdings of its own, and supplements its requirements with fruit purchased from contract growers.

Since it was founded in 1979, by businessman Morton Brown and gregarious Australian wine-maker John Hancock, Morton Estate has built its reputation on Chardonnay and Sauvignon Blanc. It was taken over in 1988 by the Australian firm Mildara, but has continued to produce excellent examples of both varieties as well as a string of other wines.

Morton Estate has been making Chardonnay since 1983, the winery's first commercial vintage. The first release won a Gold Medal, with Hancock drawing on his experience with the variety at Delegat's, and the wines have been consistently good ever since. There are three Chardonnays produced here: the light, unoaked Yellow Label; the fruity, complex, barrel-fermented White Label Winemaker's Selection; and a richer, more buttery Black Label Reserve, which is fermented and aged on its lees for up to a year in new French oak. This is a full, flavoursome wine with lots of colour and broad, peachy flavours. Morton Estate also make a highly successful sparkling wine, which contains around 15 per cent Chardonnay in the blend.

NOBILO

Station Road, Huapai, Auckland

Chardonnay production: 370,000 bottles

Labels: Gisborne; Dixon Vineyard; Tietjen Vineyard;
  Poverty Bay

Quality: 🍇🍇–🍇🍇🍇🍇 Price: ★★/★★★

Best vintages: 1986, 1987, 1989

Nick Nobilo, who bears a certain resemblance to the actor Burt
Reynolds, runs this large 2.7-million-bottle winery with his
brothers Steve and Mark. The business has had its ups and
downs over the last two decades, with a succession of different
financial partners, but after selling off most of their vineyard
land in the late eighties, the Nobilos are now back in control.

The dominant variety in the Nobilo portfolio is Müller-
Thurgau, sold on export markets under the White Cloud label,
but the winery also makes extremely good Sauvignon Blanc,
Cabernet and Chardonnay. Nobilo buys fruit from all over
New Zealand and has a small planting of its own around the
winery in Huapai. All of its Chardonnay fruit is bought in.

Nobilo produce no fewer than four different Chardonnays:
two Gisborne blends and two single vineyard wines, Tietjen
and Dixon. There are three basic styles: one unoaked (Poverty
Bay), one oak-aged (Gisborne and Tietjen) and one oak-
fermented (Dixon). The Dixon Vineyard Gisborne Chardonnay gets the full works, with a high-solids fermentation in
French and American *barriques*, lees contact and partial
malolactic. This is the star of the quartet, with full, attractive
fruit and well-integrated oak, but I have had very enjoyable
bottles of the more commercial Gisborne and Tietjen
Chardonnays, too. In top vintages, Dixon is one of New Zealand's finest Chardonnays, with an ageing potential of at least
five years.

★

TE MATA ESTATE

Te Mata Road, Havelock North

Chardonnay vineyard: 15 acres

Production of Chardonnay: 35,000 bottles

Quality: 🍇🍇🍇🍇🍇   Price: ★★★★

Best vintages: 1986, 1987, 1989, 1990

John Buck's house is a striking eyeful, a bright modern jumble of angles, surrounded by vines, on the northern slope of Hawke's Bay's Te Mata Peak. This brilliant white dwelling, which sits in the middle of Te Mata's Coleraine vineyard, feels like a statement of intent – a conscious break with the past. And so it is. One of New Zealand's oldest producers, Te Mata was in the doldrums when it was bought in the mid-seventies by John Buck and partner Mike Morris. The name and the Te Mata winery have been given a thorough face-lift since Buck arrived.

A freckled, fast-talking businessman, Buck takes an equally modern approach to selling his wines. His style, which has ruffled the odd bit of plumage, has been a demonstrable success. In a comparatively short space of time (the first vintage under the new owners was in 1980), Buck has developed two highly successful single vineyard wines at Te Mata. The Coleraine Cabernet/Merlot is among New Zealand's best reds, although it certainly has its critics, while the single-vineyard Elston Chardonnay is, for my money, the country's leading Chardonnay.

The ungrafted Elston vineyard is planted on gravel and sandy loam and yields Chardonnays that take several years to develop. The grapes are picked late and yields are on the low side. Winemaker Peter Cowley gives the must six hours' skin contact and cold settling before it is racked to barrels – 50 per cent new, 50 per cent one-year-old – for the fermentation. The wine stays in oak for four to six months, and roughly 10 per cent of it goes through malolactic. The 1989, which is the best Elston Chardonnay yet, has 13.9 per cent alcohol, grapefruity, buttery flavours and rich, toasty oak. It has the structure and finesse to age for at least five years.

VILLA MARIA

PO Box 43046, Mangere, Auckland

Chardonnay vineyard: 62 acres

Production of Chardonnay: 200,000 bottles

Quality: 🍇🍇🍇🍇   Price: ★★/★★★

Best vintages: 1986, 1987, 1989

In Australian oenologist and Master of Wine Kym Milne and viticulturist Steve Smith, Villa Maria has one of the best young wine-making partnerships in New Zealand. Villa Maria is one of the three largest wineries in the country, drawing fruit from Auckland, Gisborne, Hawke's Bay and Marlborough, but this has not stopped it winning an impressive clutch of medals over the last five years. This success, coupled with renewed financial backing, has pulled the company back from the brink of receivership, a situation occasioned by New Zealand's brutal price wars of the mid-eighties.

There are two main lines at Villa Maria: Private Bin, which is something of a misnomer since the quantities produced are considerable, and Reserve. Milne's top wines are arguably his reds, but his Chardonnays are well made too, and are consistently among the best four or five examples in New Zealand.

Chardonnay is made in two styles at Villa Maria. The Private Bin is stainless-steel-fermented, but oak-aged; while the Reserve, produced in selected vintages, is a barrel-fermented wine from the company's top Gisborne vineyard. The delicious 1989 Reserve spent nine months in barrel and went through partial malolactic fermentation. It has fattish, butter and toasty oak flavours with excellent, nutty fruit intensity.

Villa Maria also owns two Hawke's Bay wineries, Vidals and Esk Valley, which make and bottle wine under their own labels.

Vidals was acquired in 1976; Esk Valley (formerly called Glenvale) in 1987. Both wineries produce good Chardonnay. The Vidals' Reserve was particularly flavoursome in 1989, with barrel-fermentation and lees characters complemented by high natural acidity and complex fruit. The 1990 Esk Valley Reserve is lighter and more perfumed in style, but also shows a great deal of promise.

WAIPARA SPRINGS

RD 3, Amberley

Chardonnay vineyard: 28 acres

Production of Chardonnay: 20,500 bottles

Quality: 🍇🍇🍇🍇/🍇🍇🍇🍇🍇   Price: ★★/★★★

Best vintages: 1989, 1990

Mark Rattray has a distinguished wine-making pedigree. He was educated at Geisenheim Institute in Germany and has made wine for four famous names: Schloss Johannisberg, Montana, St Helena and Penfolds. He and his wife Michelle bought this 10-acre vineyard in Waipara, near Canterbury, in 1988, from a former Cabinet minister, Derek Quigley. The portion that was planted with Gewürztraminer has been grafted over to Pinot Noir (1990 being the first vintage), but the Chardonnay vines date back to 1981. Most of Rattray's Chardonnay, however, comes from a partner's vineyard nearby.

The two Chardonnay releases from this young enterprise have both shown great promise. The wine is fermented and aged for five months in Vosges oak and undergoes partial malolactic. On the 1990 the alcohol is a full-bodied 13.8 per cent, but the wine has good balance and supple, smoky fruit. Both vintages should age for four to six years. A name to watch in the South Island.

PORTUGAL

Total vineyard area: 875,000 acres
Area planted to Chardonnay: 800 acres

Chardonnay has gained little more than a toehold in Portugal, a country where traditional local varieties still hold sway (see map on p. 247). The only two varietal Chardonnays available in any quantity are Raposeira's Quinta de Valprado and João Pires's Cova da Ursa, but Chardonnay has also set out its stall in Bairrada (where it is an authorized variety), Alenquer (Quinta de Pancas) and Arrábida (Fonseca Sucessores). Fonseca and Quinta de Pancas both use Chardonnay as part of a white-wine blend: 25 per cent in Pasmados, and 40 per cent in the latter's Vinha Maior.

Raposeira, which is owned by the Canadian drinks giant Seagram, produces a clean, Mâcon-style Chardonnay, which is highly prized in Portugal but rarely seen elsewhere. It also uses a percentage of the grape in its sparkling wine, Super Reserva. The Quinta de Valprado vineyard is just outside the demarcated Douro region, and has proved such a commercial success that Raposeira have planted a second, neighbouring vineyard (Quinta da Recheca) with Chardonnay and Pinot Noir.

Cova da Ursa, Portugal's premier Chardonnay, is made by the talented, wisecracking Australian wine-maker, Peter Bright, the man who has done so much to drag Portuguese viticulture into the twentieth century. João Pires is based in the fly-blown town of Pinhal Novo near Palmela, to the south of Lisbon, and its Chardonnay grapes come from a single limestone vineyard nearby.

While it is not the best João Pires wine, Cova da Ursa has continued to improve steadily since the first vintage in 1986.

What was lumpen and rather awkward has become slightly more refined. It is possibly the only Chardonnay in the world to be fermented in Portuguese oak – though this is unlikely to set a trend. Otherwise it reflects the Antipodean training of its wine-maker. The 1989 is rich, buttery and oaky, with come-and-get-it fruit. It reminds me somewhat of an old-style Australian Chardonnay. The superior 1990 is a more balanced, complex wine.

| Best producers: João Pires, Quinta de Valprado

ROMANIA

Total vineyard area: 500,000 acres
Area planted to Chardonnay: 2,400 acres

Romania, surprisingly, is one of the world's half dozen largest wine producers, with substantial plantings of Aligoté, Sauvignon Blanc, Pinot Gris, Merlot, Pinot Noir, Cabernet Sauvignon and, of course, Chardonnay. Most of the country's Chardonnay is concentrated in the regions of Murfatlar and Tarnave.

Exports of Romanian wine to the West have increased in the last few years, but Romanian wines are still rare outside Eastern Europe. In the case of Romanian Chardonnay, this may be just as well, as the only example I have tasted, from the region of Murfatlar, was dull, heavy and oxidized. Wine writers who have visited the country have a slightly more enthusiastic tale to tell, but for the time being, Romanian Pinot Noir and Cabernet Sauvignon are a much better bet than Chardonnay. Once again, though, the potential for good white wines is considerable. All Romania needs is a few more temperature-controlled, stainless-steel tanks. Picking earlier would also help.

SOUTH AFRICA

Total vineyard area: 246,547 acres
Area planted to Chardonnay: 3,400 acres

South Africa undoubtedly has the potential to produce great wine. A combination of external political opprobrium and over-centralized control has hindered its progress over the last twenty years, but as apartheid crumbles there are signs that South Africa's wine industry is beginning to emerge as a serious contender.

The most planted white grape variety in South Africa is the workaday Steen, or Chenin Blanc, but increasingly it is Chardonnay which is producing the Cape's finest dry white wines. Historically, the grape has had problems adapting. It was first planted in the Welgevallen experimental vineyard at the University of Stellenbosch, in the 1920s, but the chosen clone proved unsuccessful. As interest in Chardonnay developed, the same clone was planted in the seventies, and continued to pro-duce unexciting wines, frequently hindered by viral problems. Throughout the decade, various ill-starred attempts were made to import better European and American clones. It was this which led to the Chardonnay scandal of the mid-eighties, when it was discovered that what most wineries had planted was not Chardonnay, but the inferior Gros Auxerrois.

Many aspects of South African life are intensely bureaucratic and the country's wine industry is no exception. Faced with rigorous quarantine regulations for their grapevine imports, most producers despaired of obtaining better clonal material through official channels. (To be fair to the authorities, the appearance of various vineyard diseases in the Cape was almost certainly due to smuggled vines.) Imports of illegal Chardonnay vines began in the late seventies. By the early eighties, most of the key wineries were bringing in illicit cuttings. At one point, groups like the Bergkelder were shipping European vines on a vast scale to South Africa.

The arrival of Auxerrois via Alsace from Germany, where it had been incorrectly identified at first, was the joint responsibility of Boschendal and the Bergkelder. While at Boschendal, wine-maker Julius Laszlo had ordered the vines from Europe with the full knowledge of his employers. He was then head-hunted by the Bergkelder, and requested that his imports, then *en route* to him at Boschendal, be sent to the Bergkelder instead.

According to one well-placed source, wine-makers associated with the Bergkelder realized what was happening by the early eighties. By this stage they were already generously distributing cuttings to growers outside the group who had been requesting the plants for some time. As a result, Gros Auxerrois was not limited to members of the group. Instead, it was widely planted in 'Chardonnay' vineyards throughout the Western Cape. This explains why there were few or no bona fide Chardonnay plantings in South Africa before the mid-eighties.

More recent vintages have witnessed a significant increase in the number of (legal) commercial plantings, as well as the arrival of new, disease-resistant clones. Hamilton-Russell vineyards, one of South Africa's leading Chardonnay producers, have no fewer than eight, and the KWV, the country's dominant cooperative, is evaluating as many as thirty.

Chardonnay, despite its history, is still a comparatively rare variety in South Africa and, as yet, there is no distinctive style. Vineyards have been replanted and are multiplying at an impressive rate, so much so that there is now talk of a glut. Nevertheless, the future of the grape looks bright in South Africa, at least at the top end of the scale. Lower down the pecking order, many of the wines seem rather one-dimensional. The pioneering Cape Chardonnays have all come from private producers, but cooperative growers have also begun to show an interest in the variety. At their best, barrel-fermented Cape Chardonnays can already stand comparison with the finest wines from Australia and California. If only there were a few more of them.

Best producers: Backsberg*, Boschendal*,
   Buitenverwachting, De Wetshof*, Fairview, Glen
   Carlou*, Hamilton-Russell*, Klein Constantia, Neil Ellis,
   Rustenberg*, Talana Hill, Vriesenhof*

BACKSBERG

PO Box 1, Klapmuts 7625

Chardonnay vineyard: 74 acres

Production of Chardonnay: 120,000 bottles

Quality: 🍇🍇🍇   Price: ★★

Best vintages: 1985, 1986, 1990

Arguably the country's leading winery, Backsberg was one of the Cape's Chardonnay pioneers. Sydney Back has completed more than fifty vintages at the winery and has long been an important innovatory force within the South African wine industry. He planted a five-acre block of Chardonnay in 1976, under contract from the centralized KWV cooperative. The first cuttings came from the Viticultural and Oenological Research Institute at Nietvoorbij, Stellenbosch, and suffered from viral infection, a persistent problem in the early days of South African Chardonnay.

Subsequent plantings have come mainly from Switzerland, according to Michael Back, Sydney's son. With each vintage the Backs – father Sydney and son Michael – have increased the number of acres under vine and now have some of the largest plantings in the country.

The first commercial Backsberg Chardonnay was made in 1980, but it was not until 1985 that the Backs began to barrel-ferment their wines. In terms of quality, the transformation has been remarkable. Since 1986, Backsberg Chardonnays have been among the best examples in South Africa, with nutty, toasty elegance and good acidity as their hallmarks. Recent vintages have been more French in style, undergoing full malolactic fermentation. The 1990 was particularly successful, and has the structure to age for at least five years. Whether it will match the glorious 1986 remains to be seen.

BOSCHENDAL

PO Groot Drakenstein 7680

Chardonnay vineyard: 200 acres

Production of Chardonnay: 36,000 bottles

Quality: 🍇🍇🍇   Price: ★★/★★★

Best vintages: 1988, 1989

Boschendal, one of the oldest wine estates in South Africa, had entered a period of relative decline until it was purchased by the giant Anglo-American Corporation in 1969. The last twenty years have witnessed a wine-making renaissance, however, and under its eccentric oenologist Achim von Arnim, Boschendal developed one of the most interesting ranges in the Cape. Since 1989, the wines have been made by von Arnim's former assistant, Hilko Hegewisch, but the quality has not suffered in the least. In fact, he has built on von Arnim's considerable achievements, introducing whole-bunch pressing, lower sulphur levels and other improvements in the winery.

Boschendal has the largest plantings of Chardonnay in the Cape. Much of the Chardonnay is used as part of the blend for an excellent *méthode champenoise* fizz, called Boschendal Brut, and to upgrade the quality of some of its other non-varietal white wines, including Grand Vin Blanc.

The estate's first varietal Chardonnay (this time without bubbles) was produced in 1986 and comes from a single vineyard on the estate, planted with no fewer than five different clones. The 1987 and 1988 vintages were only partially barrel-fermented. As a result, the integration of oak and fruit was sometimes a little clumsy. The 1989 was a vast improvement, benefiting from barrel-fermentation, seven months on the lees and regular *bâtonnage*. The oak seems softer and less aggressive, possibly the result of a move away from Limousin barrels. This is a splendid wine, full of Cape fruit, but with an elegance and balance all too rarely found in South African Chardonnays.

DE WETSHOF

Box 31, Robertson 6705

Chardonnay vineyard: 192 acres

Production of Chardonnay: 600,000 bottles

Labels: De Wetshof; Danie de Wet

Quality: 🍇🍇/🍇🍇🍇🍇   Price: ★–★★★

Best vintages: 1985, 1988, 1989

Danie de Wet studied oenology in Germany and, appropriately, was one of the first South Africans to make a varietal Rhine Riesling. He returned from Geisenheim to the family estate in 1971 and it was his decision to concentrate on three white grapes: Chardonnay, Sauvignon Blanc and Rhine Riesling. He was in the vanguard of Chardonnay producers, and has enjoyed considerable success with the variety.

The eighties were difficult times at the estate. In 1985, it was discovered that much of what was planted at De Wetshof was not Chardonnay but Gros Auxerrois. After protracted negotiations de Wet had to graft over 54 acres of vineyard and, as a result, he made smaller crops in 1986 and 1987. The great irony was that De Wetshof's 1985 Chardonnay, made almost entirely from Auxerrois, had been extremely well received, winning the Grand Prix d'Honneur at Vinexpo in 1987.

De Wet now produces no fewer than four different Chardonnays, and regards himself as something of a Chardonnay specialist. Two are fermented in barrel (De Wetshof and Danie de Wet); one in stainless steel (Danie de Wet Bon Vallon); and a fourth is fermented in stainless steel but aged in oak (Danie de Wet Clos de Roche).

The best of the four are the two barrel-fermented wines

though, to my mind, neither quite lives up to this estate's exalted reputation. In 1989, both Chardonnays had crisp natural acidity (even after malolactic fermentation), medium body and good ageing potential. The style of wine is either elegant or dilute, depending on your point of view.

GLEN CARLOU

Simondium Road, PO Box 23, Klapmuts 7625

Chardonnay vineyard: approximately 35 acres

Production of Chardonnay: 17,000 bottles

Quality: 🍇🍇🍇🍇   Price: ★★★★

Best vintages: 1989, 1990

Glen Carlou is a felicitous partnership between Walter Finlayson, who earned his wine-making stripes over a period of sixteen years at Blaauwklippen in Stellenbosch, and Johannesburg advertising executive, Graham de Villiers. Finlayson planted his ninety-acre vineyard in the foothills of the Simonsberg Mountain south of Paarl as recently as 1985, but in only three vintages, Glen Carlou has established itself as one of South Africa's leading estates.

Red wines predominate here – a Pinot Noir, a Merlot and two Bordeaux-style blends – but Finlayson also makes one white, a Chardonnay. I have not tasted the reds, but the Chardonnay is an extremely fine expression of the grape. It is barrel-fermented in three different oaks – Nevers, Allier and Tronçais – and remains on its lees for eight months. The exceptional 1990 combines subtle flavours of vanilla and nut with intense, citrusy fruit. The wine has more complexity and breed than most South African Chardonnays put together, and confirms Walter Finlayson's reputation as an exceptional wine-maker.

*

HAMILTON-RUSSELL

Hemel-en-Aarde Valley, PO Box 158, Hermanus, 7200
  Cape of Good Hope

Chardonnay vineyard: 86 acres

Production of Chardonnay: 85,000 bottles

Quality: 🍇🍇–🍇🍇🍇🍇🍇   Price: ★★/★★★

Best vintages: 1983, 1985, 1989

Tim Hamilton-Russell is a controversial figure. A polite, Oxford-educated advertising executive, Hamilton-Russell's gentlemanly demeanour belies his outspoken views on the structure of the South African wine industry. In 1990, for example, Hamilton-Russell published *Winelands Commitment*, a radical document which demanded a minimum wage, better conditions for agricultural labourers, and an end to apartheid. At the time of writing there were three fellow signatories: John Platter of Clos du Ciel, Simon Barlow of Rustenberg and Peter Younghusband of Haute Provence.

This was not the first time Hamilton-Russell had got into trouble with the authorities. His decision to plant South Africa's southernmost vines in Hermanus, 130 km to the south-east of Cape Town, was also frowned upon, and for some time he was unable to sell wine under his own label. His continuing battles with the Wine and Spirit Board probably deserve a book of their own.

It was in this cool climate that Hamilton-Russell planted that well-travelled Burgundian duo, Chardonnay and Pinot Noir, a brave move back in 1976. The first Chardonnay was released in 1981, and the wines have consistently been among the most interesting in South Africa ever since. The prices tend to be high on the domestic market, but more reasonable abroad.

Hamilton-Russell and his winemaker, Gail Kreusch-Dau, are now producing two different Chardonnays. One is lightly oaked, citrusy and intended for early drinking; the second is richer and consciously Burgundian in style. The latter wine is vinified in oak, (usually) goes through malolactic fermentation and remains on its lees for six to ten months.

Vineyard yields are low and it is no coincidence that the Hamilton-Russell Chardonnays always have good definition and depth. The wines have greater subtlety than the majority of examples produced in the Cape, although I am still not convinced of their ageing potential. It remains to be seen whether Kreusch-Dau can match the brilliant wines produced by Hamilton-Russell's previous wine-maker, Peter Finlayson, who left after the 1990 vintage to form a joint-venture with Paul Bouchard of Burgundian *négociants* Bouchard Aîné.

RUSTENBERG

PO Box 33, Stellenbosch 7600

Chardonnay vineyard: 12 acres

Production of Chardonnay: 15,000 bottles

Labels: Rustenberg; Schoongezicht (until 1989)

Quality: 🍇🍇🍇   Price: ★★/★★★

Best vintages: 1986, 1988, 1989

One of the South African wine industry's most prominent liberals, Simon Barlow, took over the running of this historic property from his mother, Pamela, in 1988. Blessed with a setting of prodigious natural beauty, Rustenberg can trace its foundation back to 1692 and has been producing wine more or less continuously ever since.

The estate specializes in deeply coloured, intense, Bordeaux-style red wines, but since 1986 has also produced a small amount of Chardonnay. Wine-maker Étienne le Riche vinified his first Chardonnays in stainless steel, ageing them in oak, but has now switched to full barrel-fermentation. The 1989, which spent more time on the lees than previous bottlings, is his best wine yet, confirming Rustenberg's potential as a producer of some of South Africa's finest Chardonnays.

The style here emphasizes tropical fruit, although the 1989 is more restrained than the 1986 and the 1988. The influence of new Allier oak is marked, but the wine has good underlying structure and should age for three to five years. Le Riche uses malolactic fermentation sparingly in order to retain the natural acid balance of the grapes.

According to the South African journalist John Platter, a large percentage of Rustenberg's Chardonnay is made with Cape clone 166, which leaves a slight Muscatty flavour in the wines. With new clones coming on stream, this character will diminish in future vintages.

VRIESENHOF

Stellenbosch, 76000

Chardonnay vineyard: 25 acres

Production of Chardonnay: 24,000 bottles

Quality: ᵽᵽᵽᵽ   Price: ★★

Best vintages: 1989, 1990

Vriesenhof is owned by the dynamic former Springbok flanker, Jan 'Boland' Coetzee. As well as making wine at his own estate, he manages to find time for a host of other activities, as rugby coach, consultant to other wineries, and vice-chairman of the Rural Foundation, which has pioneered much-needed agri-cultural reforms and better conditions for black workers.

Coetzee took over at Vriesenhof in 1980, after eleven years at the Kanonkop estate. Most of his experience had been with Cabernet Sauvignon, so that autumn he went to work for the Beaune *négociant* Joseph Drouhin to learn how to make Chardonnay. Coetzee still makes tough, muscular Cabernets that age for up to a decade, but his sojourn in Burgundy taught him how to treat Chardonnay too.

The first Vriesenhof Chardonnay was released in 1986, and was made, like subsequent vintages, in a deliberately Burgundian style: barrel-fermentation and seven months on lees. The 1986 and 1987 were a little disappointing, but as the vines have aged, so the wine has improved. The 1990 is lighter than the buttery, more clamorous 1989, but I find it the most balanced Vriesenhof Chardonnay yet.

SOVIET UNION

Total vineyard area: 2 million acres
Area planted to Chardonnay: approximately 1,000 acres

Getting reliable information out of the former Soviet Union, until recently the world's fifth largest wine producer, is an adventure, as each of the constituent republics is now acting with virtual independence. Chardonnay is certainly included in the country's enormous area under vine, but it is a comparatively unimportant variety. There are plantings in the Crimea, Moldavia and Georgia, but the only example I have tasted is an undistinguished Moldavian sparkling wine, called St Petersburg, which includes 15 per cent Chardonnay in the blend.

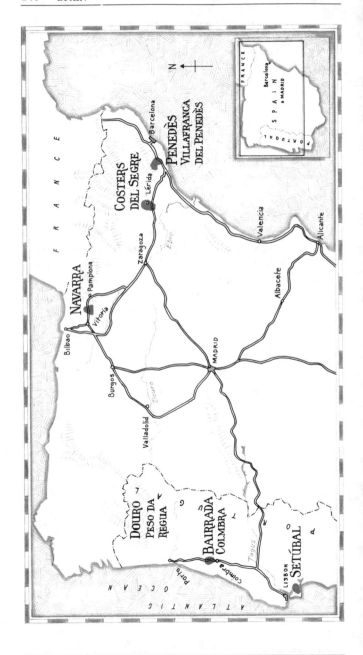

SPAIN

Total vineyard area: 3.89 million acres
Area planted to Chardonnay: 2,000 acres

Spanish Chardonnays are like Spanish vegetarians, rather thin
on the ground. In a country which harbours the world's most
planted grape, Airén, Chardonnay is swamped by lesser white
varieties. In most Denominaciones de Origen, it continues to
be a pariah, although plantings have increased considerably in
the last three years.

Chardonnay now has authorized status in Navarra, where the
local oenological station EVENA has produced some drinkable
examples, Majorca, Galicia and Somontano. It has also begun
to appear, on a strictly experimental basis, in Rioja. Nevertheless, it is in Catalonia – in the DOs of Costers del Segre, Alella
and the Penedès, to be precise – that Chardonnay has per-
formed best. The Catalans have a reputation as innovators in
Spain, and it is they who have produced the country's finest
Chardonnays. So far, though, only Torres's Milmanda is a contender in the world Chardonnay stakes.

The grape was introduced to Spain by a Basque, not a
Catalan, in the mid-sixties but, significantly, Jean León chose to
plant in the Penedès. Other bodegas have been slow to follow
his example, despite the success of León's wines. Torres didn't
release Milmanda until the mid-eighties, for example. Other
interesting Chardonnays that have surfaced in the last decade
are made by Raimat in Costers del Segre, Raventos i Blanc in
the Penedès and Marqués de Alella in, would you believe it,
Alella. The first is made in two styles, one oaked, the other
unoaked; the other two are tank-fermented. Chardonnay also
crops up, as part of the blend, in Torres's Gran Viña Sol, and in
wines made by Gran Caus and Mont Marçal.

Several Cava producers, including Vallformosa, Marqués de Monistrol and Juve y Camps are said to be considering the grape to add complexity to their sparkling wines, but there is also a strong feeling among more traditional companies that it should not be allowed to become the dominant variety. Freixenet are strongly opposed to the grape. For the time being, the only Cava group to produce varietal Chardonnays is Codorníu, who make one under their own label, and another at Raimat.

Best producers: Codorníu*, Jean León*, Marqués de Alella, Raimat*, Raventos i Blanc, Torres*

CODORNÍU

Asuera SN, Sant Sadurni de Noya 08770

Production of Chardonnay: not released

Quality: 🍇🍇/🍇🍇🍇   Price: ★★

Best vintages: 1986, 1990

Codorníu is Spain's largest, and most innovative, sparkling-wine producer. As well as running its gigantic Cava business, the Raventós family owns two further wineries in Catalonia, Masia Bach and Raimat. It has extensive vineyard holdings, but also works with growers in the Penedès region. Apart from Raimat, Codorníu has no Chardonnay vineyards of its own, but it controls more than three hundred acres under contract.

Codorníu's promotion of Chardonnay (to complement the three traditional white varieties of the Penedès, Parellada, Macabeo and Xarel-lo) has met with opposition from other local producers over the last few years. It may be coincidental, but the firm's sparkling wines have improved enormously in the last decade – about the length of time they have been working with Chardonnay.

Four of Codorníu's Cavas use a proportion of Chardonnay: Première Cuvée has 6 per cent, Blanc de Blancs 10 per cent,

Anna de Codorníu 15 per cent and Jaume de Codorníu 50 per cent. Only one, the aromatic, creamy Chardonnay Brut, is close to being a varietal wine (it also has 10 per cent of Parellada). At least some of the Chardonnay used in this wine comes from the Raimat estate, but the Codorníu cuvée is the more elegant of the two varietal Cavas.

JEAN LEÓN

C/Pau Claris, 106 Entlo, 2a, 08009 Barcelona

Chardonnay vineyard: 25 acres

Production of Chardonnay: 12,000 bottles

Quality: ♛♛♛/♛♛♛♛   Price: ★★/★★★

Best vintages: 1979, 1981, 1982, 1986, 1987

Jean León's story is straight out of a Hollywood film script. He was born in the Basque port of Santander, but emigrated to California as a teenager. After a succession of jobs, he found work as a waiter at La Villa Capri, a restaurant owned by baseball star Joe DiMaggio and Frank Sinatra. Old Blue Eyes took a shine to him and, three years later, León set up his own restaurant, the first of four in and around Beverly Hills.

In 1962, León went on holiday to the Penedès region, not far from the Catalan capital, Barcelona. He had been looking to purchase a vineyard in Italy or France, but had had no luck. In the Penedès, his fortunes changed. He saw an old vineyard that was up for sale, and bought it the same day.

Back in California, he enrolled at the University of California to study oenology. It was on the advice of the University that he grubbed up traditional Catalan grapes in his vineyard, and replaced them with Chardonnay, Cabernet Sauvignon, Cabernet Franc and Pinot Noir. The Chardonnay cuttings came from Burgundy in 1966, and were Spain's first commercial plantings of the variety. Jean León's Chardonnays have not scaled the same peaks as the bodega's Cabernet Sauvignons. Production is small but increasing.

Wine-maker Jaime Rovira ferments his Chardonnay in American oak (up to 25 per cent of which is new), then racks it to stainless-steel tanks after four months for 'stabilization'. This allows the wine and the strong flavour of American oak to marry (the influence of oak has certainly been toned down in the last five years). After bottling, the wine is aged for two years before release.

The 1987 Jean León Chardonnay was more restrained than the 1986, with lemony, toasty fruit and firm acidity. It should age as well as the top vintages, though it lacks the complexity of Torres's Milmanda, the Iberian peninsula's best Chardonnay.

RAIMAT

Bodegas Asuera SN, Raimat 25111, Lérida

Chardonnay vineyard: 800 acres

Production of Chardonnay: not released

Quality: 🍇🍇/🍇🍇🍇

Best vintages: 1983, 1989, 1990

The Raimat estate, situated 200 km to the west of Barcelona in the denomination of Costers del Segre, was a vast expanse of semi-desert until the Raventós family (of Codorníu fame) persuaded the Spanish government to build the Catalonia and Aragón canal through the middle of the estate in 1916. Irrigation, strictly speaking illegal in Spain, made it possible to grow vines at Raimat, but it was not until the mid-seventies that, on the advice of the University of California, Davis, the first plantings of French varieties (Chardonnay, Cabernet Sauvignon and Merlot) were made. There were initial problems, but these were mainly due to the choice of poor rootstocks and clones, rather than the inherent unsuitability of French grapes.

Today the Raimat estate is a self-contained model of Spanish paternalism with its own school, railway station, church and football pitch. Here, just outside the rather dull town of Lérida, some of Spain's most exciting varietal wines are being produced, with the emphasis firmly on Chardonnay and Cabernet Sauvignon. So far, the reds have been more consistent than the whites.

Raimat produces three Chardonnays – one sparkling and two still – and all of them are respectable, if one-dimensional, examples of the grape. The sparkling Chardonnay is a full-bodied, fruity Cava that is best drunk young. The still wines show more promise, but are produced in much smaller quantities. In recent vintages Raimat has released an unoaked as well as a barrel-fermented wine, both of which taste like New World Chardonnays, with ripe, blowsy tropical-fruit flavours. Of the two, I prefer the oaked version. Lower yields would probably produce more concentrated, balanced wines. Certainly, Raimat has still not hit top form with Chardonnay.

TORRES

C/Comerç. 22, 08720 Vilafranca del Penedès

Chardonnay vineyard: 222 acres (Penedès, 25 of which are Milmanda); 36 acres (Sonoma); 50 acres (Chile)

Production of Chardonnay: 24,000 bottles (Penedès); 36,000 bottles (Sonoma); 60,000 bottles (Chile)

Quality: 🍇🍇–🍇🍇🍇🍇🍇   Price: ★★–★★★★

Best vintages: 1985, 1986, 1988

There is a rust-coloured bottle in the Torres family's ancestral home in Vilafranca del Penedès, bearing the words 'Spanish Chablis'. Was this the first commercial Spanish Chardonnay, made long before Jean León planted the grape? Unfortunately not. The wine was made in the 1950s from Parellada, not Chardonnay. In fact, it took Miguel Torres, Spain's leading wine-maker, until 1974 to plant Chardonnay. The first release of the varietal Milmanda was the 1985, although the grape has been used as part of the Gran Viña Sol blend since the late seventies.

Milmanda was worth the wait. One of four '*pago*' (individual vineyard) wines, it has established itself as the finest (and most expensive) Chardonnay in the Iberian peninsula. The Milmanda vineyard at Poblet in the Central Penedès comes under the Conca de Barberá sub-appellation and was planted in 1979. Picking is done early to preserve acidity and cut down the risk of botrytis. Yields are considerably lower than at Pacs, the source of the Chardonnay used in Gran Viña Sol.

Miguel Torres believes that great Chardonnay must be barrel-fermented so, unsurprisingly, Milmanda is vinified in new Nevers oak. It goes through malolactic and remains on its lees until mid-May. It is early days, and Torres himself admits that the wine is not yet firing on all cylinders, but recent vintages have confirmed Milmanda's early promise. If there is a question mark in my mind, it concerns the wine's longevity. Some of the early wines have aged prematurely.

Chardonnay is also planted in Torres's outposts in Chile and Sonoma County in California. The Chilean example is clean, fresh and unoaked; more interesting is the Marimar Torres Sonoma County, Green Valley, Don Miguel Vineyard, which is managed by Miguel's sister, Marimar. The 1989 was the first release and represented a very auspicious début. Judging by its crisp, oaky concentration and excellent balance, the Sonoma wine could yet rival Milmanda as Torres's top white wine.

SWITZERLAND

Total vineyard area: 34,000 acres
Area planted to Chardonnay: approximately 200 acres

Chasselas, also known in confusing, rather un-Swiss fashion as Fendant and Dorin, is the dominant white-grape variety in Switzerland. It makes clean, dry, appealing wines that are sometimes a little flabby. Chardonnay is not a popular local style, although international fashion is having its effect here, too. The *négociant* firm of Hammel have experimental plantations of the grape at Mont-sur-Rolle and Chablais. Ville de Lausanne produces a pricey late-harvest Chardonnay and Château de Luins, also in the Vaud, claims to have been making Chardonnay on Lake Geneva for nearly twenty years. The wine is fermented in old oak casks, has something of the character of a Chablis and should be drunk young. In the Valais, the climate is warmer and the Chardonnay produced is fuller and fruitier. The best grower is Michel Clavien, whose unoaked Chardonnay has something of the character of Alsace Pinot Blanc.

USA

Wine is made in at least forty of America's fifty states and, given the way Chardonnay has captured the public imagination, Chardonnay is probably grown in most of them. California is the heart of the wine industry but, increasingly, good Chardonnays are being produced in Oregon, Washington State, New York State and other, less likely places such as Texas, Idaho and Pennsylvania.

California

Total vineyard area: 327,455 acres
Area planted to Chardonnay: 52,157 acres

Does anyone remember a time when there was no California Chardonnay? The two words may appear inseparable today, like Bonnie and Clyde or fish and chips, but the rise of America's favourite varietal is a comparatively recent, even breathless phenomenon. Thirty years ago, to plant Chardonnay in the Napa Valley was to court ridicule. According to Professor Harold Olmo at the University of California, Davis, the man who did so much to improve the health and vigour of Chardonnay clones in the fifties, there were fewer than two hundred acres of the variety planted in the entire state in 1959. Three decades later that figure has expanded to over 50,000 acres (making California a more substantial producer of Chardonnay than the whole of France) and continues to increase. Significantly, nearly half of the total has been planted since 1985.

Most of California's Chardonnay is situated in Napa, Sonoma, Monterey and Santa Barbara counties, but there are also expanding vineyards in Madera, Fresno, Kern and San Joaquin, all irrigated areas in the Central Valley producing large volumes of cheap Chardonnay for immediate consumption. Nevertheless, Chardonnay plantings are still dominated by the North Coast regions, principally Napa and Sonoma, with 25,279 acres. This is well ahead of the Central and South Coast (17,572 acres), the North Central Valley (5,350), the South Central Valley (1,017) and other areas of the state (2,939 acres).

The Chardonnay planting craze shows no sign of abating. By the mid-nineties, Chardonnay will overtake French Colombard as the state's number one grape. Consumer demand, too, continues to increase. In a little over twenty years, Chardonnay has become America's favourite generic white-wine style. Not so long ago, Randall Grahm, the innovative and eccentric owner of Bonny Doon winery in California, launched a tongue-in-cheek campaign called 'Just Say "No" to Chardonnay'. Support for his initiative has been slight.

For all its success, the exact time and place of Chardonnay's arrival in California is open to debate. Some maintain that cuttings of Chardonnay were among the original *vinifera* vines planted by settlers in the late eighteenth century, although this seems highly unlikely. The Hungarian Agoston Haraszthy, known as the father of California viticulture, certainly imported Sémillon, Sauvignon Blanc, Riesling and Gewürztraminer in 1856, but of Chardonnay there is no record.

Even if a few vines made it to California, Chardonnay did not prove popular with pre-Prohibition growers, possibly because it was comparatively low-yielding and, in many cases, virus-infected. In a census of over five hundred wineries carried out at the turn of the century, not one of the respondents admitted to making a Chardonnay, or Pinot Chardonnay, as it was almost certainly called then.

Charles Wetmore, who became chief viticultural officer of the newly founded State Viticultural Commission in 1880, is a

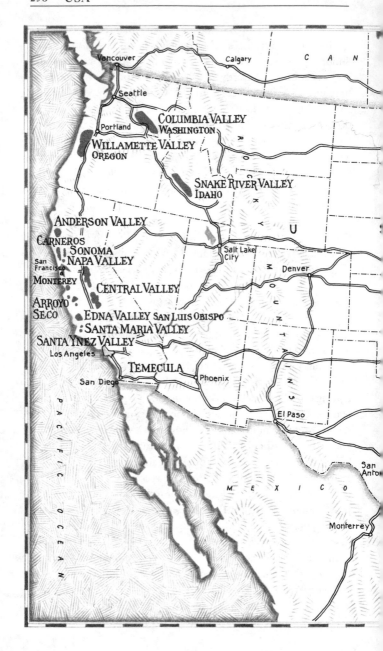

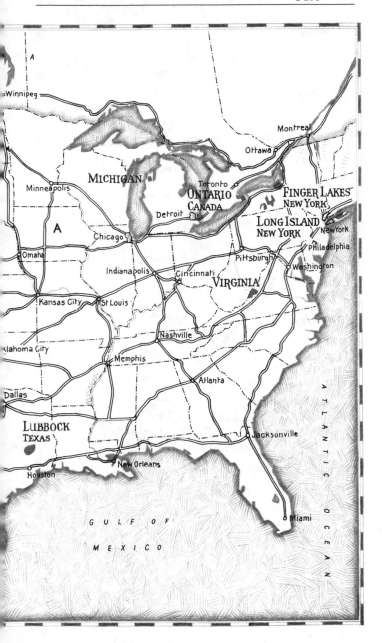

Winnipeg

Montreal

Ottawa

MICHIGAN

Minneapolis

Toronto

ONTARIO
CANADA

FINGER LAKES
NEW YORK

Detroit

A

Chicago

LONG ISLAND
NEW YORK

NewYork

Omaha

Pittsburgh

Philadelphia

Indianapolis

Cincinnati

Washington

Kansas City

St Louis

VIRGINIA

Nashville

klahoma City

Memphis

Dallas

Atlanta

LUBBOCK
TEXAS

Jacksonville

New Orleans

Houston

A T L A N T I C   O C E A N

GULF OF

Miami

MEXICO

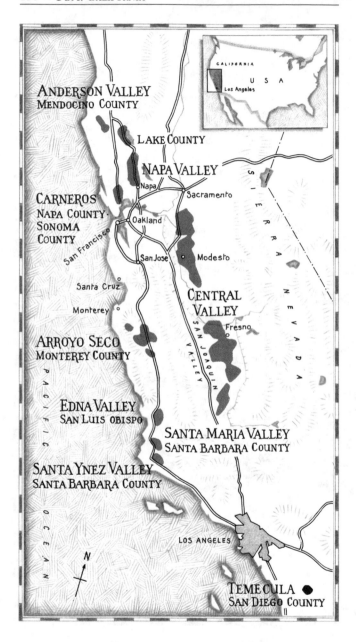

ANDERSON VALLEY
MENDOCINO COUNTY

CALIFORNIA

USA

Los Angeles

LAKE COUNTY

NAPA VALLEY

Napa

Sacramento

CARNEROS
NAPA COUNTY·
SONOMA
COUNTY

Oakland

San Francisco

San Jose   Modesto

Santa Cruz

Monterey

CENTRAL
VALLEY

Fresno

ARROYO SECO
MONTEREY COUNTY

SAN JOAQUIN VALLEY

SIERRA

NEVADA

PACIFIC

EDNA VALLEY
SAN LUIS OBISPO

SANTA MARIA VALLEY
SANTA BARBARA COUNTY

SANTA YNEZ VALLEY
SANTA BARBARA COUNTY

OCEAN

N

LOS ANGELES

TEMECULA
SAN DIEGO COUNTY

key figure in the development, if not necessarily the origins, of California Chardonnay. It was Wetmore who travelled, with state funds in his wallet, to Europe in 1882 to acquire new clones of the best *vinifera* varieties, Chardonnay among them. He distributed them to California producers on his return.

Whatever its reputation among growers at the time, Chardonnay seems to have made an impact on the young Ernest Wente, who was studying at the University of California, Davis in 1912. Wente obtained cuttings from two sources – the Gier vineyard in Pleasanton, which was already producing Chardonnay-based wines under the Giersburger label, and the Montpellier Nursery, run by a Frenchman called Léon Bonnet – and planted them in his family's Livermore Valley vineyards.

The Wente Chardonnay plantings survived Prohibition and became a source of vine material for the next generation of Chardonnay pioneers, such as Louis Martini and Fred McCrea of Stony Hill. As recently as 1960, Wente owned one-third of all the Chardonnay planted in California. Wente, incidentally, probably produced the first varietal Chardonnay in the state, way back in 1934.

For the main part, the post-Prohibition Chardonnay producers were maverick operations like Hanzell, Stony Hill, Mount Eden and Chalone, but the big boys were not far behind, and by the early seventies Chardonnay plantings had reached just over 7,000 acres. As the bandwagon slipped into second gear, more and more people began to join it, tempted on board by new, virus-free clones that promised higher yields. By the mid-seventies, the great Chardonnay boom was well and truly under way.

While some of the early producers had consciously followed Burgundian methods, the style of Chardonnay which developed in the late seventies was distinctively Californian. In most cases, the wines tended to be high in alcohol, full of flavour, and destined for a short life. Extremely ripe grapes coupled with skin contact to extract every ounce of character, stainless-steel fermentation and ageing in (predominantly new) wide-grained Limousin oak barrels were the order of the day. Some of these wines (Chateau Mòntelena in particular) have stood the demanding test of time, but most have faded into premature senility.

With hindsight, California's early successes with Chardonnay – over-oaked, over-alcoholic and even, it must be said, a little coarse – are surprising. As Bill Bonetti of Sonoma Cutrer puts it: 'Twelve to fifteen years ago, the wine-making ethos was that the wine-maker was a babysitter, whose highest calling was to take the optimum ripe fruit character and get it through into the bottle undisturbed. In those days, the stronger the varietal flavour the better, because it was easy to recognize. We were striving more for varietal character than for balance or finesse. Now Chardonnay is a "made wine" in which we try to bring out notes of complexity.'

Greater complexity has come from two main sources: first, a greater understanding of vineyard location and *terroir* (largely rejecting the much-publicized 'soil is dirt' school of thought, which maintained that you could plant grapes virtually anywhere); and second, the adoption of Burgundian techniques (lees contact, barrel-fermentation, partial or full malolactic) in the winery, moderated by rigorous scientific know-how.

There has been a general tendency over the last decade to plant Chardonnay in cooler climates with longer growing seasons – Carneros on the San Pablo Bay, Russian River Valley in Sonoma, Monterey, Edna Valley near San Luis Obispo and the lower Santa Ynez Valley near Santa Barbara – producing wines that have better structure than wines from the Napa Valley floor, although there has also been a corresponding move towards warmer, irrigated areas as the demand for $5 Chardonnay has increased.

Carneros, which spans the southern end of Napa and Sonoma Counties, is the buzz word in California Chardonnay at the moment. The big local names are all busy buying vineyards or securing long-term contracts there, and the last five years have witnessed an influx of foreign sparkling-wine producers, of whom Taittinger is the most prominent. Not bad for an area where the sheep used to outnumber the people by a factor of ten.

Carneros Chardonnays, like those from the valleys of the Central and Southern Coast, tend to have better levels of natural acidity and so can sustain malolactic fermentation without 'the finish falling off a cliff' as one wine-maker put it. It is no coincidence that the majority of California's most elegant Chardonnays are made in these areas. Those from the Napa Valley and warmer parts of Sonoma like the Alexander Valley are usually more generously upholstered, with tropical- rather than citrus-fruit flavours to the fore.

Carneros is one of a number of AVAs (Approved Viticultural Areas) that have been established in the United States by the splendidly named Bureau of Alcohol, Tobacco and Firearms over the last decade. AVAs are not as strict as French *appellation contrôlée* regulations, as they do not include things like vineyard yields or authorized grape varieties, but they are an attempt to establish viticultural boundaries of sorts. (To qualify for AVA status, a varietal wine has to be made 95 per cent from the stated vintage, 85 per cent from the designated area, and 75 per cent from the grape named on the label. Cheaper California Chardonnays, not necessarily covered by AVAs, often include varieties like Chenin Blanc and French Colombard in their make-up, but most of the top wines are pure, unadulterated Chardonnays.)

Some of these AVAs, particularly outside California, seem a little vague (the Ohio Valley AVA, for example, covers something like 5 million acres), while others are intensely political (Napa County and the Napa Valley AVA are practically synonymous), but they do represent the beginnings of a sense of regional identity. Whether they are of much use (or interest) to the consumer is, as yet, a moot point.

Irrespective of where their grapes come from, wine-makers are coming round to the idea that technology cannot compensate for poor or unripe fruit. For Dick Ward of Saintsbury: 'You've got to be in the right area to pick grapes when they reach maturity of flavour – you can't just pick early in the wrong place. The big challenge for California Chardonnay is to achieve richness with delicacy.'

It no longer makes sense to talk of a single style of California

Chardonnay, if it ever did. Chardonnay covers everything from cheap, medium-sweet varietal plonk to some of the finest wines in the world – bottles that can stand comparison with the best of Burgundy and the rest of the overseas producers.

As growers have begun to explore new areas and winemakers have developed greater experience of handling Chardonnay, so dozens of different wines have begun to emerge. There is only one fundamental: the idea of unoaked Chardonnay is almost heretical, notwithstanding the success of Calla Lees, the only California Chardonnay I know of with no oak character at all. Otherwise, wine-makers (and marketeers) have a free hand.

Too many California Chardonnays taste alike to me, particularly at the cheaper end of the spectrum. These are quaffing Chardonnays, and do the Americans quaff them! In the space of a few years, basic Chardonnay has become America's favourite white wine. As Adam Tolmach, former co-partner at Au Bon Climat, says, 'Americans only know two grape varieties, and Chardonnay is one of them.'

At this most simple level, details of producer and provenance are virtually irrelevant, though much of the fruit in fact comes from the warmer areas. Basically, the more you pay the more complexity you are likely to encounter. Chardonnay needs what John Thacher at Cuvaison calls 'flavour tools' to make it interesting, and such things cost money.

California Chardonnay is approaching the end of a troubled adolescence, during which it has done and learnt a good deal. Mistakes have been made in the past, but there is now a welcome tendency to make wines that allow the fruit to peek out from behind the oak. For the top wineries, a greater understanding of climate, *terroir* and viticulture will further accentuate individual differences.

So where does California Chardonnay go from here? A major constraint is the high price of some of the best wines, partly the result of the high cost of vineyard land (and consequently, grapes) in California compared with other newcomer countries. Nevertheless, the quality of the Chardonnays from the likes of Au Bon Climat, Saintsbury, Cuvaison, Chalone, Ric

Forman, Flora Springs and Mount Eden is exemplary. These wines will continue to find a market, whatever happens to public taste in the USA. If American consumers ever get tired of drinking Chardonnay, other (lesser) producers may not be so fortunate.

Best producers: Acacia*, S. Anderson*, Arrowood*, Au Bon Climat*, Beaulieu, Beringer*, Bouchaine, Buena Vista, Carneros Creek, Chalk Hill, Chalone*, Chateau Montelena*, Chateau St Jean*, Château Woltner, Clos du Bois*, Clos du Val, Congress Springs, Crichton Hall, Cuvaison*, De Loach*, Dry Creek, Edna Valley*, Far Niente*, Ferrari-Carano*, Fetzer, Flora Springs*, Forman*, Frog's Leap*, Glen Ellen*, Grgich Hills*, Hanzell*, William Hill, Iron Horse*, Jordan, Kendall-Jackson*, Kistler*, La Crema, Leeward, Long*, Matanzas Creek*, Mayacamas, Peter Michael*, Robert Mondavi*, Morgan, Mount Eden*, Newton*, Patz & Hall, Joseph Phelps, Pine Ridge, Qupe, Raymond, Ridge, Round Hill, Saintsbury*, Sanford*, Santa Barbara, Sequoia Grove, Silverado*, Simi*, Sonoma-Cutrer*, Stag's Leap*, Sterling, Stony Hill*, Swanson*, Torres*, Villa Zapu, Mark West, ZD*

California Chardonnay Vintages

1991. One of the latest vintages on record. A cool summer was followed by unusually hot weather in September and October. Initial fears were allayed by the high autumn temperatures, which (in most cases) belatedly ripened the grapes. Potentially an outstanding vintage for Chardonnay.

1990. Generally a very fine year. Smaller-than-average crop because of rain during flowering in some areas, but this was a great Chardonnay harvest in California, producing luscious wines with good structure. Like 1988, only more so.

1989. A difficult vintage, dubbed 'the harvest from hell' by one grower. At the end of a cool growing season, many wineries were hit by heavy rain in September and had to deal with a large, botrytis-affected crop. Some of the wines are surprisingly good, particularly from the small number of producers who picked before the rains, but these are still Chardonnays for the short to medium term.

1988. One of the best vintages of the eighties. Like 1990, this was a smaller-than-average crop because of rain during flowering in some areas. A warm but even growing season produced forward, balanced wines that tasted well when young but are also ageing gracefully.

1987. Many of the Chardonnays produced in this vintage, like 1988 a drought year, tend to be on the lean side by California standards. The best producers made wines with elegance and ageing potential; others were less successful and their Chardonnays lack generosity as a result.

1986. A fairly cool year in some areas which produced wines high in natural (malic) acidity, particularly in Carneros. Warm regions made better-proportioned Chardonnays, some of which were very fine indeed. Structure is the hallmark of the best wines. Many of the Chardonnays were lighter in alcohol than the 1985s, but with more apparent fruit, making them very attractive when young. A good rather than great vintage, for medium-term drinking.

1985. A vintage to rival, and possibly surpass, 1988. A relatively cool, trouble-free growing season produced wines with good structure, concentration and more elegance than the 1986s. The best wines will age for at least a decade.

ACACIA

2750 Las Amigas Road, Napa, 94558 California

Chardonnay vineyard: 50 acres

Production of Chardonnay: 360,000 bottles

Labels: Carneros; Marina Vineyard

Quality: 🍇🍇🍇🍇   Price: ★★★

Best vintages: 1983, 1986, 1987, 1988, 1989

Larry Brooks, Acacia's appealingly garrulous wine-maker, lists his hobbies as 'literature, art, music, bicycling and cigars'. Whatever Brooks does in his spare moments, wine is clearly his consuming daytime passion. He describes Chardonnay as 'something to pay the bills', enabling him to concentrate on his first love, Pinot Noir, but the wines that Brooks has made at Acacia over the last decade have been consistently fine.

Acacia has been producing Chardonnay in Carneros since 1979, although the wines were not made at Acacia until 1981. Initial vintages saw releases of a Napa Valley and a blended California Chardonnay, but since Chalone purchased the winery in 1986, Acacia has concentrated solely on Carneros fruit. One-third of its needs come from its own vineyards, the rest is purchased from local growers.

Brooks makes two Chardonnays: Marina Vineyard, from the 42 acres in front of the winery, and a Carneros blend. Whereas Edna Valley, Carmenet and Chalone (the other three wineries in the Chalone group) all favour 100 per cent barrel-fermentation for their Chardonnays, Acacia uses a combination of stainless steel and oak; the wine is fermented half in new and one-year-old French oak barrels, and half in stainless steel. All of it sees some oak maturation.

It is partly a question of space, according to Brooks, but mainly one of style. At Acacia he is aiming to produce lighter, more floral Chardonnays than Chalone and Edna Valley, although his wines can still weigh in at over 13 per cent alcohol by volume. The percentage of malolactic varies from none at all (in 1987) to 35 per cent.

The Marina Vineyard is usually the more complex of the two Acacia Chardonnays, but both wines have good structure and age well. In their youth, Acacia Chardonnays can seem quite austere, but as Brooks says 'most California wines are made to taste good when they're bottled. We're aiming for something with integrity that will hold up for much longer.' Acacia was one of the few California wineries to make an outstanding Chardonnay in 1989.

*

S. ANDERSON

1473 Yountville Crossroad, Yountville, 94558 California

Chardonnay vineyard: 60 acres

Production of Chardonnay: 60,000 bottles of Chardonnay;
9,000 bottles of Blanc de Blancs

Labels: Estate; Proprietor's Reserve

Quality: 🍇🍇🍇   Price: ★★★

Best vintages: 1984, 1985, 1988

Stan Anderson, a tanned, white-haired dentist from Southern California, planted his first vines near the junction of Yountville Crossroad and the Silverado Trail as long ago as 1971. One of the varieties he decided upon, much against the advice of local growers, was Chardonnay: 22 acres of it. 'When we harvested our first crop in 1975, I drove up and down Silverado Trail with the grapes, and no one would buy them. It's funny, if I'd chosen Sauvignon Blanc or Riesling, I'd be bankrupt now.'

Anderson's Chardonnay did not go unsold in subsequent vintages. Until he decided to make his own Chardonnay, in 1980, the grapes were bought by Cuvaison, among others. Anderson called his new winery S. Anderson to avoid confusion with the Anderson Valley in Mendocino County. Today it still sits just behind his house and English rose garden – a small, homely operation producing some very decent wines.

There are two main styles at S. Anderson: full, toasty Chardonnays and a range of sparkling wines. The Chardonnays are much more interesting in my view. Two-thirds of the wine is barrel-fermented, in 20 per cent new oak: 'I'm terrified of the stuff,' says Anderson. 'Too many California Chardonnays taste like packing cases.' Anderson does not use malolactic fermentation, except on his Proprietor's Reserve, produced in exceptional years, but he does give his wines up to twelve hours of skin contact. These are Chardonnays with lots of alcohol and flavour, but which nevertheless age well. The 1981 was still enjoyable when I tasted it eight years after release.

ARROWOOD

14347 Sonoma Highway, Glen Ellen, 95442 California

Chardonnay production: 78,000 bottles

Quality: 🍇🍇🍇/🍇🍇🍇🍇   Price: ★★★

Best vintages: 1986, 1987, 1988, 1989

Richard Arrowood spent twelve successful years at Chateau St Jean before moving eight miles south to create his own winery, in 1986. For the first four vintages, Arrowood continued to act as a consultant at Chateau St Jean but, since 1990, he has cut the lifeline, focusing his attention entirely on Arrowood Vineyards and producing just three wines: Cabernet Sauvignon, Merlot and Chardonnay.

Arrowood's declared intention is to produce Chardonnay that constitutes 'an attack on neutrality, that has a flavour statement to make'. He is convinced that vineyard site has an important influence on Chardonnay and buys his fruit from a range of growers in the Alexander, Russian River and Sonoma Valleys.

Arrowood's own Chardonnays have richly fulfilled his intentions. At an international Chardonnay conference held in Beaune, the Burgundians were hugely impressed by Arrowood's wines. Entirely fermented in French oak, they also go through partial malolactic, which may explain the Burgundians' enthusiasm. So far the Arrowood Chardonnays have been made in a leaner style than Chateau St Jean's, surprisingly so since the St Jean wines have no malolactic character. However valid the comparison, the 1988 Arrowood Chardonnay is a superb wine in its own right, with elegant, structured fruit and great length. A very promising winery.

AU BON CLIMAT

PO Box 113, Los Olivos, 93441 California

Chardonnay production: 45,000 bottles

Quality: 🍇🍇🍇🍇🍇   Price: ★★★/★★★★

Best vintages: 1986, 1988

After the stylized winery tours and PR flunkeys of the Napa Valley, Au Bon Climat comes as a delightful, understated surprise. Situated in the northern part of Santa Barbara County, it is a difficult place to find. A sign at the turn-off on the main road says 'Sawyer Construction'; no mention of Au Bon Climat. The winery itself sits at the end of a dirt track in a large grey metal warehouse surrounded by barren land. When I visited in 1989, partners Adam Tolmach and Jim Clendenen had just moved into the new building (having been evicted from their former premises by the owners of Los Alamos vineyard) and were being overrun by earwigs.

The two friends founded Au Bon Climat in 1982, after winemaking stints elsewhere in California, in Australia and (most significantly) in France. Their intention was to produce Burgundian-style Pinot Noir and Chardonnay. 'We don't always succeed,' says Tolmach, 'but it's something to aim for.' Others, including this writer, would disagree, for Au Bon Climat's Chardonnays and Pinot Noirs are some of the most complex wines in California.

Au Bon Climat does not own any vines of its own. All of its Chardonnay is bought from local Santa Barbara growers in the Santa Maria and Santa Ynez Valleys. The inland valleys of the Central Coast are cooler than Carneros in many cases, according to Tolmach, but 'because it's not Napa, people have been very slow to recognize this as a quality region'. The source of Au Bon Climat's Chardonnay has changed over the years, as it has lost fruit from the Los Alamos and Benedict vineyards, but the quality of the wine has not suffered. Most of the Chardonnay is now sourced from the Bien Nacido and Rancho Viñedo vineyards near the winery.

Three Chardonnays are produced at Au Bon Climat: a regular, a Reserve and (until 1990) a single-estate Benedict Vineyard. Michael Benedict's vineyard is now owned by the Sanford winery, but it is possible that some of the grapes will again be sold to Au Bon Climat in the future.

Vinification for all three wines follows Burgundian methods, with barrel-fermentation, extended lees contact and full malolactic. The Reserve and Benedict see a higher proportion of new oak. Yeast stirring is not usually practised – 'we get plenty of lees character without it,' says Tolmach.

Unlike many California Chardonnays, those at Au Bon Climat are not particularly alcoholic; most are kept below 13 per cent. The richest of the trio of Chardonnays is the Reserve wine; Benedict (produced in 1987, 1988 and 1989) tends to be leaner and more restrained.

In June 1991 Adam Tolmach sold his interest in Au Bon Climat to Jim Clendenen. Perhaps the earwigs were getting to him.

BERINGER

PO Box 111, St Helena, 94574 California

Chardonnay vineyard: 700 acres

Production of Chardonnay: 1.3 million bottles

Labels: Proprietor Grown; Private Reserve

Quality: 🍇–🍇🍇🍇🍇🍇   Price: ★★/★★★

Best vintages: 1985, 1986, 1988

On a Monday morning in May, the three car parks were packed with coaches, confirming Beringer's standing as one of the Napa Valley's great tourist attractions. Its ugly German Rhine house, allegedly brought piece by piece to California in the early 1880s by founders Jacob and Frederick Beringer, receives more than 350,000 visitors a year.

Beringer is more than a T-shirt shop, however. For a winery

which produces in excess of 1 million cases a year, its standards are commendably high, a tribute to the continuing investment of multinational Nestlé, which bought the run-down operation in 1971. Beringer's reputation has been built on Cabernet Sauvignon and Chardonnay, particularly its Private Reserves, but it also makes one of the more palatable White Zinfandels, as well as good Sémillon and Sauvignon Blanc.

In the Chardonnay stakes, Beringer is a considerable presence. Its basic Chardonnay, blessed with the snappy title of Proprietor Grown and produced from the winery's own vineyards in Yountville and the southern Napa Valley, is always reliable – all 100,000 cases of it. This is usually fermented, half and half, in stainless steel and French oak, with 25 per cent going through malolactic.

More impressive is the company's Private Reserve, which gets a higher percentage of barrel-fermentation (in one-third new oak). The wine, first released in 1978, is a big, flavoursome Chardonnay that combines depth with finesse. Under wine-maker Ed Sbragia, an extensive research programme was launched in 1984, to study such things as yeast strains, lees contact and oak ageing. The results are impressive if the 1986 Private Reserve, one of the best wines of the vintage, is any-thing to go by.

CHALONE

PO Box 855, Soledad, Monterey County, 93960 California

Chardonnay vineyard: 110 acres

Production of Chardonnay: 95,000 bottles

Quality: 🍇🍇🍇🍇/🍇🍇🍇🍇🍇   Price: ★★★★/★★★★★

Best vintages: 1982, 1984, 1986, 1988, 1989

Chalone is one of California's least accessible wineries, perched high above the Salinas Valley on an isolated hillside near the Pinnacles National Monument in Monterey County. The first vines were planted here (appropriately enough, by a

Frenchman) at the beginning of this century, but went through a succession of owners before Dick Graff persuaded his mother to buy the property in 1965.

As self-styled president of the fledgeling venture, Graff studied oenology at the University of California, Davis for a year. Unimpressed by what he learnt, he applied for a credit card and took himself off to France to study Burgundian wine-making techniques. On his return, he became the first American to import French barrels for sale in the USA. Graff put his Burgundian experience to good use in other ways: Chalone's Chardonnay and Pinot Noir soon began to develop a cult following in California. To this day, they remain some of the most sought-after bottles in the state.

The microclimate at Chalone is extremely hot and dry, with as little as 14 inches of annual rainfall. The soil is thin and rocky and, unusually for California, contains a significant proportion of limestone. Perhaps that Frenchman knew what he was up to after all. Yields are extremely low here – rarely more than 1.8 tons to the acre – and this is reflected in the wines.

Chalone's style of Chardonnay has followed a consistent path since the first vintage in 1965, give or take the odd experiment with skin contact in the late seventies and a more recent tendency to reduce the amount of time in oak. The wine is barrel-fermented (in 35 per cent new oak), goes through malolactic and spends up to seven months on its lees. Since 1980, Chalone has released small amounts of Reserve Chardonnay, as well as its regular bottling.

Chalone's Chardonnays are built for the long haul, with good acidity and structure. The best wines will age for at least ten years and tend to be less forward than those produced at Edna Valley, Chalone's stable-mate. The other big difference between the two wines is the source of their oak: Chalone's comes mainly from the cooper Sirugue, while Edna Valley favours François Frères.

In vintages like 1982 and 1984, Chalone produced some of California's most complex, densely flavoured Chardonnays. If there is a question mark against the wines, it concerns a musty flavour that sometimes develops in bottle. Some have put this down to *terroir*, others to bad corks, but the most likely explanation is a barrel fault. The winery changed its entire cooperage in 1988, and this seems to have solved the problem.

CHATEAU MONTELENA

1429 Tubbs Lane, Calistoga, 94515 California

Chardonnay vineyard: 15 acres

Production of Chardonnay: 210,000 bottles

Labels: Alexander Valley; Napa Valley

Quality: 🍇🍇🍇   Price: ★★★★

Best vintages: 1984, 1985, 1986, 1988

'Everyone has gone off to Carneros, so we've come jumping back out of the bushes,' says Bo Barrett, the joke-a-minute wine-maker at Chateau Montelena, one of the Napa Valley's most northerly wineries. Montelena's gothic stone château was established here at the foot of Mount St Helena by a California state senator, called Alfred Tubbs, in 1882, although its modern post-Prohibition reincarnation dates back to only 1972. Under successive wine-makers – Mike Grgich, Jerry Luper and now Bo Barrett – Montelena has stuck to a consistent house style; hence Barrett's withering comment about the fashionability of Carneros.

The early Chardonnays at Montelena were made by Mike Grgich – his legendary 1973 beat a number of famous French wines in Steven Spurrier's 1976 Paris tasting and this, in Barrett's words, 'was the first time a California wine had been placed on a par with the great wines of the world'. Luper and Barrett have followed Grgich's lead, producing old-style California Chardonnays: big, brassy and full of fruit.

Since 1981, Montelena has produced two different Chardonnays – one from Alexander Valley, in Sonoma County, the other from Napa – with a high percentage of purchased fruit from a total of four growers and a small amount of grapes from its own vineyards. Before that, its wines had been labelled as

'Napa Alexander', 'Napa' or simply 'California' Chardonnay.

Of the two wines, the Napa bottling tends to be the better balanced, but the softer, more forward Alexander Valley wine can also age well. The latter bottling is usually released before the Napa Chardonnay.

Both wines are made in a consciously California style – with stainless-steel fermentation, oak (7 per cent new) ageing and no malolactic or lees contact. Barrett's aim is to produce wines that will age for at least five years, but which emphasize varietal character – the wines can seem surprisingly lean in their youth, but they do mature with considerable grace. The 1983 was still fresh when I tasted it in 1989.

CHATEAU ST JEAN

8555 Sonoma Highway, Kenwood, 95452 California

Chardonnay vineyard: 45 acres

Production of Chardonnay: 1.2 million bottles

Labels: Sonoma County; Robert Young Vineyards; Belle Terre Vineyards; Estate Selection

Quality: ♦♦♦/♦♦♦♦   Price: ★★★/★★★★

Best vintages: 1983, 1985, 1986, 1987, 1988

At the height of its obsession with vineyard-designated Chardonnays, Chateau St Jean produced no fewer than nine different bottlings, a brave move in a country where simplicity is revered as a supreme virtue. Dick Arrowood, who made the wines here from the first vintage (in 1974) until his departure in 1986, is one of California's great Chardonnay specialists. As well as wines from individual vineyards, Arrowood made sparkling Chardonnay and, in 1977, a Late Harvest style. 'One of the worst wines I've ever made,' he says. 'It was a nice dry sherry.'

Chateau St Jean draws Chardonnay fruit from 245 acres in Sonoma County – 45 of its own and a further 200 leased from growers. Arrowood reckons these include something like eighteen different soil types, and his vineyard bottlings were an attempt to reflect a Burgundian sense of *terroir*. With hindsight, Arrowood admits that 'maybe we should have blended as many different vineyard lots as possible to achieve complexity'; in effect, this is what he has done at Arrowood Vineyards. Suntory, which bought Chateau St Jean in 1984, would appear to share his opinion for the Japanese drinks giant immediately rationalized the number of labels to four.

The two best Chardonnays here are both from single vineyards – Belle Terre and the legendary Robert Young plantings – both in the Alexander Valley. In recent vintages, there has also been a Robert Young Reserve. All three wines are fermented in (one-third new) French oak, with lees ageing but no malolactic.

In my experience, the Belle Terre wines tend to be tighter than those from the Young vineyard. Both sites can produce superb wines: the 1987 Robert Young Reserve is a fantastic Chardonnay, rich, toasty and complex; recent vintages of Belle Terre have been equally impressive. It remains to be seen how Chateau St Jean will manage without the wine-making genius of Dick Arrowood. Certainly the 1989 Estate Selection was a disappointment.

CLOS DU BOIS

PO Box 339, Healdsburg, 95448 California

Chardonnay vineyard: 270 acres

Production of Chardonnay: 1.7 million bottles

Labels: Barrel Fermented; Calcaire Vineyard; Flintwood Vineyards; Winemaker's Reserve

Quality: ♟♟–♟♟♟♟   Price: ★★/★★★

Best vintages: 1983, 1984, 1986, 1987, 1988, 1989

Clos du Bois was set up in the late sixties by a group of investors, who purchased a 500-acre prune and plum ranch in Sonoma County's Alexander Valley. Until 1974, when the partnership decided to bottle wines under its own label (punning on the French translation of the name of one of its founders, Frank Woods), it sold grapes to a number of California wineries, including the Gallo brothers.

Clos du Bois released a Chardonnay in its first vintage, but it was not until the arrival of John Hawley (in 1981) that the winery started to produce great wines. Expansion has proceeded apace ever since, with no apparent effect on quality. 'I've gone from being a rubber-boots-hanging-out-in-the-cellar kind of wine-maker to someone who spends a week a month on the road,' Hawley told me in 1989. Hawley left to go to Kendall-Jackson in 1990 and was replaced by his former assistant, Margaret Davenport, but Clos du Bois continues to go from strength to strength. Hiram Walker, which bought the winery in 1988, has just constructed a new hi-tech winery in the Alexander Valley to replace the jerry-built premises on a suburban street in Healdsburg.

Clos du Bois makes four different Chardonnays. It produces large quantities of its Barrel Fermented brand, and smaller lots of Calcaire (a single vineyard in the Alexander Valley), Flintwood Vineyards (from a number of growers in Dry Creek Valley) and (in exceptional vintages) a Winemaker's Reserve.

All four wines are entirely vinified in French oak, but are markedly different in style. Barrel Fermented is a balanced, extremely reliable drop of Chardonnay, with a lower percentage of malolactic and new barrels than the three top wines. Calcaire, which despite its name is not grown on limestone, is a big, oaky, complex wine, while Flintwood tends to be a little more austere. All of the Flintwood goes through malolactic fermentation, compared with 65 per cent for the Calcaire. Winemaker's Reserve, which John Hawley made in 1987 and 1988, was 'my attempt to bring Burgundy production to California', with full malolactic and extended lees ageing. The wine was not produced in 1989 or 1990. For my money, Calcaire is the most intense of this quartet of Chardonnays, but the other wines are all very well made indeed.

CUVAISON

4550 Silverado Trail, Calistoga, 94515 California

Chardonnay vineyard: 200 acres

Production of Chardonnay: 450,000 bottles

Labels: Reserve; Carneros

Quality: ♛♛♛♛/♛♛♛♛♛   Price: ★★★

Best vintages: 1985, 1986, 1987, 1988, 1990

'To make the best wines you have to take risks, and most of the big risks are in the vineyard,' says John Thacher, the engagingly intelligent wine-maker at Cuvaison. This belief lies at the heart of Cuvaison's recent success. Although it is situated towards the warmer, northern end of the Napa Valley, Cuvaison sources nearly all of its grapes from its own 300-acre vineyard, half an hour to the south, in the fashionable district of Carneros.

The Carneros plantings were not made until 1980, the year after the near-dormant winery was bought by a family of Swiss industrialists. Since 1985, when the Carneros grapes began to come on stream, Cuvaison's wines have improved dramatically. Its range of Merlot, Pinot Noir, Zinfandel, Cabernet Sauvignon and Chardonnay is now one of the most exciting in California, displaying clear, focused flavours and great elegance. The 1990 Chardonnay is Thacher's best yet.

At 200 acres, the parcels of Chardonnay account for the majority of Cuvaison's Carneros vineyard. Thacher makes two styles of Chardonnay: a regular Carneros blend and (since 1986) an oakier, less forward Reserve. He works with five distinct clones and harvests grapes from a number of different exposures. Controlling his own grapes is a crucial factor: 'People have begun to realize that you either have the grapes or you don't.'

In the winery, Thacher favours a policy of minimal intervention. 'We are almost religious about how much we touch our Chardonnay,' he says. 'A vintage has its own intrinsic nature. You can rein it in a bit, but you can't alter it fundamentally.'

Most of Cuvaison's Chardonnay is barrel-fermented (using oak from six different coopers): 90 per cent for the Reserve, 70 per cent for the Carneros blend. Malolactic varies from vintage to vintage, between 5 and 50 per cent, with a higher percentage in the Reserve. Both wines stay in (30 to 80 per cent new) oak for up to six months, but never seem excessively woody. Like all Cuvaison's wines, they are complex, well-structured and have the ability to age. As the Carneros vineyard matures, the wines should improve even further.

DE LOACH

1791 Olivet Road, Santa Rosa, 95401 California

Chardonnay vineyard: 54 acres

Production of Chardonnay: 264,000 bottles

Labels: Russian River Valley; Chardonnay OFS

Quality: 🍇🍇🍇   Price: ★★★/★★★★

Best vintages: 1984, 1985, 1987, 1988, 1989

Cecil De Loach gave up his job as a San Francisco fireman to found this excellent Sonoma County winery in 1975, producing his first wines four years later. The fire brigade's loss was our gain, as De Loach produces some of the most intense Chardonnays in California, with a sweet, but balanced tropical-fruit and oak character that makes them easy to appreciate when young. Levels of residual sugar were excessive in the first few vintages, possibly because of De Loach's failure to select a suitable fermentation yeast, but have been toned down in recent years. Some tasters still find the wines a little cloying.

De Loach makes two Chardonnays – Russian River Valley and a Reserve wine called OFS (Our Finest Selection) – using grapes from his own Russian River vineyards. OFS is made with free-run juice, is entirely barrel-fermented and goes through 70–100 per cent malolactic; the Russian River Chardonnay is only 50 per cent barrel-fermented with no more than 60 per cent malolactic.

OFS tends to mature better than the early-drinking Russian River bottling but, given their depth of flavour, both wines display a surprising amount of finesse. This is California Chardonnay at its most seductive, with delightful, easy-drinking fruit and considerable concentration.

EDNA VALLEY

2585 Biddle Ranch Road, San Luis Obispo, 93449 California

Chardonnay vineyard: 305 acres (505 acres by 1994)

Production of Chardonnay: 600,000 bottles; 1 million bottles by 1994

Quality: 🍇🍇🍇   Price: ★★★

Best vintages: 1982, 1984, 1987, 1988, 1989

Steve Dooley is convinced that the Edna Valley, just south of the town of San Luis Obispo, on the Central Coast of California, is the ideal region for growing Chardonnay. Given that he makes the wine at Edna Valley, the largest member of the four-strong Chalone group, he could be accused of partiality, but this cool, fog-bound basin, 10 kilometres from the Pacific, has certainly proved its worth as a source of Chardonnay over the last decade.

The first Chardonnay was planted here, by the Paragon Vineyard Company, in 1973, and from 1977 (the initial vintage) to 1979, the wine was made at Chalone in Monterey County. Edna Valley work with a number of clones, including one from the Stony Hill vineyard, all of which are planted on their own roots in well-drained alluvial soil.

In 1980 Chalone formed a partnership with Paragon and set up a winery at Edna Valley. Edna specializes, like Chalone and Acacia, in Pinot Noir and Chardonnay. I find its Pinot Noirs rather jammy, but the Chardonnays are consistently good. The whole winery was designed to produce Chardonnay in a French style and, as Dooley puts it, 'with grapes like this, you'd have to try to screw it up'.

Production has increased considerably over the years, from 12,000 bottles to a projected 1 million by 1994, but this has not had an adverse effect on quality. The wine-making at Edna Valley follows the pattern established by Dick Graff at Chalone in the early sixties, with barrel-fermentation in new, one- and two-year-old oak, lees contact and full malolactic. The wine remains in barrel for nine months and is racked only once.

The Edna Valley style is for rich, full-bodied wines, sometimes with as much as 10 per cent botrytis, that nevertheless have good levels of natural acidity. The climate is much cooler here than in Northern California, and the grapes are often not picked until the second week of October. There are two wines: the basic estate Chardonnay and a Reserve, fermented entirely in new Sirugue oak. If anything, the wines have improved since Dooley's arrival in 1987: the oak is more subtle, the fruit more complex. Can he work the same magic with a million bottles? We shall have to wait and see.

FAR NIENTE

PO Box 327, Oakville, 94562 California

Chardonnay vineyard: 100 acres

Production of Chardonnay: 290,000 bottles

Labels: Napa Valley; Estate (in 1982 and 1983)

Quality: 🍇🍇🍇   Price: ★★★★

Best vintages: 1981, 1982, 1985, 1987, 1988

The name of this historic stone winery, situated just south of Oakville, comes from an old Italian saying, *dolce far niente*, or 'idling is sweet'. In one sense, nothing could be less apposite. Far Niente, which looks like an imposing Highland distillery, is one of California's oldest estates and you don't stay in production that long without expending a bit of effort. In another, the name given to the winery by founder John Benson, way back in 1885, proved curiously prophetic. Far Niente stopped making wine during Prohibition and lay idle for more than sixty years.

Since the winery reopened in 1979, with Oklahoma entrepreneur Gil Nickel in charge, the emphasis has been on Chardonnay and (more recently) Cabernet Sauvignon. Far Niente's production of the latter variety accounts for two-thirds of its output. Initially the grapes were bought in, but with successive vintages the percentage of production from Far Niente's own three vineyards – one in Oakville behind the winery and two in Coombsville, to the east of Napa (the city, not the region) – has increased. Since 1991 Far Niente has been self-sufficient.

The winery's fresh-faced oenologist, Dirk Hampson, has done wine-making stints at Schloss Vollrads, Château Mouton-Rothschild and Labouré-Roi, but the style of Chardonnay he has produced here since 1982 is distinctly Californian. The grapes are given prolonged skin contact, begin their fermentation in stainless steel and complete it in one-third new oak barrels. The wine is aged on its lees for approximately seven months and does not go through malolactic fermentation.

The Far Niente style is at the big and fruity end of the California spectrum, often showing too much oak when young, but with enough underlying acidity to age. I sometimes find the wines lacking in finesse, although a vertical tasting going back to 1979 proved that, in some vintages, the wines can age superbly. Far Niente's Chardonnays are almost among the most expensive in the Napa Valley. In years like 1988, 1985, 1982 and 1981, they're definitely worth the money.

FERRARI-CARANO

8761 Dry Creek Road, PO Box 1549, Healdsburg, 95448 California

Chardonnay vineyard: 180 acres

Production of Chardonnay: 380,000 bottles

Labels: Alexander Valley; California Reserve

Quality: 🍇🍇🍇🍇   Price: ★★★—★★★★★

Best vintages: 1985, 1986, 1987, 1988, 1989

In the best American tradition, Ferrari-Carano has come a long way in a very short space of time, producing a string of spectacular Chardonnays since its first release in 1985. This modern Dry Creek Valley winery is the creation of Don Carano, a Nevada lawyer and casino-owner, and his wife Rhonda. The couple have big plans for Ferrari-Carano, including a huge Italianate villa adjoining the winery. The flower budget alone is bigger than some wineries' entire marketing spend. They have also been buying up prime vineyard land over the last decade as if it were going out of fashion, and now own well over five hundred acres in Alexander Valley, Dry Creek and Carneros.

The style of Chardonnay here emphasizes complexity. Wine-maker George Bursick blends nearly a dozen distinct vineyard lots and works with a number of different fermentation yeasts and sources of oak. He produces two Chardonnays: Alexander Valley and smaller quantities of Reserve wine, most of which comes from Carneros. Bursick uses 85 per cent French barrel-fermentation, up to 30 per cent malolactic and prolonged lees contact to make nuanced, multifaceted wines.

The Reserve, made with fruit from a cooler climate, tends to be tighter-knit. The Alexander Valley Chardonnay is sweeter and ready to drink on release, but will keep for two to five years. The 1989 has a wonderfully dense, chewy texture with oak and fruit in mellifluous harmony. It confirms Ferrari-Carano's standing as one of California's top Chardonnay producers. The 1988 Reserve is better still, with more structure and length.

FLORA SPRINGS

1978 West Zinfandel Lane, St Helena, 94574 California

Chardonnay vineyard: 98 acres

Production of Chardonnay: 160,000 bottles

Labels: Estate; Barrel Fermented

Quality: 🌿🌿🌿🌿   Price: ★★★/★★★★

Best vintages: 1983, 1985, 1986 (Estate only), 1987, 1988, 1989, 1990

Situated midway between the towns of St Helena and Ruther-ford, Flora Springs' old stone cellar is a Napa Valley landmark. Originally known, pre-Prohibition, as the Rennie Brothers winery, it subsequently served as Louis Martini's sherry store, but had fallen into disrepair by the time Jerry and Flora Komes bought the abandoned property in 1977, and renamed it Flora Springs.

The Komes and Garvey families, associated by marriage, own more than 400 acres of Napa Valley vineyard between them, and Flora Springs creams off the best grapes, using approximately 20 per cent of the total production. Most of the winery's Chardonnay comes from two sources: the P&J Ranch in St Helena and the Crossroads Ranch in Oakville. 'Our grapes are from mid-valley vineyards,' says long-time wine-maker Ken Deis, 'that's the deck of cards we've been dealt. If we ignored the fruit character, we'd be passing up what the vineyard gives us.'

Flora Springs specializes in rich, fruity Chardonnays. There are two separate bottlings: an early-drinking Estate wine and a more leesy, buttery reserve, called Barrel Fermented. The Estate Chardonnay completes its fermentation in two- to five-year-old French oak, whereas the Barrel Fermented is entirely vinified in new and one-year-old oak. Neither wine goes through malolactic, although the Barrel Fermented has ben-efited from extensive lees stirring since 1987.

The latter wine is one of California's most flavoursome Chardonnays, packed with flavours of honey, peach and butter-scotch; the Estate is more tropical in character, with mango, pineapple and guava. Flora Springs' Barrel Fermented is the supreme expression of forceful, densely textured Napa Chardonnay, but it is also a wine that can age for up to eight years. The superlative 1983 is still very much alive and kicking.

FORMAN

PO Box 343, St Helena, 94574 California

Chardonnay vineyard: 35 acres

Production of Chardonnay: 24,000 bottles

Quality: 🍇🍇🍇🍇   Price: ★★★/★★★★

Best vintages: 1985, 1986, 1988, 1990

Ric Forman worked at Stony Hill, Robert Mondavi, Sterling and Newton wineries (not a bad grounding in Chardonnay) before setting up his own one-man operation on the western slopes of Howell Mountain in 1983, after falling out with former partner, Peter Newton. The winery was set up on a patch of land that was literally blasted out of the mountainside – a suitably dramatic opening chapter for a highly individualistic wine-maker – although most of Forman's Chardonnay comes from the Napa Valley floor.

Forman makes two wines – a Chardonnay and a Cabernet Sauvignon – and both have garnered high praise over the last decade. The Chardonnay, definitely one of California's finest, is barrel-fermented and aged in new oak, but the splinters never seem to get in the way of the fruit. Not a toothpick wine. The Chardonnay spends up to seven months on its lees, but does not go through malolactic. It certainly has the ability to age in bottle, although its complex, spicy fruit is very attractive when young. Forman says that, if he had his way, he wouldn't make any white wine at all. Nevertheless, the 1986 and 1990 are two of the finest California Chardonnays I have tasted.

FROG'S LEAP

3358 St Helena Highway, St Helena, 94574 California

Chardonnay production: 45,000 bottles

Quality: 🍇🍇🍇   Price: ★★★

Best vintages: 1984, 1986, 1988, 1990

Frog's Leap is a rare find, a winery with a sense of humour. Despite the joke name, this is a serious Napa Valley operation, making excellent Chardonnay and Cabernet Sauvignon and fresh, drinkable Sauvignon Blanc. Frog's Leap (whose motto is 'Time's Fun When You're Having Flies') is situated on the site of a nineteenth-century frog farm, and the current owners – Larry Turley and John Williams – came up with the spoof name sitting in a hot tub one afternoon. Today, the winery is covered in frogs: paper frogs, metal frogs, plastic frogs, stone frogs. Even the telephone is frog-shaped.

John Williams worked at Stag's Leap and Spring Mountain wineries before setting up with Turley, a local casualty doctor, in 1981. The winery is run by three people: Turley, Williams and his wife, Julie. They buy most of their grapes from Napa Valley growers, although John Williams does have two vineyards of his own, planted with Cabernet Sauvignon and Zinfandel.

John Williams makes two different Chardonnays, one from the Napa Valley, the other from Carneros. Both wines are pleasingly restrained, although the influence of French oak is quite marked. Williams ferments his wine, using wild-yeast strains, in 25 per cent new *barriques*. Neither wine goes through malolactic fermentation.

Of the two, the Napa Chardonnay is generally fatter and more pineappley; the superior Carneros Chardonnay is closer to a wine from the Côte de Beaune, with toasty cinnamon and apple fruit. The 1988 Carneros Chardonnay was particularly good.

GLEN ELLEN

1883 London Ranch Road, 95442 California

Production of Chardonnay: 15.5 million bottles

Labels: Proprietor's Reserve; Benziger of Glen Ellen

Quality: 🍇   Price: ★/★★

Best vintages: 1984, 1985, 1987, 1990

Any operation that sells over 15 million bottles of Chardonnay a year has got to have something going for it and, sure enough, this dynamic, family-owned Sonoma County winery produces one of the most appealing, inexpensive brands available. Glen Ellen does not own any Chardonnay vineyards, preferring to work with 102 different growers in Sonoma, Napa, Monterey and Mendocino. The aim is to blend wine from various sources to achieve a consistent style.

The formula is clearly a success. The Proprietor's Reserve has introduced numerous people to wine in general, and to Chardonnay in particular. It's clean, off-dry and tastes like a cross between Muscat and ripe, tropical-fruit Chardonnay. The wine is stainless-steel-fermented, though a small percentage is aged in heavily toasted French oak for three to four months.

In an attempt to break out of the lower 'fighting varietal' end of the market, the Benziger family, which owns Glen Ellen, has introduced a range of upbeat wines dedicated to Bruno Benziger, the man who founded this incredibly successful winery a little over a decade ago. The first, barrel-fermented Chardonnay release was the 1987. The 1989 is a dry, ripe commercial style with good acidity.

GRGICH HILLS

PO Box 450, Rutherford, 94573 California

Chardonnay vineyard: 170 acres

Production of Chardonnay: 300,000 bottles

Quality: 🍇🍇🍇   Price: ★★★★

Best vintages: 1985, 1986, 1988

Miljenko 'Mike' Grgich is one of the great old characters of the California wine industry, a small dynamic Yugoslav distinguished by his natty French beret and creative use of the English language. Grgich's contribution to Chardonnay production in California is significant. It was he who made the 1973 Montelena Chardonnay which defeated a host of well-known Burgundies in Steven Spurrier's famous Paris tasting in 1976. Before that he worked at the Robert Mondavi Winery and at Beaulieu Vineyard under André Tchelistcheff.

Grgich Hills was set up in 1977 and has produced a string of highly rated Chardonnays. Whereas the Montelena Chardonnay was fermented in stainless steel, the Grgich Hills style is built on barrel fermentation in 35 per cent new Limousin oak. Grgich used Limousin at Mondavi and at Montelena and is happy with the results. Most people agree with his taste – Grgich Hills has attained cult status in California – but I find the wines less interesting than many top Napa Chardonnays.

The origin of the wood is significant. Limousin is a coarse oak, rarely employed for anything but spirits in France, and I find it gives an aggressive, sawdusty character to Grgich's Chardonnays. The wine stays in barrel for up to ten months, but does not go through malolactic fermentation. With this amount of new oak, it is too long.

The fruit that Grgich uses comes from four different vineyards, in Carneros, Yountville, Napa and Rutherford, with Carneros fruit accounting for half of the blend. The resulting wines are crisp, well-structured and long-lived, but they never lose that Limousin oak flavour. Pity.

HANZELL

18596 Lomita Avenue, Sonoma, 95476 California

Chardonnay vineyard: 17 acres

Production of Chardonnay: 21,600 bottles

Quality: 🍇   Price: ★★★★

Best vintages: 1980, 1982, 1985, 1990

When the American diplomat James Zellerbach planted his first Chardonnay and Pinot Noir cuttings in the hills overlooking the town of Sonoma, way back in 1952, he could hardly have imagined the effect he would have on the California wine industry. Zellerbach, the modern pioneer of Burgundian varietals in California, died in 1963, before the state's romance with Chardonnay had really begun, but his winery still stands and under its British owners, the De Brye family, it has continued to produce wines that are true to the spirit of its founder.

Zellerbach's greatest contribution to California wine was the introduction of stainless-steel fermentation and French-barrel ageing. Hanzell's Chardonnays have never been entirely Burgundian in style, however: malolactic fermentation never goes above 30 per cent and lees contact is kept to a minimum. Wine-maker Bob Sessions has also persevered with eight to ten hours' skin contact before the juice is racked to the original stainless-steel tanks, a practice that would find little favour in Burgundy.

Since 1965, Hanzell has produced only one Chardonnay bottling from its sloping, spectacularly sited Sonoma vineyards. These wines have been remarkably consistent over the years: rich, ripe, alcoholic and flavoursome. These are old-fashioned Chardonnays that age better than one would expect, developing an unctuous, almost honeyed character. There are two problems here: the site is too warm for Chardonnay, and the wines are a little too rustic for my taste.

IRON HORSE

9786 Ross Station Road, Sebastopol, 95472 California

Chardonnay vineyard: 80 acres; 105 acres by 1995

Production of Chardonnay: 12,000 bottles of Blanc de Blancs; 85,000 bottles of Chardonnay

Quality: 🍷🍷🍷🍷   Price: ★★★

Best vintages: 1984, 1985, 1987 (Blanc de Blancs); 1987, 1989, 1990 (Chardonnay)

Iron Horse, California's finest sparkling-wine producer, is situated in Green Valley, one of California's coolest growing regions. Known locally as Sonoma's answer to Siberia, Green Valley gets so cold in spring that frosts are a real danger. This

marginal climate is ideal for the production of premium sparkling wines, yielding intensely flavoured grapes. 'To make
sparkling wines,' says partner and wine-maker Forrest
Tancer, 'you've got to be in the right area. You can't just pick
early in the wrong place.'

When the first vineyards were planted here in 1971, there
was a good deal of local consternation, on account of the
marginal climate. This did not discourage corporate lawyer and
prominent Democrat Barry Sterling, who bought the 300-acre
property in 1976 and built his own winery three years later. It
was not until the early eighties that Iron Horse began to produce fizz, however.

Tancer makes five different sparkling wines as well as a range
of table wines from Green Valley and his own vineyard in the
much warmer Alexander Valley. There are two Chardonnays at
Iron Horse: an elegant, sparkling Blanc de Blancs, aged for four
years before release; and a tight, lean Green Valley Chardonnay
that resembles a Chablis in structure. The latter Chardonnay
has improved enormously in recent vintages. It is barrel-
fermented with a maximum of 10 per cent malolactic, which
can make the wine a little austere when young. It does, on the
other hand, give the wine good ageing potential. It certainly
demonstrates the superb quality of Iron Horse's Green Valley
fruit, although the best place to taste it is unquestionably in the
Blanc de Blancs.

KENDALL-JACKSON

600 Matthews Road, Lakeport, 95453 California

Chardonnay vineyard: 1,200 acres

Production of Chardonnay: 7.2 million bottles

Labels: Vintner's Reserve; The Proprietor's Grand
   Reserve; Durell Vineyard; Dennison Vineyard; DuPratt
   Vineyard; Camelot Vineyard; Stone Street Vineyard

Quality: 🍇🍇🍇   Price: ★★/★★★

Best vintages: 1986, 1987, 1988, 1990

In under twenty years Jess Jackson, a successful constitutional lawyer, has turned an 80-acre pear and walnut ranch just south of Lakeport into one of the California wine industry's great success stories. Jackson planted his first 30 acres in 1975, produced his first 200,000 bottles of Chardonnay (from growers all over California as well as his own vines) in 1982, and now makes something in the region of 600,000 cases of Chardonnay per annum. From a standing start, Kendall-Jackson's Vintner's Reserve has become one of the five largest Chardonnay brands in the United States.

Kendall-Jackson's phenomenal success can be put down to four things: the business acumen of Jess Jackson, consistency, reasonable prices and the wine-making of Jedediah Tecumseh ('Jed') Steele, who joined the winery in 1983. In 1990, Kendall-Jackson further strengthened its wine-making team by hiring John Hawley from Clos du Bois. Steele left in 1991 to set up his own winery in Lake County.

Jess Jackson has always believed that blended is best, at least as far as Chardonnay is concerned. The 1990 Vintner's Reserve, with its soft, gluggable fruit, was made from thirty different vineyards in no fewer than five coastal counties. In 1987, Jackson bought 700 acres of the Tepusquet Vineyard in Santa Barbara, which has become the winery's main source of Chardonnay. Jackson also owns vines in Sonoma, Monterey, Lake and Mendocino Counties, but continues to supplement his considerable requirements by buying grapes from all over the state.

Kendall-Jackson's most famous wine is its Vintner's Reserve, but it also makes 25,000 cases of The Proprietor's Chardonnay and (since 1984) much smaller bottlings from individual vineyards in the Sonoma, Anderson and Redwood Valleys, as well as some pretty decent reds.

Every single drop of Chardonnay is barrel-fermented, with at least 70 per cent of each blend undergoing malolactic fermentation. The winery has been criticized for leaving around six grams of residual sugar in some of its wines, making them more appealing when young. The criticism seems irrelevant to me. The Vintner's Reserve is clearly a style of wine that people like

– at an affordable price. Kendall-Jackson is also more than a single brand. In good vintages, its Proprietor's Grand Reserve and Durell Vineyard wines are up there with the best Chardonnays in California.

KISTLER

2207 Morningside Mountain Drive, Glen Ellen, 95442 California

Chardonnay vineyard: 42 acres (23 at Kistler Estate, 19 at Vine Hill Road)

Production of Chardonnay: 140,000 bottles

Labels: Kistler Estate Vineyard; Durell Vineyard; Dutton Ranch; McCrea Vineyard; Sonoma County; Vine Hill Road Vineyard

Quality: ♥♥♥–♥♥♥♥♥   Price: ★★★/★★★★★

Best vintages: 1986, 1987, 1988, 1989

In a characteristically quiet, unassuming way Steve Kistler has emerged as one of California's Chardonnay superstars over the last few years. Kistler and partner Mark Bixler made their first three Chardonnays (with purchased fruit from Dutton Ranch in Green Valley, Sonoma-Cutrer's Cutrer Vineyard and Winery Lake in Carneros) in 1979, and the wines received enthusiastic critical support. The 1980 vintage, which was eventually withdrawn from sale, was marred by a pronounced sulphide character, but since that nadir, Kistler Vineyards has recovered to establish itself as a top-notch Chardonnay specialist.

Kistler makes no fewer than six different Chardonnays: two from his own vines, Kistler Estate and Vine Hill Road Vineyard; three from outstanding Sonoma County growers (Durell Vineyard, Dutton Ranch and McCrea Vineyard); and a cheaper Sonoma County blend.

All six wines are extremely fine Chardonnays, produced in a deliberately Burgundian style, although a bit of rationalization would not necessarily be a bad thing. 'Our wines', says Kistler, 'reflect our commitment to the art of wine-making in Burgundy.' Accordingly, Kistler uses barrel fermentation, full malolactic and extended lees contact. His faith in *terroir* is also very Burgundian: the differences between the wines, he feels, are the result of vineyard location, soil and microclimate.

Six Chardonnays may seem too many, not least in commercial terms, but Kistler remains dedicated to the idea of single-vineyard wines. He made his first Kistler Estate Chardonnay in 1986, using an old clone from Martin Ray's Mount Eden Vineyard, and a second estate wine, from his Vine Hill Road Vineyard, in 1990. Throughout the eighties, he also turned out a series of vineyard-designated Chardonnays from bought-in fruit. The McCrea Vineyard is a comparatively recent supplier (1988 being the first vintage), as is the Durell Vineyard (1986), but Dutton Ranch has been a Kistler source since the start.

Kistler favours low-yielding clones, and produces correspondingly well-structured wines. My favourites are the Dutton Ranch and Kistler Estate Chardonnays, but you can't go wrong with any of these wines. My only caveat is Kistler's Burgundian-style prices.

LONG VINEYARDS

PO Box 50, St Helena, 94574 California

Chardonnay vineyard: 14 acres

Production of Chardonnay: 24,000 bottles

Quality: 🍇🍇🍇🍇   Price: ★★★★★

Best vintages: 1985, 1986, 1987, 1988

Tucked away in the hills above St Helena, with a spectacular view of Lake Hennessy, Long Vineyards has developed a remarkable following for its elegant, well-balanced Chardonnays. It was founded by Bob Long and his then wife Zelma (of

Simi winery fame) in the late sixties, releasing its first wine in 1977. The couple are divorced now, but they continue to work amicably together as business partners.

'When we planted here,' says Bob Long, 'very little was known about hillside vineyards. We picked it because it was a nice place.' Sure is. The initial plan was to specialize in Riesling and 'some high-risk Chardonnay'. The risk paid off. Long continues to produce a little bit of Cabernet Sauvignon, Sauvignon Blanc and Riesling, but the winery's main focus is Chardonnay. At 40 hl/ha, Chardonnay yields are low here, and the wines have a corresponding intensity of flavour. Most of the vineyard is planted with an old Louis Martini clone, which imparts a pronounced spicy, almost Muscatty, flavour to the wines.

Bob Long's Chardonnay is entirely barrel-fermented, in a consciously Burgundian style. He uses little or no new oak, and puts the wine through full malolactic fermentation. The wines have good natural acidity, none the less. There are two reasons for this. First, most of the Chardonnay vineyard is north-facing; and, second, it is usually a few degrees cooler up in the hills than down on the Napa Valley floor. Long's Chardonnays are not cheap, but they can be very fine indeed. They are definitely wines that age well – the 1986 still has some life in it, and the superlative 1988 will take at least eight years to reach its peak.

MATANZAS CREEK

> 6097 Bennett Valley Road, Santa Rosa, 95404 California
>
> Chardonnay vineyard: 30 acres
>
> Production of Chardonnay: 200,000 bottles
>
> Quality: 🍇🍇🍇🍇   Price: ★★★
>
> Best vintages: 1985, 1987, 1988, 1989

Matanzas Creek makes some of the most elegant, understated Chardonnays in California. The style has evolved considerably since Sandra and Bill MacIver produced their first Chardonnay in 1979. The blowsy richness of the early wines has been toned down, resulting in wines with better structure and ageing potential.

The winery's reputation as a Chardonnay producer owes much to the talents of Dave Ramey, who made the wines between 1984 and 1987. It was Ramey who introduced barrel-fermentation and other Burgundian techniques learned at Simi winery. The spectacular 1987, made in Ramey's last vintage, was the first to benefit from full malolactic fermentation, and still has a long life ahead of it. Since 1988 the wines have been made by Susan Reed and Bill Parker.

One-third of Matanzas Creek's Chardonnay comes from their own vineyards in Sonoma County's Bennett Valley; the rest is bought from growers in Carneros, Sonoma Mountain and the Russian River Valley. The recent increase in production does not appear to have affected the winery's high standards.

PETER MICHAEL WINERY

16485 Highway 128, Calistoga, 94515 California

Chardonnay vineyard: 17 acres

Production of Chardonnay: 120,000 bottles

Labels: Mon Plaisir; Howell Mountain Cuvée; Cuvée Indigène

Quality: 🍇🍇🍇/🍇🍇🍇🍇   Price: ★★★

Best vintages: 1987, 1988, 1989

Sir Peter Michael, English multimillionaire and chairman of Cray Electronics, bought a 600-acre estate at the foot of Mount St Helena, in Sonoma County's picturesque Knight's Valley, in 1982. He planted vines – a 25-acre vineyard of Cabernet Sauvignon, Merlot and Cabernet Franc called Les Pavots and a smaller, 20-acre plot of Chardonnay (Adobe II) in Sonoma Valley – the following year, producing his first wines in 1987. A second 30-acre Chardonnay vineyard, Peregrine, has been planted at 1,800 feet and will be in full production by 1993. The eventual aim is to produce a maximum of 15,000 cases of Chardonnay and Cabernet Sauvignon.

The Peter Michael winery complex, completed in 1989, is housed in the former town hall and schoolhouse of the old town of Kellogg, and was the first such building to be constructed in Knight's Valley in more than one hundred years. Initial vintages of Chardonnay have been extremely promising, with rich but well-balanced fruit and oak. The wines were made in 1987, 1988 and 1989 by Helen Turley, sister of one of the partners at Frog's Leap, but Mark Aubert is now in charge. He has continued the tradition of 75 per cent new barrels, full malolactic fermentation and lees stirring. An estate to watch.

ROBERT MONDAVI WINERY

7801 St Helena Highway, Oakville, 94562 California

Chardonnay vineyard: 77 acres (Oak Knoll); 258 acres (Carneros); 137 acres (Santa Barbara)

Production of Chardonnay: 1.2 million bottles (Robert Mondavi); 1.8 million bottles (Woodbridge)

Labels: Napa Valley; Barrel Fermented Reserve

Quality: 🍇🍇–🍇🍇🍇🍇🍇   Price: ★★★/★★★★

Best vintages: 1983, 1985, 1986, 1987, 1988

With its college-style lawns, Mediterranean architecture and summer jazz festivals, the Robert Mondavi Winery is a Napa Valley showpiece. In the best theatrical tradition, the relaxed atmosphere front of house conceals a hive of off-stage activity. Mondavi may feel like a cosy, boutique operation but, make no mistake, this is the big league, with a total production of more than 2 million cases. At Oakville alone, the smaller of its two wineries, there are eight full-time tour guides.

Set up by Robert Mondavi in 1966, his eponymous creation has consistently been at the forefront of research, development and marketing in California. If California wines enjoy international standing today, it is Mondavi who can take much of the credit. This is not to say that his wines are always the finest in the state – the volumes are simply too large for that – but Mondavi wines are rarely anything less than drinkable. In the case of three of the Reserve wines (Pinot Noir, Chardonnay and Cabernet Sauvignon), they are a good deal more complex than that.

If much of the winery's early reputation was based on its Cabernet Sauvignons, it has invested a good deal of time and effort in improving its Chardonnays over the last decade. The style has moved around a bit but, since 1987, all Mondavi's Chardonnay has been barrel-fermented. There are three different bottlings: a Napa Valley blend; a Reserve; and, since 1989, a cheaper Woodbridge Chardonnay, mainly from Santa Barbara County fruit.

The grapes for all three wines come from Mondavi's own plantings in Yountville and Santa Barbara, and from contract growers. In 1988, the winery purchased a large area of land in Carneros, and will have a further 258 acres of Chardonnay to play with by 1993.

The Reserve is the richest, most interesting wine, with full malolactic and a high percentage of new oak. Delicious when young, the wine does not always age particularly well, but as the Carneros plantings mature, the structure of the wine (and its ability to develop in bottle) may change. Whatever happens, you can be sure that Robert Mondavi's son Tim and his large team of oenologists will continue to ask questions. So far, they've come up with most, but not all, of the right answers.

MOUNT EDEN VINEYARDS

22020 Mount Eden Road, Saratoga, 95070 California

Vineyard: 25 acres

Production: 12,000 bottles (Mount Eden); 60,000 bottles (Edna Valley)

Labels: Mount Eden; MacGregor Vineyard (Edna Valley)

Quality: 🍇🍇🍇🍇🍇   Price: ★★/★★★★★

Best vintages: 1981, 1984, 1986, 1987, 1988, 1990

By Californian standards, where the 1950s are considered ancient history, Mount Eden is an old winery. Created by the late Martin Ray, Mount Eden continues to produce excellent Chardonnay and Pinot Noir, although it now belongs to an investment group called the MEV Corporation.

Ray played an important part in the development of California Chardonnay. He was, according to Dick Graff at Chalone, the first person in California to ferment and age his wine in small new French oak barrels. As long ago as the early sixties, Ray was making his Chardonnay in a Burgundian style. It took most Californians another twenty-five years to catch up.

The Chardonnay vines at Mount Eden, beautifully situated in the Santa Cruz Mountains to the south of San Francisco, are some of the oldest in the state, and produce wines of low yield and great concentration. Some of the Chardonnays from the early seventies have begun to fade now, but the best vintages of the eighties, produced by oenologist Jeffrey Paterson, have the structure to age for at least a decade. The 1981 was still full of life when tasted in October 1991.

Paterson's wine-making follows broad Burgundian precepts. The grapes are picked ripe, then fermented in new and one-year-old barrels. All the wine goes through malolactic, with racking off the gross lees in November, and bottling the following June.

The estate-bottled Chardonnay is much sought-after and sells at an elevated price. Deservedly so, for this is a truly brilliant wine. Since 1985, Mount Eden has also produced a second wine, MacGregor Vineyard, from bought-in grapes in the Edna Valley. The MacGregor Chardonnay sees less new oak and receives only 75 per cent malolactic, and tends to be a more forward, easy-drinking wine than the Mount Eden estate Chardonnay.

NEWTON VINEYARD

2555 Madrona Avenue, PO Box 340, St Helena, 94574 California

Chardonnay production: 72,000 bottles

Labels: Newton Chardonnay; Lot 2

Quality: 🍇🍇🍇🍇   Price: ★★/★★★

Best vintages: 1987, 1988, 1989, 1990

Peter Newton is an unusual figure to come across in the Napa Valley. A former *Financial Times* leader-writer, he has lived in California since 1964, but remains every inch an Englishman, right down to his polka-dot cravat and fondness for Latin quotations. Newton founded a paper-manufacturing company, Sterling International, in 1953 and, by now a wealthy man, set up Sterling Vineyards, in the Napa Valley, eleven years later.

Newton sold his 75 per cent interest in Sterling Vineyards in 1979 to create a new venture, overlooking the valley in the hills above St Helena. The pagoda-style winery, designed by Newton's energetic, polymathic Chinese wife, Su Hua, is extremely striking; so are the vineyards, carved out of the forest and, in some cases, so steep that they remind you of the Mosel in Germany.

Newton specializes in Bordeaux-style red wines, but its Chardonnays are also impressive. Since 1988, the wines have improved dramatically. None of the winery's 110 acres is planted with the grape; an early, unsuccessful vineyard was grafted over to Cabernet Sauvignon. All Newton's Chardonnay is purchased from contract growers, mainly in Carneros.

The first Chardonnay was made in 1981, and some of the early bottlings (particularly the 1983) have held up well. The wine today is (50 per cent new) barrel-fermented, goes through full malolactic and remains in oak for as long as twenty months. The 1988 and 1987 are extremely promising, with enough citrus and pineapple fruit and concentration to balance the pronounced flavour of oak. Both wines have a surprising amount of finesse and should age for at least five years. The 1989 is even better – a real achievement in a difficult vintage. In 1988, Newton introduced a second label Chardonnay, called Lot 2, which is also well up to scratch.

PINE RIDGE

PO Box 2508, Yountville, 94599 California

Chardonnay vineyard: 56 acres

Production of Chardonnay: 160,000 bottles

Labels: Knollside; Stag's Leap Vineyard

Quality: 🍇🍇🍇/🍇🍇🍇🍇   Price: ★★★/★★★★

Best vintages: 1985, 1987, 1990

Gary Andrus, a former Olympic skier, moved to the Napa Valley with his wife Nancy in 1978, purchasing one of California's oldest Chardonnay vineyards. Andrus produced his first Stag's Leap Vineyard Chardonnay in 1979, although the wine was actually made at Clos du Val in Sonoma: Andrus's own winery was not constructed until the following year.

In 1981, he introduced a second Chardonnay (called Oak Knoll until 1984 and, subsequently, Knollside). This is a blend of grapes (some of them purchased) from a marginally cooler area to the south of Yountville, and tends to be the more restrained of the two bottlings. Andrus also makes good Bordeaux blends and an outstanding Chenin Blanc.

Chardonnay vinification techniques at Pine Ridge are very Burgundian: barrel-fermentation in (one-third new) French oak, full malolactic and extended lees contact. But Andrus is not a formula wine-maker by any means; he is constantly experimenting with fermentation yeasts and different types of oak, and his care is reflected in the wines.

These are rich, complex, multifaceted Chardonnays which can develop a character impressively close to fine White Burgundy. The Stag's Leap Vineyard, produced in part from low-yielding vines planted in 1964, is particularly good. The wines will usually age for four to five years, but not much more. Recent vintages, namely 1988 and 1989, have been marred by a certain amount of bottle variation. The 1990s are back on song.

SAINTSBURY

1500 Los Carneros Avenue, Napa, 94559 California

Chardonnay production: 200,000 bottles

Quality: 🍇🍇🍇🍇   Price: ★★★

Best vintages: 1981, 1984, 1985, 1986, 1987, 1988, 1990

'Beaune in the USA' reads the slogan on this winery's bright blue T-shirts. Named after the famous English literary critic and wine writer, Professor George Saintsbury, it has more than lived up to its Burgundian role model since the amusing duo of David Graves and Richard Ward made their first Pinot Noir and Chardonnay in 1981. According to Ward, they chose the name Saintsbury because 'we kind of liked the old codger'.

Both varieties have been extremely successful at Saintsbury, and have settled in to an attractive house style: elegant, easy-drinking wines with lots of flavour but enough structure to age gracefully. The first Chardonnay release was still full of life when I last tasted it in 1991. The 1981 and the 1982, incidentally, were labelled Sonoma County, as Carneros did not become a delimited appellation until two years later.

Saintsbury does not own any Chardonnay vineyards of its own; instead it buys grapes exclusively from local Carneros growers, most of whose vines are on clay and loam soils. The source of fruit is significant: comparatively cool growing conditions produce Chardonnay that has excellent levels of natural acidity, something that Graves and Ward were among the first to realize. It is generally harder to find good Pinot Noir than Chardonnay on the open market, which is why Saintsbury's vineyards are all planted with Pinot Noir, but there are plans to extend the winery's vineyard holdings to include Chardonnay as well as Pinot Noir in the next few years.

Since 1986, Saintsbury has released a Reserve as well as its regular Carneros bottling. The only recent exception was 1989, the so-called 'harvest from hell', when the regular Carneros Chardonnay was still surprisingly good.

The two wines are made in much the same way, although the Reserve has a higher percentage of new oak and spends an additional two months on its lees. The Chardonnay is barrel-fermented in (30 per cent new) French oak, goes through full malolactic and, in the case of the Reserve, has up to eleven months on its lees. Despite going through malolactic, the wine never seems fat or unbalanced. In fact, Richard Ward thinks that malolactic actually helps the wine to age better.

Of recent vintages, 1988 and 1990 are the richest Chardonnays. The 1985, 1986 and 1987 are leaner and have taken longer to develop their full potential. The 1988 Reserve was one of the best California Chardonnays of the vintage, with exuberant, toasty fruit and wonderful poise. Of the older wines, the stars are the 1984 and the 1981.

SANFORD

7250 Santa Rosa Road, Buellton, Santa Barbara, 93427 California

Chardonnay vineyard: 8 acres

Production of Chardonnay: 240,000 bottles

Labels: Santa Barbara County; Barrel Select

Quality: 🍇🍇🍇🍇   Price: ★★★

Best vintages: 1985, 1986, 1987, 1988

Situated in a parking lot, a few feet from Highway 101, Sanford's unprepossessing location has not stopped it producing a string of excellent Chardonnays over the last few years. Not many of the world's great Chardonnays are made next door to something like the Valley Automotive Service.

Bruno D'Alfonso, the swarthy young wine-maker, worked at Edna Valley before moving to Sanford in 1983. The winery had already completed its first two vintages of Chardonnay, mostly using the same growers in Santa Barbara County's Sierra Madre and Santa Maria Hills as it does now. Owner Richard Sanford has subsequently added a 15-acre vineyard of his own which, once it matures, should give the winery more control over its raw material.

D'Alfonso likes to pick his grapes 'real ripe, preferably with sunburn and a bit of botrytis'. He acidifies when necessary, but the grapes usually have good natural acidity, thanks to the cool nights in the valleys of the Central Coast. It is significant that acidification has enabled him to make better wines in recent vintages.

The Sanford Chardonnay style is similar to that at Edna Valley, although D'Alfonso tends to settle and clean the juice more before fermentation. Sanford produces two Chardonnays: a regular bottling and, since 1985, a reserve wine called Barrel Select. Both wines are barrel-fermented, go through malolactic fermentation and spend time on their lees. The Barrel Select stays in (entirely new) Sirugue oak for as long as eighteen months; the regular Chardonnay nine months in 25 per cent new oak.

The winery really got into its stride in 1985, since when D'Alfonso has produced a string of concentrated, richly textured Chardonnays, with bags of nutty, butterscotch and vanilla flavours, proof that top-notch California Chardonnay doesn't have to be made north of San Francisco.

SILVERADO VINEYARDS

6121 Silverado Trail, Napa, 94558 California
Chardonnay vineyard: 150 acres
Production of Chardonnay: 500,000 bottles
Labels: Napa Valley; Limited Reserve
Quality: 🍇🍇🍇/🍇🍇🍇🍇   Price: ★★★
Best vintages: 1986, 1987, 1988, 1989

Known affectionately as 'the house that Mickey built',
Silverado is the creation of Walt Disney's widow, Lillian, and
her daughter and son-in-law, Diane and Ron Miller. The
partners originally bought two vineyards in the Napa Valley
(one in Stag's Leap, the other in Yountville) in the mid-
seventies, adding Sauvignon Blanc to the Chardonnay and
Cabernet Sauvignon already planted. They sold their grapes to
other producers before setting up their own picturesquely sited
winery overlooking the Silverado Trail in 1981.

Under wine-maker John Stuart, Silverado's Chardonnays
have got better and better since the first vintage. Stuart now
draws fruit from vineyards in Stag's Leap, Yountville, Coombsville and Carneros and the Silverado style of Chardonnay is still
evolving. The wine is 80 per cent barrel-fermented (in 20–25
per cent new oak) and half of it goes through malolactic fermentation. It stays on its lees for seven months, with
occasional *bâtonnage*, or stirring. Since 1986, Stuart has also
produced a Limited Reserve Chardonnay.

These are attractive, medium-priced wines for comparatively
early drinking. 'I don't want to impose a style on the wine,' says
Stuart, 'I want to learn its style from working with it.' He is
clearly listening – his Chardonnays are complex, often under-
rated, wines. Recent vintages have produced a string of rich,
harmonious Chardonnays. Mickey Mouse may have helped to
build Silverado, but these are very serious wines indeed.

*

SIMI

16275 Healdsburg Avenue, PO Box 698, Healdsburg,
95448 California

Chardonnay vineyard: 140 acres

Production of Chardonnay: 900,000 bottles

Quality: 🍇🍇🍇–🍇🍇🍇🍇🍇   Price: ★★★

Best vintages: 1980, 1982, 1985, 1986, 1987, 1989

The fortunes of this old Sonoma Valley winery have been
revived in the last decade by two things: money (in the shape of
the French luxury-goods giant Louis Vuitton Moët-Hennessy)
and the arrival of Zelma Long. It was Simi's then president,
Michael Dixon, who had the foresight to lure Long away from
the Robert Mondavi Winery where, as chief oenologist, she had
developed an impressive research programme as well as producing some superb wines.

When Long moved to Simi, she created a similar set up, with
considerable investment in stainless-steel tanks, new French
barrels and California's first must chiller. Next, Simi employed
the services of a full-time viticulturist, Diane Kenworthy. The
following year (1982) it started buying vineyard land in the
rolling hills of the south-eastern Alexander Valley. A more
recent purchase is a large 110-acre parcel, intended primarily
for Chardonnay, in the cool Russian River Valley. By 1993, this
property will be providing over half of Simi's Chardonnay
needs, the rest being bought in from Sonoma, Mendocino and
Napa growers.

Long and Kenworthy are committed to experimentation in
the winery and the vineyard, and there are ongoing trials with
trellising, clones, rootstocks, oak-ageing and malolactic. In
1989, Long was promoted to president of Simi, but she retains
an enormous influence over the Simi style.

There are two Chardonnay bottlings here: a very good basic
Sonoma/Mendocino blend and a Reserve. The Reserve is
entirely barrel-fermented, whereas the regular Chardonnay is

vinified half and half in stainless steel and oak. Both wines are aged in barrel, on their lees, for up to seven months. The portion of Chardonnay which goes through malolactic varies from 60 to 90 per cent.

Of the two wines, the one to look out for is the Reserve. Production is small at 24,000 bottles, but in recent vintages this has emerged as one of California's top dozen Chardonnays, a wine that is fit to stand alongside the great white Burgundies. I attended a Chardonnay conference in 1990 at which Gérard Boudot of Étienne Sauzet confidently identified a 1985 Simi Reserve as one of his own wines in a blind tasting. High praise indeed. The 1990 is the best Simi Reserve yet.

SONOMA-CUTRER

4401 Slusser Road, Windsor, 95492 California

Chardonnay vineyard: 520 acres

Production of Chardonnay: 900,000 bottles

Labels: Les Pierres; Cutrer Vineyard; Russian River Ranches

Quality: 🍇🍇🍇–🍇🍇🍇🍇🍇   Price: ★★★/★★★★

Best vintages: 1985, 1986, 1987, 1988

When Brice Jones, a former Vietnam fighter pilot and graduate of Harvard Business School, went looking for California vineyard land in the early seventies, he did so with a view to planting Cabernet Sauvignon. As there was nothing available in the warmer parts of Napa and Sonoma Counties, Jones bought land in the cooler climates of the Russian River Valley and Carneros. To his consternation, he discovered that the areas were best suited, not to Cabernet Sauvignon, but to Chardonnay, then a comparatively unimportant variety.

Fortuitously, his discovery coincided with the great white-wine boom of the mid-seventies, and as the vines started to bear fruit, Jones found that it was easy to find a market for his grapes. In 1981, he decided to sell wines under his own label and employed veteran California wine-maker Bill Bonetti to help him realize his ambition.

From the start, Jones resolved to specialize in Chardonnay. His elegant winery, north-west of Santa Rosa, despite its manicured croquet lawns and country-club patio, was designed to produce premium Chardonnay, and nothing else. 'You do not make great wines by chance,' says Bonetti, and at Sonoma-Cutrer, nothing is left to chance. The grapes are handled with obsessive care: sorted, chilled and pampered like starlets. Even the vineyards were planted so that, at one o'clock on 1 September, the sun shines right down the middle of the rows.

Sonoma-Cutrer produces three different Chardonnays from a total of five vineyards: four in the Russian River Valley and the fifth, Les Pierres, at the southern end of the Sonoma Valley, on the edge of the Carneros district. The most forward of the three is the Russian River Ranches Chardonnay, a blend of the Kent, Shiloh, Mirabelle and Cutrer vineyards. The second bottling comes entirely from the Cutrer vineyard, yielding full but well-structured wines. And Les Pierres, as its label suggests, is from the vineyard of the same name. Les Pierres is consistently the best wine of the three, often displaying a flinty character reminiscent of Chablis.

The differences between the three wines reflect Sonoma-Cutrer's comparatively un-Californian belief in the importance of *terroir*. All three are treated identically, although Les Pierres usually sees more new oak. Fermentation is carried out, at low temperatures, in Limousin oak, with 20–40 per cent malolactic and five months' lees contact. It may or may not be attributable to *terroir*, but Les Pierres is always the longest-lived of the Sonoma-Cutrer Chardonnays. Even so, it is best drunk after three to five years.

STAG'S LEAP

5766 Silverado Trail, Napa, 94558 California
Chardonnay production: 300,000 bottles
Labels: Stag's Leap; Hawk Crest
Quality: 🍇🍇–🍇🍇🍇🍇🍇   Price: ★★★
Best vintages: 1986, 1987, 1988

Warren Winiarski, one of the Napa Valley's great autodidacts, is better known for his concentrated, finely grained Cabernet Sauvignons than for his white wines, but the improvement in Stag's Leap's Chardonnays has been extremely impressive in recent vintages. Winiarski made his first Chardonnay as long ago as 1975, but has only struck gold since 1985, when he launched a Reserve wine made with primarily Carneros fruit.

Winiarski markets a total of five Chardonnays: three at Stag's Leap, and two called Hawk Crest, the winery's second label, which are made in Healdsburg. Stag's Leap owns no Chardonnay vineyards of its own, but buys fruit from the Beckstoffer Ranch, Cuvaison and assorted Napa growers. The grapes from the Beckstoffer vineyard are bottled separately, and sold at the winery. The other two Stag's Leap labels are a Napa Valley blend and a Reserve Chardonnay.

The Napa Chardonnay sees 50 per cent barrel-fermentation, whereas the Beckstoffer and the Reserve get the full treatment, with malolactic fermentation thrown in for good measure. The oak at Stag's Leap is either new or one-year-old; after it has done service for white wines, it does the same for the winery's reds.

All three wines can be very fine, with crisp, elegant flavours and great length. The rich 1988 Reserve is Stag's Leap's finest Chardonnay yet. It was still closed when I tasted it in May 1991, but harboured the promise of great things to come. The 1989 Napa Valley Chardonnay is also surprisingly good for the vintage.

*

STONY HILL

3331 St Helena Highway, St Helena, 94574 California

Chardonnay vineyard: 25 acres

Production of Chardonnay: 36,000 bottles

Labels: Stony Hill; SHV

Quality: 🍇🍇🍇🍇/🍇🍇🍇🍇🍇   Price: ★★★/★★★★

Best vintages: 1976, 1980, 1981, 1983, 1985, 1986, 1987, 1989

The death of Eleanor McCrea in the spring of 1991, at the grand old age of eighty-three, robbed the Napa Valley of one of its great characters. Eleanor and her husband Fred set up Stony Hill winery in the late 1940s, and were among the first to plant Chardonnay in the Napa Valley, a decision which was regarded as highly eccentric at the time. When Fred McCrea died in 1977, Eleanor took over the running of the winery full-time.

Stony Hill's Chardonnays have achieved almost mythical status in California and regularly fetch high prices at auction. Old wines from Hanzell and Chalone – two other California Chardonnay pioneers – are almost cheap by comparison. The Stony Hill wines, it must be said, are relatively inexpensive when released, certainly when placed alongside the likes of Grgich Hills, Far Niente and Château Woltner. Most of the Chardonnay is sold to mail-order customers; the stuff that isn't flies off the shelf.

The original Chardonnay vineyard was planted in 1948, using the Wente Livermore Valley clone and it is these old vines, coupled with a northerly aspect, low yields and the avoidance of new oak, which account for the extraordinary Stony Hill style, according to Mike Chelini, the estate's wine-maker for the last two decades.

Stony Hill is the exception that proves the rule about California Chardonnay. Most Napa Chardonnays have fallen to pieces by the time their tenth birthday comes around, but some of the old Stony Hill wines are still lively after fifteen years or more. The wines are often closed when young, with few of the rich butter and oak flavours of many Napa wines, but develop an extraordinary elegance with age. As much as 50 per cent of the wine is stainless-steel-fermented. Stony Hill Chardonnays have something of the character of ripe Chablis, although the winery released a series of more forward wines in the eighties.

Since 1988 Stony Hill has released two Chardonnays: an estate wine and the cheaper SHV, made from young vines replanted (with the original clone) in the last few years. Both wines will reward the patient wine-lover.

SWANSON VINEYARDS

1271 Manley Lane, PO Box 459, Rutherford, 94573 California

Chardonnay vineyard: 29 acres

Production of Chardonnay: 100,000 bottles

Quality: 🍇🍇🍇 Price: ★★★—★★★★★

Best vintages: 1988, 1990

It is early days for this recently established Napa Valley venture, but the first Swanson Chardonnay, released in 1990, was an extremely impressive début. W. Clarke Swanson, the winery's owner and guiding light, owns Chardonnay vineyards in three sites – two in Oakville and one 17-acre parcel in Carneros – but sells off two-thirds of the fruit. All three vineyards are over fifteen years old, although Swanson's vineyard manager, Jim Lincoln, has also been experimenting with a selection of new clones and pruning and trellising techniques. The Carneros vineyard is mainly planted with the established, low-yielding Abbot/Wente clone.

Swanson released two 1988 Chardonnays – a Napa Valley and a Napa Valley Reserve – both of which are entirely barrel-fermented. The straight Chardonnay is on the oaky side, but has superb fruit/acid structure, with flavours of lemon, honey and apple and no malolactic character. It is best drunk in the

first five years of its life. The Reserve bottling sees a greater
percentage of new oak and is made almost entirely from Carneros fruit. After a disappointing year in 1989, the 1990 releases
are a vast improvement. For me, they are wine-maker Marco
Cappelli's best Chardonnays to date.

ZD

8383 Silverado Trail, Napa, 94558 California

Production of Chardonnay: 220,000 bottles

Quality: 🍇🍇🍇🍇   Price: ★★★

Best vintages: 1981, 1982, 1984, 1985, 1988

When Norman deLeuze and partner Gino Zepponi founded
what was then a Sonoma Valley winery in 1969, they borrowed
the name ZD from a rocket engine programme (called 'Zero
Defects') that deLeuze was working on at the time in
Sacramento. Since Gino Zepponi's death in 1985, the winery
has been run entirely by the deLeuze family: Robert makes the
wine, Brett is the marketing director, Julie the office manager
and Norman and his wife Rosa Lee oversee the whole
operation.

ZD moved to the Napa Valley in 1979, but has continued to
produce Chardonnay in a remarkably consistent, opulent style
since its first vintage in 1971. The consistency is even more
remarkable when you consider that ZD has never owned any
vines. Its Chardonnay is bought in from a dozen different
growers, as far apart as Napa and Santa Barbara, a tricky logisti-
cal feat. As far as possible, deLeuze likes to source grapes from
cool areas and pick late, although recent vintages have seen a
greater percentage of warmer Napa Valley fruit in the ZD
Chardonnay, as some of his growers have sold their grapes to
higher bidders.

There is one particularly interesting wine-making peculiarity
at ZD. After extensive barrel experiments in the early 1980s,
deLeuze concluded that, after ten months, the wine tasted as
good in American oak as it did in more expensive French *bar-*

riques. To this day, the Chardonnay is fermented in a mixture of one-third new American and French barrels. The wine spends up to ten months in oak, but as soon as the alcoholic fermentation is finished, it is racked off its lees. There is no malolactic.

ZD Chardonnays are good value by California standards, and can age for up to eight years. They are full of pineapple and pear flavours when young, but develop a delicious, smoky, honeyed complexity in bottle.

New York State

Total vineyard area: approximately 17,500 acres

Area planted to Chardonnay: approximately 800 acres

Not many people know this, as Michael Caine once said, but New York State is the second most densely planted wine region in America. The area has traditionally played host to a jamboree bag of peculiar hybrids and native *Vitis labrusca* varieties: Seyval Blanc, Baco Noir, Maréchal Foch and de Chaunac among the former, Delaware, Catawba, Concord, Diamond and Ives among the latter.

Vinifera grapes, including Chardonnay, are a more recent phenomenon. It was long believed that New York State's thermal-underwear winters were too cold, even for the likes of Riesling. It took the pioneering work of a Russian émigré called Dr Konstantin Frank, first at the Geneva Research Station and then at Gold Seal Cellars, to change people's minds, although *labrusca* and hybrid grapes still account for a substantial proportion of the area under vine in New York State. Following his father's death in 1986, Frank's son Willy makes the wine at the family's Vinifera Wine Cellars.

The two best areas for Chardonnay are around four of the Finger Lakes – Keuka, Canandaigua, Cayuga and Seneca –

immediately south of Lake Ontario, and Long Island, a few miles from the centre of New York. The Finger Lakes is generally the colder of the two regions, although the Chardonnay produced by Wagner does not taste like a cool-climate wine. The area is also home to Hermann Wiemer, an expatriate German who makes a more European style of Chardonnay: he was the first to use French oak, for example.

Long Island, play-pen of New York's rich and famous, is arguably even more promising for Chardonnay. The climate here, with its moderating maritime influence, is a good deal more benign, particularly on the North Fork. Vines were first planted here in the seventeenth century, but the industry was long dead by the time Alex Hargrave came to replant a potato field with grapes in 1973. Chardonnay has flourished here and now makes up around 40 per cent of the island's estimated 1,500 acres. Foreign interest is also growing. The Italian producers Villa Banfi have 75 acres of Chardonnay on the Brookville estate, Long Island, for example. There are a number of interesting Chardonnays emerging, most of them with oak ageing and/or barrel-fermentation and full malolactic. The top wines – Hargrave, Bedell, Bidwell, Pindar and Peconic Bay – manage to combine the oak character with good underlying structure. A region to watch.

> Best producers: Bedell, Bidwell, Finger Lakes Winery, Hargrave/Long Island Vineyard, Lenz, Palmer, Peconic Bay, Pindar, Vinifera Wine Cellars, Wagner*, Hermann Wiemer

WAGNER VINEYARDS

> Route 414, Lodi, 14860 New York
> Chardonnay vineyard: 12 acres
> Production of Chardonnay: 30,000 bottles
> Quality: 🍇🍇   Price: ★★/★★★
> Best vintages: 1984, 1986, 1987

Even though it has nothing to do with the German composer of the same name, this Finger Lakes winery has produced some distinctly Wagnerian wines over the years – big, rich and full of dramatic flavours. Bill Wagner, a local grape grower and lifelong resident of upper New York State, decided to start bottling his own crop in 1978, although he did not make his first *Vitis vinifera* wine (a Chardonnay) until 1980. Production has grown from the initial 3,000 bottles of Chardonnay to ten times that figure, with the grapes still coming from Wagner's own vines on the eastern shore of Lake Seneca. Wagner also produces a curious barrel-fermented Seyval Blanc, which is well worth a taste.

The style here is surprisingly rich for such a cool region. After six hours' skin contact, the Chardonnay is fermented and aged in American oak, with full malolactic, lees contact and *bâtonnage*. The 1987 Barrel Fermented was a wonderful wine, creamy, nutty and complex. I have not tasted more recent releases, however.

Oregon

Total vineyard area: 5,250 acres

Area planted to Chardonnay: 1,200 acres

Oregon may share a border with northern California, but this wonderful region, full of bearded eccentrics and home-spun wineries, has little or nothing in common with most of the Golden State. Oregon's wine industry picked up post-Prohibition (around the same time as California's, though on a slightly smaller scale) in 1963 when UC Davis graduate Richard Sommers planted Riesling in the Umpqua Valley. He was followed three years later by David Lett of the Eyrie Vineyards ('named after a family of red-tailed hawks with whom we share our 20-acre vineyard'), who bravely set up the first winery in the cooler Willamette Valley, which was to become Oregon's most important wine region.

It was probably Lett who brought the first Chardonnay cuttings to Oregon from California. He chose a selection from the Draper vineyard, unlike subsequent growers, most of whom tended to plump for the more productive UCD 108 clone. Chardonnay has not been as successful in Oregon as Pinot Noir, and many producers blame UCD 108. 'It's terrible,' says Dick Erath of Knudsen Erath. 'It was selected in California for Californian conditions, but it doesn't work here. It's like a big pineapple. I've seen clusters over 1 lb.'

Not everyone is as enthusiastic about the Draper clone, or clones, as David Lett. David Adelsheim of Adelsheim Vineyard says that 'Draper isn't much better than UCD 108; if the grapes aren't ripe, the wine tastes like old sweat-socks.' Whatever the relative merits of these two clones, it is perhaps significant that Oregon's best Chardonnay (from Eyrie) is made entirely with the Draper variety, though even here David Lett's Chardonnay is a good deal less interesting than his Pinot Noir. The release of new Burgundian clones from quarantine in 1989 should see a marked improvement in Oregon's Chardonnays over the next decade.

So far, there have been some good, if not great, examples of the variety. 'With Chardonnay we go through the motions,' says Craig Broadley of Broadley Winery, 'but deep down we hate Chardonnay and it hates us.' This may be putting it a little strongly, but Chardonnay does not seem to have captured the imagination of Willamette Valley wine-makers in the same way as Pinot Noir.

David Adelsheim identifies three stages in the development of Oregon's uneasy relationship with Chardonnay. The first, in the early seventies, produced wines that were clean if unexciting. This gave way to what Adelsheim calls 'power wine-making' – an attempt to emulate the big, blockbuster styles of California with lots of new oak, and lees and skin contact. In Oregon, which has a much cooler climate than most of California and produces leaner, more acid Chardonnays as a result, this approach effaces the basic character of the fruit.

Fortunately, according to Adelsheim, a third development is now under way – a more sensitive approach to the variety, using less vigorous clones and toning down the influence of new oak. With the new Dijon clones just about to come on stream, Oregon is set to become an excellent source of cool-climate Chardonnay. I just hope the prices stay sensible.

> Best producers: Adelsheim*, Amity, Bethel Heights (from 1990 vintage), Cameron*, Eyrie*, Ponzi*, Rex Hill, Tualatin, Veritas*, Yamhill Valley

ADELSHEIM VINEYARD

> 22150 NE Quarter Mile Lane, Newberg, 97132 Oregon
>
> Chardonnay vineyard: 5 acres
>
> Production of Chardonnay: approximately 35,000 bottles
>
> Labels: Oregon; Yamhill County Reserve
>
> Quality: 👑👑👑   Price: ★★★
>
> Best vintages: 1985, 1986, 1988, 1989, 1990

David Adelsheim is a vociferous advocate of the Oregon wine industry. Educated at the 'Viti' (Lycée Viticole) in Beaune, among other places, Adelsheim worked for a vintage at Eyrie Vineyards before setting up his own winery in the mid-seventies. He is a much-respected authority on all aspects of viticulture in the North-West and, more significantly, makes some of Oregon's best Pinot Noir and Chardonnay.

Since 1989, Adelsheim has released two distinct Chardonnays, both of which tend to be at the fuller end of the spectrum. His Oregon blend is made mainly from bought-in grapes, while the Yamhill County Reserve is produced from Adelsheim's own vineyards. The area planted to Chardonnay at Adelsheim will increase to 20 acres by 1993: the original UCD 108 will be supplemented by clones imported from Dijon.

'My philosophy is that if you can get away without doing it, don't do it,' says Adelsheim. His approach to Chardonnay, which he made for the first time in 1978, has increasingly reflected this belief. The 1987 was a watershed vintage in this respect; Adelsheim switched to whole-bunch pressing and stopped using skin contact on his Chardonnay. Adelsheim picks his fruit as late as possible and acidifies if necessary.

Mindful of criticism, he has also cut back the proportion of new oak to a maximum of 25 per cent, and done away with lees stirring, or *bâtonnage*. In true Burgundian fashion, Adelsheim does not inoculate with dry yeast cultures, allowing the wine to take its own course.

His Chardonnays have benefited from the changes. The fruit seems cleaner and richer on the palate, but wines have lost none of their structure. They tend to take three to four years to come together, although of recent vintages, the 1988 was comparatively forward. The 1989s and 1990s are Adelsheim's best Chardonnays to date.

CAMERON

8200 Worden Hill Road, PO Box 27, Dundee, 97115 Oregon

Chardonnay vineyard: 8 acres, Abbey Ridge; 8 acres, John Paul

Production of Chardonnay: 18,000 bottles

Quality: 🍇🍇🍇   Price: ★★★

Best vintages: 1985, 1988, 1989

Wine-makers, like lion-tamers, are an eccentric bunch. And they don't come much more eccentric than John Paul, former marine biochemist and now one of Oregon's finest producers. Paul is a small, garrulous fellow who likes to sport loud shirts and clashing, criss-cross ties. With the easy charm so typical of the region, Paul is winningly honest about his approach to Chardonnay. 'Someone asked me the other night what I am trying to achieve. The honest answer is that I don't know. When you plant in Oregon at the moment it's a real craps shoot.'

Paul describes himself as an 'incurable Burgundophile'; as well as working in Burgundy, Paul has done wine-making stints in New Zealand and at Carneros Creek, in California. It was natural, then, that Paul would choose Chardonnay and Pinot Noir when he planted his first vines in 1984. His Chardonnay comes from two main sources: Abbey Ridge, which belongs to his business partner and is the main source for the Cameron Reserve, and Paul's own vines on the lower slopes of the Dundee Hills. Yields are very low here – 'barely economical but it makes what I like'.

Both the Reserve and the 'Vintage' Chardonnay follow broadly Burgundian vinification techniques, with fermentation in French oak, malolactic and extended lees contact (up to twenty months). The wines are unfiltered and retain a markedly individual character. Racking takes place according to the phases of the moon. Paul breaks with Burgundian tradition on one point only – he uses a combination of dry yeast strains from as far afield as New Zealand.

Of the two bottlings, the Reserve is the more substantial; the 'Vintage' tends to be more fruity, but lacks the concentration and ageing potential of the more expensive wine. Both Chardonnays are marked by firm acidity. The style is still evolving at Cameron and, while the Chardonnays are not yet as good as the Pinot Noirs, they are still interesting wines with real personality.

EYRIE

PO Box 697, Dundee, 97115 Oregon

Chardonnay vineyard: 4 acres

Production of Chardonnay: 18,000 bottles

Quality: 🍇🍇🍇/🍇🍇🍇🍇   Price: ★★★/★★★★

Best vintages: 1983, 1985, 1986, 1988, 1990

With his white beard and slightly hooded eyes, David Lett
bears more than a passing resemblance to the great novelist
Ernest Hemingway. Hemingway would certainly have
approved of Lett's pioneering spirit. He was the first man to
plant *vinifera* grapes in the Willamette Valley, very much
against the advice of his former teachers at the University of
California, Davis, and he was the first wine-maker to concentrate on Pinot Noir, the variety which has done so much to
establish the state's reputation as a major wine-producing
region. In the early days, according to wine writer Ted Jordan
Meredith, Lett and his family lived in a tent in the middle of the
vineyard. He still runs Eyrie from an unmarked former turkey-
processing plant down by the railroad tracks in McMinnville.

Lett's faith in Pinot Noir has been vindicated, and his wines
have gained a considerable reputation, not least for their per-
formance in blind tastings. He also produces an interesting
range of white wines: Pinot Meunier, Muscat Ottonel, Pinot
Gris and Chardonnay.

Unlike many Oregon Chardonnays, Lett's is not made with
the bland, widely planted UCD 108. His original vines came
from Jerry Draper's Spring Mountain vineyard in the Napa
Valley, in 1964. The wine has followed a more or less consistent style since its initial vintage in 1970, with barrel-fermentation and as much as eleven months on its lees, although it has
gained in complexity as Lett has developed more experience
with the variety. He started putting the wine through malolactic fermentation in 1977. In some years, Lett also produces
a Reserve, which tends to see more new oak.

Eyrie's Chardonnays are the best in Oregon, with a lean,
citrus fruit character that helps the wine to age. Lett's emphasis,
as always, is on subtlety. 'We have a marginal climate here,' he
says, 'so what's the point of making wines that come out tasting
like California Chardonnay?' Quite so.

PONZI

Route 1, Box 842, Beaverton, 97007 Oregon

Chardonnay vineyard: 5 acres

Production of Chardonnay: 36,000 bottles

Labels: Willamette Valley; Reserve

Quality: 🍇🍇🍇   Price: ★★★

Best vintages: 1982, 1985, 1986, 1988, 1989

Dick Ponzi worked as an engineer for Disneyland before dropping out, in popular sixties fashion, and moving to Oregon to become the third wine pioneer in the Willamette Valley. He planted his 12-acre vineyard, 24 km from Portland, in 1970, producing his first wines four years later. Ponzi supplements his Chardonnay requirements with fruit from an additional 12 acres belonging to local contract growers.

Ponzi's best wine is his superlative Pinot Noir, but he also makes Pinot Gris, Riesling and two of Oregon's finer Chardonnays. There are two different labels: a regular Willamette Valley Chardonnay and a Reserve, in effect a selection of the best barrels.

Ponzi's Chardonnay is barrel-fermented in 20 per cent new French oak, spends six months on its lees and goes through full malolactic fermentation. In good years, it reflects two decades of experience with the grape, with the fresh natural acidity of Oregon balanced by toasty oak and sweet, creamy fruit. The Reserve is consistently more interesting than the Willamette Valley blend.

VERITAS

31190 NE Veritas Lane, Newberg, 97132 Oregon

Chardonnay vineyard: 12 acres

Production of Chardonnay: 18,000 bottles

Quality: 🍇🍇🍇/🍇🍇🍇🍇   Price: ★★/★★★

Best vintages: 1988, 1990

John Howieson spends most of his working week as a physician at the Oregon Medical School, but combines his day job with the running of his own winery, Veritas vineyard. 'This was intended to be a retirement project,' he says, 'but I got drawn into a larger-scale operation because it was so much fun.' In 1983, John and his wife Diane bought a 30-acre prune and hazelnut farm at the northern end of the Willamette Valley, and planted Pinot Noir, Chardonnay, Pinot Gris, Riesling and Müller-Thurgau.

The Howiesons and their wine-maker John Eliassen, who trained at the University of Dijon, have been more successful with Chardonnay than most Oregon wineries. It may be the warmer microclimate, or Eliassen's French background, but Veritas Chardonnays have a depth of flavour that is all too rare in the North-West. Since 1988, Veritas has produced two Chardonnays: a Reserve, which is made from their own grapes, and a crisper, more citrusy regular release. The 1990 (there was no Reserve in this vintage), which was barrel-fermented and left on its lees for nearly a year, is its best Chardonnay yet.

Texas

Total vineyard area: 3,209 acres

Area planted to Chardonnay: 732 acres

The common image of Texas as hot, dusty and unsuitable for anything but the production of sultanas is, like most generalizations, only partly true. There are more than thirty wineries in Texas, a state which is larger than France, and some of them are producing very drinkable *vinifera* wines. The best areas are the high plains, centred on the 'dry' town of Lubbock, and the Hill Country, to the north-west of Austin. The climate here is cool – by Texan standards anyway – with some vineyards planted as high as 3,000 feet above sea level. Drip irrigation enables wine-makers to overcome low rainfall, but lack of acidity is often a problem as far as Chardonnay is concerned.

In one sense, Texas has a more ancient wine-making tradition than California – the first grapes were planted here by Spanish missionaries in 1662 – but the modern wine industry (using grapes that are a little more acceptable to twentieth-century tastes) dates back to the mid-seventies. One of the first latter-day producers was Austin lawyer Ed Auler, whose Fall Creek Chardonnay is one of the best in the state. Auler and his wife Susan planted vines in 1975, inspired by a visit to Clos de Vougeot.

Chardonnay is only just getting into its stride here, as wine-makers begin to experiment with oak ageing and barrel-fermentation, but give Texas another decade, and its Chardonnays could rival California's. Production costs are certainly cheaper here – the one thing Texans aren't short of is land.

Best producers: Fall Creek, Llano Estacado, Pheasant Ridge

Washington State

Total vineyard area: 12,000 acres
Area planted to Chardonnay: 2,000 acres

In the best tradition of hackneyed travel writing, Washington could, with some justification, be described as a region of contrasts. The main contrast is created by the Cascade Mountain Range, which runs north to south down the middle of the state, producing two quite distinct climates. To the west of the Cascades, as anyone who has ever spent a damp week in Seattle will confirm, the weather tends to be cool and invariably wet. To the east, mile upon mile of virtual desert stretches away to the horizon.

Grapes (mainly *Vitis labrusca*) were certainly grown in Washington, on both sides of the Cascades, before Prohibition, but the modern renaissance of the Washington wine industry is comparatively recent. Washington has only been back in business for a little over twenty years. Two groups – one of growers (American Wine Growers, now called Chateau Ste Michelle), the other of university academics (Associated Vintners, subsequently renamed Columbia Winery) – did most to bring it about, but a host of other producers have followed in their steps, making Washington State a vibrant, exciting wine region.

The state's earliest successes were with Riesling, still its most important grape, and in the seventies, producers tended to vinify Chardonnay in a similar fashion, with low-temperature fermentation in stainless steel and little or no oak ageing. Other grapes that have done well here are Sémillon, Cabernet Sauvignon and Merlot.

Many of Washington's leading wineries have their headquarters in Seattle, but the only name of any consequence which grows grapes on the western side of the Cascades is Salishan, down in Clark County, in a microclimate remarkably similar to that of Oregon's Willamette Valley. Almost everyone else grows or buys grapes in the Columbia River basin, the area which contains 99 per cent of the state's *vinifera* plantings.

The Columbia Valley is surprisingly well suited for grape growing. Here, in the rain shadow of the Cascades, irrigation is essential, but a combination of hot days and cold nights produces grapes that are high in sugar yet also have good levels of balancing acidity. The only risk as far as Chardonnay is concerned is spring frosts, which is why some growers prefer the more doughty Riesling. The 1991 harvest, in particular, was severely reduced by frost. It is early days, but the two best areas for Chardonnay appear to be the Yakima and Walla Walla Valleys, both sub-appellations within the Columbia Valley.

It is also too soon to talk of a distinctive Chardonnay style, as Washington produces everything from light, crisp wines to big oaky brutes. But it is surely no coincidence that the most complex Chardonnays (Woodward Canyon, Salishan and Columbia Winery's Wyckoff Vineyard) are all entirely barrel-fermented. Rick Small's Woodward Canyon Chardonnays (for my money the best example of the grape in the North-West) are proof of the grape's enormous potential in Washington.

Best producers: Arbor Crest, Chinook, Columbia Winery*, Hogue, Chateau Ste Michelle, Salishan*, Woodward Canyon*

COLUMBIA WINERY

14030 NE 145th, Woodinville, 98072 Washington
Chardonnay production: 200,000 bottles
Labels: Columbia Valley; Wyckoff Vineyard
Quality: 🍇🍇🍇   Price: ★★/★★★
Best vintages: 1988, 1989, 1990

Columbia Winery, known until 1984 as Associated Vintners, is one of Washington's oldest wineries. It was started, on an informal basis, by a group of academics from the University of Washington in the early sixties. They muddled along for a few years, earning the praise of eminent wine critics like Leon Adams, before deciding to produce their first commercial vintage in 1967.

The arrival of Canadian-born Master of Wine David Lake in 1979 was an important step in the winery's development. So was the decision to sell off its vineyards to finance further expansion a few years later. Columbia buys in all of its grapes from growers in the Columbia and Yakima Valleys, but rather than undermining the quality of the wines, the greater freedom has worked to Lake's advantage. The stars here are the reds, particularly the Red Willow Cabernet Sauvignons, but Columbia has also developed a reputation as a good producer of whites.

There are two main Chardonnays: a Columbia Valley blend, from four different sources, and the single-estate Wyckoff Vineyard. The Columbia Valley wine is 50 per cent barrel-

fermented and goes through partial malolactic, while the
Wyckoff is entirely barrel-fermented in one-third new French
oak and spends six months on its lees. Recent vintages of the
Wyckoff Chardonnay, drawn from a cool site in the Yakima
Valley, have been particularly impressive, confirming Lake's
progress with the variety. Along with the wines of Woodward
Canyon and Salishan, Wyckoff is now among the best
Chardonnays in the state. The 1990 is the most successful to
date.

SALISHAN

Route 2, Box 8, La Center, 98629 Washington

Chardonnay vineyard: 3 acres

Production of Chardonnay: 3,600 bottles

Quality: 🍇🍇🍇   Price: ★★

Best vintages: 1986, 1987, 1989

Salishan's address is misleading – viticulturally, it is closer to
Oregon's northern Willamette Valley than to the main bulk of
Washington's vineyards, east of the Cascades. 'Washington's
answer to Oregon Pinot Noir' reads the winery's T-shirt.
'Yeah,' says owner and wine-maker, Joan Wolverton, 'I feel a
bit schizophrenic. I've got the same growing climate, but I can't
join them for promotions and things like that.'

The Wolvertons – Joan and husband Linc – planted their
first grapes in 1971, convinced that south-western Washington
was an ideal spot for Pinot Noir and Chardonnay. The couple
ran the winery at weekends, pursuing full-time jobs in Seattle –
she as a journalist on the *Seattle Times*, he as an economist –
until 1982.

From 1976 to 1981, the wine was made by other people, Dick
Ponzi among them. Joan Wolverton took over the following
year, and the wines have improved dramatically since.
Salishan's range (Pinot Noir, Chardonnay, Riesling and
Chenin Blanc) seems to get better with every vintage. Pinot

Noir is Salishan's top wine, but the well-structured Chardonnay is also interesting.

Original plantings were with the UCD 108 clone, but Joan Wolverton supplemented these with cuttings from David Lett's Draper selection in 1980. After a period of experimentation, she has now settled on a definite Chardonnay style: barrel-fermentation in one-third new Nevers oak, full malolactic and up to eight months on the lees. 'Sort of by default,' she adds, 'as it can take that long for some of the barrels to go through malolactic.' Appropriately enough, the wines taste quite Oregonian, with firm natural acidity and a touch of spice. The 1989, made in a warmer year, had the depth of flavour to match.

WOODWARD CANYON

Route T, Box 387, Lowden, 99360 Washington

Chardonnay vineyard: 10 acres

Production of Chardonnay: 30,000 bottles

Labels: Columbia Valley; Roza Bergé Vineyard; Walla Walla Valley

Quality: 🍇🍇🍇🍇/🍇🍇🍇🍇🍇   Price: ★★★/★★★★

Best vintages: 1988, 1989, 1990

This small, unprepossessing winery is situated east of the Cascade mountains in the Walla Walla Valley, now a recognized viticultural area. Of the major Washington wineries, only Preston Vineyards is further from Seattle, but in this isolated spot, amid rolling grain fields, the eccentric, fast-talking Rick Small is producing some of Washington's finest wines, concentrating on Sémillon, Cabernet Sauvignon and Chardonnay. Not bad for a man who started out making wine in his garage.

As well as drawing Chardonnay from its home vineyard, Woodward Canyon purchases fruit from selected local growers. In 1990, three different Chardonnays were made here: a basic Columbia Valley blend and the more expensive Roza Bergé

Vineyard and Walla Walla Valley Chardonnays, the latter from Small's own vines. The Roza Bergé, which comes from a cool site in the Yakima Valley, tends to be the leanest of the three, while the Walla Walla is the most open when young. In 1991, thanks to the frost, there was no Walla Walla and very little Roza Bergé Chardonnay.

Small's Chardonnays are made in time-honoured Burgundian fashion, with (60–100 per cent new) barrel-fermentation, full malolactic, *bâtonnage* and extended lees contact. He has followed this oenological path for over a decade and, while his Chardonnays can seem quite oaky when young, they are certainly among the most complex and age-worthy in the state. Recent vintages have been particularly good, with considerable depth and length on the palate. Small thinks that 'Merlot and Cabernet Sauvignon are the grapes that will make Washington famous', adding that most of Washington is too warm for great Chardonnay. I beg to disagree.

YUGOSLAVIA

Total vineyard area: 600,000 acres
Area planted to Chardonnay: 18,500 acres

Compared with the ubiquitous (and consistently unpleasant) Laski Rizling, Chardonnay is a relatively minor grape in the former republic of Yugoslavia. Some plantings date back to the mid-seventies although, as in Italy, Chardonnay has frequently been confused with Pinot Blanc. The majority of the Chardonnay in what was Yugoslavia comes from Slovenia, along the country's north-western border with Italy. The climate here is cool and the wines ought to be a lot more exciting than they are, given the quality of the Chardonnay produced on the other side of the border. Yields are high and there appears to be little or no interest in making good Chardonnay. All of the Yugoslavian Chardonnays I have tasted have been unoaked, but tend to lack freshness. Once more, lack of investment has not helped matters.

GLOSSARY

APPELLATION CONTRÔLÉE

French laws controlling the origin and style, but not the quality, of wines. VDQS, *Vin de Pays* and *Vin de Table* come below it in the pecking-order.

BARRIQUE

French term used to describe the Bordeaux cask of 225 litres and the Burgundy cask (sometimes called a *pièce*) of 228 litres.

BÂTONNAGE

Stirring the lees at the bottom of a barrel to keep them in suspension. The resulting wines, adherents claim, display a richer, creamier texture. A Burgundian technique, now widely practised in other countries.

BOTRYTIS CINEREA

Also known as noble rot, a fungus that attacks grapes under certain (usually humid) conditions. Its effect is beneficial for the production of sweet wines, as it dehydrates the grapes, concentrating their sugars. A percentage of botrytis-affected grapes can be used to add complexity to dry white wines, too.

CENTRIFUGE

Machine used to separate grape solids from juice or wine.

CHAPTALIZATION	The addition of sugar to grape juice before (or during) fermentation to increase the alcohol content of the resulting wine. Widely practised in Burgundy and Champagne. Generally illegal in southern Europe. Unnecessary in the New World.
DENOMINAZIONE DE ORIGINE CONTROLLATA (DOC)	Approximate Italian equivalent of France's *appellation contrôlée* system.
FEUILLETTES	Traditional 132 litre barrels used in Chablis.
FINING	Clarification of wine after fermentation. Various fining agents can be used, from egg-whites to bentonite.
FOUDRES	Large oak barrel used for storing or maturing wine.
FÛTS	Small oak barrel. See *barrique*.
LEES	Sediment that settles to the bottom of a vat, tank or barrel after fermentation. Chardonnay wines are often left on their lees to pick up added complexity and richness.
MALOLACTIC FERMENTATION	Secondary fermentation, occurring during or (more often) after the primary, alcoholic fermentation, in which malic acid is transformed by the action of bacteria into softer, lactic acid. Not to be confused with the second fermentation (effectively a re-fermentation) responsible for the bubbles in sparkling wine.

MÉTHODE CHAMPENOISE	Known in English as the Champagne method, a technique widely used for the production of sparkling wines in Champagne and elsewhere. Its distinguishing feature is that the second fermentation, which produces the bubbles, takes place in bottle. Sometimes described as 'bottle fermentation'.
MUST	Unfermented grape juice.
MUST CHILLER	Machine used to cool the must, giving the winemaker more control over the timing and temperature of fermentation. Particularly useful in warm climates, when grapes have been picked in the heat of the day.
NÉGOCIANT/ NÉGOCE	A merchant who buys, matures and sells wine. Some, but not all, have their own vineyards and wineries.
PHYLLOXERA	Vine louse which devastated European vineyards in the late 19th century. Now present in most wine regions of the world. Vinifera vines grafted on to American rootstocks are generally phylloxera-resistant.
RACKING	Moving clear wine off its lees by transferring it from one container to another.
RESIDUAL SUGAR	Natural grape sugar left behind in a wine when fermentation is arrested by means of sulphur dioxide addition, chilling or microfiltration. Used by some producers (particularly in the New World) to give their wines 'mouth-feel'.

SKIN-CONTACT

Leaving the juice on its grape skins to extract flavour and (usually) colour. Once used widely in the New World, now out of fashion for anything but cheap, commercial styles of Chardonnay.

SULPHUR DIOXIDE

Preservative, antiseptic and antioxidant used at various stages of the winemaking process. It is virtually impossible to make top quality wine without it.

TOAST

The charring on the inside of a barrel. Can be light, medium or heavy.

VIN DE PAYS

Literally, a country wine. The category of French wines between VDQS and the more lowly *Vin de Table*. Used with the name of a region or *département*, such as *Vin de Pays d'Oc*.

VDQS

Vin Délimité de Qualité Supérieure. The category of French wines between *appellation contrôlée* and *Vin de Table*.

INDEX